Faulkner's Art
and Characters

◈◈◈◈◈◈◈◈◈◈◈◈◈◈◈◈◈◈◈◈◈◈◈◈◈◈◈

BY WALTER K. EVERETT

ASSISTANT PROFESSOR OF ENGLISH
UNIVERSITY OF SOUTHERN MISSISSIPPI

Barron's Educational Series, Inc., *Woodbury, New York*

ACKNOWLEDGMENTS

The Dictionary of Characters section was first developed in 1962 at Mississippi College, Clinton, Mississippi, under the direction of Dr. Louis E. Dollarhide and Dr. Sarah A. Rouse.

Quotations from *Faulkner in the University* are reprinted through the courtesy of The University Press of Virginia.

Quotations from *Soldiers' Pay* and *Mosquitoes* are reprinted through the courtesy of Liveright Publishing Corporation.

All other quotations from the works of Faulkner are reprinted through the courtesy of Random House, Inc.

Specific notations of the editions and of the page numbers occur with the individual analyses.

All inquiries should be addressed to:
Barron's Educational Series, Inc.
113 Crossways Park Drive
Woodbury, New York 11797

Library of Congress Catalog Card No. 68-31478

PRINTED IN THE UNITED STATES OF AMERICA

Preface

◆◆◆◆◆◆◆◆◆◆◆◆◆◆◆◆◆◆◆◆◆◆◆◆◆◆◆◆◆◆◆◆◆

The variety and the complexity which characterize the literary canon of William Faulkner serve not only to compliment the genius that was his but also to arouse the interest of readers and the speculations of critics. Certainly no American writer thus far in the twentieth century has created a larger number of memorable characters, employed more diverse techniques, or presented in his work a broader spectrum of universal human experience.

This book attempts to aid the student of Faulkner in two ways. It seeks, even at this dangerously early date, to give some evaluation of the basis for Faulkner's permanent reputation and endeavors to emphasize important aspects of his novels and stories. And it presents an index of characters to aid the reader in identifying and noting the development of Faulkner's characters.

The discussions of all of Faulkner's novels and of all the collected short stories seek to call attention to peculiar and important facets of the work in question. They are arranged alphabetically within two subsections: one for novels, one for short stories. The comments found here aim at presenting insights into a fuller understanding of the work and at emphasizing the literary merits of the work.

Because Faulkner created such a large number of characters, many of whom appear repeatedly in works concerned with Yoknapatawpha, an index of characters (based on all of Faulkner's work) is included. As a good storyteller, William Faulkner constantly refers to characters who live in Yoknapatawpha as if he were among old friends who would immediately recognize the name of a familiar personality from the past.

BIOGRAPHICAL NOTE

No literary man of worthwhile stature stands or falls by the details of his personal life. His work is its own excuse for its existence and the best defense not only of its own merit but also of the greatness of the writer. The legends which often surround a public figure seem to have found extremely fertile ground in the biography of William Faulkner. He apparently was a somewhat diffident man in life who, while undeniably sensitive, did not enjoy the self-seeking literary visitor or the fatuous admiring poseur. The number of people who, during his lifetime, could have or would have presumed to label themselves his close personal friends seems to have been small. Shortly after his death, when reporters and people of genuine literary interest invaded Oxford, Mississippi, almost everyone who had ever sat at the table next to him in a restaurant, or who had said good morning to him on the street, felt free to refer to him affectionately as "dear old Bill."

Conflict over his "real" personality has led to claims that he continually drank too much and often fled the presence of people, and even sometimes ignored serious admirers. Other attempts have been made to rewrite his biography, giving him angelic proportions, making him into an apotheosis. Fortunately the tremendous task of separating the truth from the legend, of separating facts from the calumnious gossip and the whitewash, can be left to the official biographers. The Faulkner of importance to posterity lives in his work. Below is a sketch of the general facts of his life.

William Faulkner was born on September 25, 1897, at New Albany, Mississippi. He was the first son of Murray Cuthbert Falkner and Maud Butler Falkner. Later the family moved to Oxford, Mississippi, some thirty-five miles away, where after running a livery stable, Murray became the Business Manager for the University of Mississippi.

William's attendance in school was desultory from the junior high grades onward. He did not complete the requirements for a high school diploma, nor was he successful in his try at college work at the University.

Rejected by the U. S. Army Air Corps during the First World War, Faulkner went to Canada and enlisted in the Canadian branch of the Royal Air Force. It is reported that the war was over before he actually received his commission, and that the knee injury he received while flying was sustained in an accident.

After an unsuccessful term as postmaster at the University post office (1921–1924), Faulkner decided to go abroad. His friend Phil Stone felt that Faulkner might more easily attain fame in another country. In 1924, the year that a book of verse, *The Marble Faun,* was published and not very well received, William Faulkner started for Europe via New Orleans.

He remained in the Crescent City, however, for six months. There he met Sherwood Anderson through Mrs. Anderson (formerly Elizabeth Prall) whom Faulkner had met on a previous trip to New York. During this period of time he wrote sketches which appeared in *The Times-Picayune,* a New Orleans newspaper, and in the *Double Dealer,* a little magazine. In 1925 in the company of William Spratling, an artist friend from New Orleans, William Faulkner went to Europe.

In 1926 *Soldiers' Pay* was published and though it received some favorable reviews, it was not financially successful. *Mosqui-*

toes, set in New Orleans, came out in 1927 and *Sartoris* in 1929. Neither of these books were particularly well received, critically or financially.

The Sound and the Fury which Faulkner also published in 1929 proved to be a tremendous critical success. In this same year he married a childhood sweetheart, Mrs. Estelle Oldham Franklin, two years divorced from the father of her two children, a boy and a girl. The first child of William and Estelle Faulkner was a daughter whom they named Alabama after Faulkner's favorite aunt, but, unfortunately, this child died shortly after birth. A second child, a daughter, was born to them. She is now Mrs. Paul D. Summers of Charlottesville, Virginia.

Faulkner's next book, *As I Lay Dying* (1930) was written while he was working as a night superintendent at a power station. This book also proved popular with the critics but to no large degree with the buying public. Then came *Sanctuary* (1931), which, according to his own admission, Faulkner originally intended as a money-maker. It was a tremendous financial success. In 1931, also, was published *These Thirteen,* a collection of short stories. There followed limited editions of *Idyll in the Desert* (1931) and *Miss Zilphia Gant* (1932). During the 1930's and 1940's Faulkner at various times wrote or adapted scenarios for Hollywood, ostensibly to make enough money to allow himself to write his own work as his art demanded.

Building upon the setting of *Sartoris* and earlier stories, Faulkner continued to utilize the Yoknapatawpha milieu with *Light in August* (1932), *Absalom, Absalom!* (1936), *The Unvanquished* (1938), *The Hamlet* (1940), *Go Down, Moses and Other Stories* (1942), *Intruder in the Dust* (1948), *Knight's Gambit* (1949), *Requiem for a Nun* (1951), *The Town* (1957), *The Mansion* (1959), and his final book, *The Reivers* (1962).

Nineteen-hundred-and-fifty was a year of awards for Faulkner. In that year he was given the National Book gold medal for his *Collected Stories* (1950), and the Nobel Prize for Literature. In

1955 he received the Pulitzer Prize for *A Fable* (1954). In 1957 he began a series of annual appearances (from February to June) as Writer-in-Residence at the University of Virginia.

In June of 1962, *The Reivers* was published and was chosen as a Book-of-the-Month selection for June. On July 6 of the same year at 2 A.M. William Faulkner died of a heart attack at the age of 64.

Not only has Faulkner left, within the confines of his own writing, a rich legacy to the readers and writers of the future, but he has also left material encouragement for them. The William Faulkner Foundation, established in December of 1960, is dedicated to promoting literature and its understanding. It provides scholarships for worthy students, mostly Negroes of the Deep South, and an annual award for the best first novel.

SOME ASPECTS OF FAULKNER'S ART

One element which creates more difficulty for would-be Faulkner readers than any other is Faulkner's style, that composite of highly variable factors including his psychological and physical point of view, his intricate rhetoric, his philosophical proclivities, and his sense of comedy and pathos.

Sometimes Faulkner's style is complicated by his ability to weld the grammar of the English sentence into increasingly intricate forms. This sort of obstacle is most often encountered in the prose which is ostensibly the ordered meditations of a general in the French army or of Gavin Stevens, M.A., Harvard, Ph.D., Heidelberg. *A Fable, The Town,* and *Pylon* often include passages in which the prose seems capable of an unending flow of words. Such sections are often Faulkner's attempt to deal with the rationalizations of an intelligent, frequently sophisticated, character. As the mind of the character becomes more and more absorbed by the problem he is attempting to solve, Faulkner's prose parallels the involvement, entangling the reader so that he too feels some of the pressure of the situation. The more deeply involved personally the character is with the problem, the more difficult the prose becomes for the reader. For example, "The Bear" in *Go Down, Moses* contains perhaps the most grammatically perplexing passages in Faulkner's writing, passages in which Ike McCaslin and McCaslin Edmonds argue the facets of the Negro-white relationship. Ike is seeking to extricate himself from the most potent problem of the South, a problem of the greatest personal commitment for young Ike. Consequently the explication of the problem becomes so entangled grammatically as to be virtually incoherent at times. The meditations of Gail Hightower, D.D., in *Light in August* present this sort of problem because Gail has isolated himself from the present reality, and the throes of recognizing his situation are psychically painful for him; thus the prose recounting his analysis of the moral condition becomes involved and abstruse. In *A Fable,* the prose reflects the scope of the problems broached in the work, the problems of man's inhumanity to man for the sake of ordered civilization, and as a result, the expanse of words frequently exceeds the limits of the dramatic tension. In *Absalom, Absalom!* something of the same difficulty is employed with excellent success. The prose not only reflects the concern of the particular narrator with the Sutpen story, but it also develops into a montage capable of impacting the reader in the element of prose, forming in his mind the desired experience. The reader then is made to experience the fantasies of the narrators as they create the Sutpen myth, giving the reader a share of the creative artistic moment. In general the complexity of Faulkner's grammar parallels the depth of the ideas involved or the involvement of the character in a problem.

Complexity of grammar does not, however, account for an especially perplexing aspect of Faulkner's style. Point of view does. *The Sound and the Fury* is the prime example of this problem. Confusion develops for many readers in the Benjy section and in the Quentin section, but not because the grammar is complicated. For the most part it is rather simple. The problem here is the shifting point of view that leaves sentences, thoughts, or words unfinished. The incoherence here is a result of the mind which Faulkner is depicting. On one hand, Benjy is a mentally retarded character who is incapable of distinguishing chronological compartments. His mind ranges freely over the whole of his thirty-three years, or whatever portion of it is immediately subject to recall. His associational arrangement of persons and ideas is confusing during the first reading because the reader must stop and order the sequences of thought into some pattern of manageable chronology. Quentin's section presents a problem of a different order. Since Quentin is deranged to the point of committing suicide, his mind fails to distinguish reality from illusion, a task the reader's mind must accept. Occasionally the grammar does become fairly complicated, but usually not for very long passages. Once the reader learns to differentiate Quentin's thoughts from the realities of his situation, the section yields meaning and esthetic pleasure.

Similarly in *As I Lay Dying* the point of view offers some difficulty when Faulkner is working with the deranged mind of Darl Bundren or with the naive mind of Vardaman Bundren. In "The Leg" the mind of a manic depressive, Davy, provides some enigma for the reader.

Another salient facet of Faulkner's style is his vocabulary. He apparently loved words and never forgot a word that he had read or heard. When the language did not offer the exact term for his purpose he did not hesitate to telescope, to forge, or to coin the necessary implement of his trade; profanity and vulgarisms were employed where artistically appropriate. The telescoped words are more characteristic of his work through 1933 or 34 than they are of his later writing. His choice of words frequently includes expressions no longer in common use and a goodly number of words he appropriated from French or Latin bases. His last novel has as its title a word so unfamiliar to the general public that the publishers included a definition of it on the dust cover.

Faulkner's delicate sense of comedy and pathos also contributes manifestly toward his style. He often chose a young, naive narrator to tell his story because with such a tool Faulkner could more effectively play upon incongruity and irony. "That Will Be Fine" is an example of such a device, as are some of Chick Mallison's sections in *The Town* and Lucius Priest's parts in *The Reivers*. At other times his humor is developed through the lack of awareness on the part of a participant in the action. Such is the case with Wilfred Midgleston who in "Black Music" fails to adequately evaluate his own actions, and with Claude Hope who in "Turnabout" miscalculates the bravery of American flyers. In perhaps his best comic episode, "Spotted Horses" in *The Hamlet,* Faulkner develops a humorous situation principally by his precise choice of word, the exact turn of phrase that captures the awkward, helter-skelter confusion of the scene. In this passage also he touches the comedy with pathos, as Mrs. Armstid begs Henry not to waste the pittance she has saved to buy shoes for the chaps. In "Mule in the Yard" from *The Town,* the same capacity to choose the exact word to evoke the reader's sense of humor prevails. In "Two Soldiers" as perhaps nowhere else in his work, Faulkner employs a superb blend of the humorous with the pathetic to move the reader.

Another complicating factor in Faulkner's style is his penchant for the flashback and the caterpillar device. Hardly a piece of Faulkner's writing, short story or novel, does not contain numerous flashbacks. Generally the flashbacks are necessary for filling in the background because the author has begun his tale *in medias res.* Occasionally the flashbacks are employed as a means of developing an involution which carries the reader further and further into the story. *Absalom, Absalom!* and *Go Down, Moses* utilize the flashback thus. The caterpillar device is the technique of skipping ahead in the chronology of the story only to bring up the skipped portion later, as a caterpillar propels himself by moving his head forward and then bringing the rest of his body up to consolidate the gain. *Light in August* and *Sanctuary* noticeably utilize this device.

If Faulkner's style presents difficulties to his readers, then his use of recurring themes provides a convenient approach for dealing with his writing. The themes do not occur in every novel and short story, but they reappear often enough for one to be aware that Faulkner is concerned with them and that he often views them from differing vantage points.

Time and its cumulative nature is a continually reappearing theme in Faulkner. For him time was not an element which could be divided into compartments, neatly labeled, and stacked away in a closet. It was a compilation of all that a character had ever done or been or read or known. Nothing is ever lost or wasted because a character or person is the product not only of his heritage but of his past, his present, and his future. Time, for Faulkner is *IS*. No past or future exists; everything is now.

Benjy Compson typifies this theme. He was incapable of making the tense distinctions which people generally recognize. Joe Christmas was a cumulation of all his days and nights of fighting the miscegenated blood, the guilt complexes which others sought to instill in him. The Southerners—Quentin Compson, Bayard Sartoris, Gail Hightower, Emily Grierson, Ike McCaslin—could never be free of the Civil War or slavery because it was a part of the Time which is always Present. One might seek to escape time as Quentin Compson did or remain static at some moment as Gail Hightower did, but such efforts were doomed from their inception. Faulkner often viewed characters in their ability or inability to adjust to the continuum of Time. Lucas Beauchamp successfully recognized the immediacy of time without seeking to push it back or pull it forward. Thomas Sutpen could not accommodate himself to the cumulative effect of time, and in trying to obliterate the past, he was himself destroyed.

Faulkner did not avert his attention from the historic evils of the South; one recurring theme is Negro-Caucasian relationships. No novel or short story set in the South, with the possible exception of *Mosquitoes,* is free of this concern. Faulkner does not attempt to whitewash the South; he portrays all Southerners, the bigoted, the ignorant, the moderate, the intelligent, the violent, and the humane. Nowhere is the issue so squarely faced as in "The Bear" from *Go Down, Moses.* Here both sides of the issue, the idealistic and the pragmatic, are discussed. Faulkner describes the Negro-white relationship because it is an inherent factor in the milieu he has chosen for the most of his work, and a part of this complex problem is miscegenation. The McCaslin family is the principal source of Faulkner's miscegenated characters, but many other families—the Sartorises, the Sutpens—have branches composed of mixed Negroes. The miscegenated characters are almost universally counted among the ranks of the Negroes in Faulkner's work because that is the position that such unfortunate people held in the society he was depicting. The problems posed by the miscegenated character are admirably dramatized in Lucas Beauchamp, and the problems posed for the miscegenated character are apotheosized in Joe Christmas.

The problem of race relations, though he wrote much about it per se, serves Faulkner as a focal point for a broader theme with which he was greatly concerned: man's common humanity. Faulkner conceived of Man as one race, one family, and he was frequently concerned with injustices which one man inflicted upon another, and with the elements that constituted basic humanity. This theme does not make its first appearance in the Nobel Prize address of 1950, but it is a basic tenet of Faulkner's artistic philosophy, incontrovertibly appearing in "Dry September" (1931) and *Light in August* (1932). It receives its most obvious discussion in *A Fable,* published in 1954 but begun in the early forties. In some of his work, notably "The Bear" and *The Sound and the Fury,* Faulkner implies that the more primitive repre-

sentatives of the human race are near the universal elements
of man's common humanity. This idea is not prevalent in the
later works, though Faulkner maintains almost throughout his
canon a distrust of highly educated or sophisticated characters.
Faulkner has persistently stressed the idea that a man can only
do what he can with what he has, but Faulkner has constantly
affirmed that this effort will be enough to insure that man will
prevail.

William Faulkner has been one of the most successful of
American writers in the twentieth century. The current critical
interest in his literary canon attests to his popularity with scholars
and contemporary readers. Faulkner's future reputation will rest
upon a solid foundation of excellent novels and short stories. In
the opinion of this writer, the following works are among
Faulkner's best, the ones which will possess enduring popularity
because of their literary merit, and ones which will provide the
basis of Faulkner's permanent reputation. *The Sound and the
Fury* (1929) should hold its position as Faulkner's most ambitious
undertaking and his most magnificent achievement. Other superior novels are *Light in August* (1932), *Absalom, Absalom!*
(1936), *As I Lay Dying* (1929), *The Hamlet* (1940) which includes "Spotted Horses," *Go Down, Moses* (1942) which includes
"The Bear," *The Wild Palms* (1939)—especially the "Old Man"
sections. Among Faulkner's best short stories are "A Rose for
Emily" (1930), "Two Soldiers" (1942), "Turnabout" (1932),
"The Leg" (1934), "Red Leaves" (1930), "An Error in Chemistry"
(1946), "Uncle Willy" (1935), "There Was a Queen" (1933),
"That Will Be Fine" (1935), "Artist at Home" (1933), and
"Black Music" (1934). Though they are included as portions of
novels, "An Odor of Verbena" from *The Unvanquished* (1938)
and "Mule in the Yard" (1934) from *The Town* (1957) are two
of Faulkner's better short prose selections.

Table of Contents

◆◆◆◆◆◆◆◆◆◆◆◆◆◆◆◆◆◆◆◆◆◆◆◆◆◆◆◆◆◆◆◆◆◆◆◆

Novel
Commentary

◈◈◈◈◈◈◈◈◈◈◈◈◈◈◈◈◈◈◈◈◈◈◈◈◈◈

ABSALOM, ABSALOM! [1]

The South, with its tradition of castes, its ghosts of heroes and ladies, and its history of lost grandeur, is a complicated region, an intense and somewhat unrealistic frame of mind. Shreve says that the South is fine, better than the theater (p. 217), and that it is something which his people (Canadians, i.e., non-Southerners) do not have (p. 361). The novel *Absalom, Absalom!* seems dedicated to telling about the South, but Quentin Compson says, "You can't understand it. You would have to be born there" (p. 361). This attempt to explain the South is itself a complex endeavor, utilizing an involved point of view to present the story

First published New York: Random House, 1936. Quotations here (marked with page numbers in parentheses) are from the Modern Library Edition, New York: Random House, 1951.

of Thomas Sutpen and sharpening the concluding focus so that the reader becomes concerned with Quentin's relationship to the South.

In addition to the omniscient narrator who begins the telling of the novel and seems to stand in the shadows manipulating the various accounts, four other narrators are employed in the presentation of *Absalom, Absalom!* Miss Rosa Coldfield, sister of Mrs. Ellen C. Sutpen and herself the erstwhile fiancée of Thomas Sutpen, is the first narrator to tell the story. She engages Quentin to accompany her to the old Sutpen's Hundred plantation to investigate an intuition that someone is hiding there. On the afternoon before they drive out, she summons Quentin to her house and describes her family's affiliations with Thomas Sutpen and its share in his curse. Later in section five, more of the afternoon conversation (or more accurately, the monologue) is remembered by Quentin, and the reader listens as Miss Coldfield recounts her infatuation with Thomas Sutpen, and her experiences at the plantation during the Civil War. She describes her own poverty, and Sutpen's attempt to rebuild his plantation after the war. The sections which she relates emphasize her antipathy toward Thomas Sutpen and her assumption that he was accursed and that his children would suffer the consequences of his curse.

The second narrator is Mr. [Jason III] Compson, who presents details of Sutpen's background revealed to him by General Compson, Quentin's grandfather. An account of Thomas Sutpen's wedding to Ellen Coldfield is recalled; Miss Rosa's hatred for her father and for Thomas Sutpen is described with Mr. Compson's sardonic pessimism. Mr. Compson narrates the occurrence of Sutpen's building the plantation and of the Bon-Sutpen affair. These details had come to Quentin's father through the friendship of General Compson and Thomas Sutpen. Many particulars of Mr. Compson's vividly imagined account of the Bon-Sutpen conflict are contradicted later by Quentin after he has accompanied Miss Rosa to the dilapidated plantation and learned the accurate story.

Quentin is the third and most important narrator for the novel. Miss Rosa Coldfield requests him to visit in her parlor on a hot afternoon and listen to the story, then to accompany her on an evening's expedition. Later in Cambridge, in January of 1910, a letter from his father, informing him of Miss Rosa's death, stirs the memories of the Sutpen affair and causes Quentin to relate the myth to his Harvard roommate, Shreve McCannon. Many of the details presented by Mr. Compson or Miss Rosa are displayed to the reader through the device of Quentin's memory. Sometimes Quentin simply meditates on the Sutpen saga, and the reader is permitted to overhear Quentin's thoughts. At other times the reader listens as Quentin muses over the tale for the benefit of his roommate.

The fourth narrator is Shrevlin McCannon, who is intrigued with Quentin's account of the South. Shreve is employed to emphasize the delayed information which is being given to the reader. He calls attention to details which have not been revealed in any of the previous accounts of the story. He himself occasionally introduces incidents or facts implied by earlier versions but never explicitly stated, e.g., the proposition Thomas Sutpen made to Rosa Coldfield. These are usually elements that Quentin is assumed to have told Shreve in a prior discussion of the Sutpen family. But Shreve is more important as a narrator of imagined incidents in the Charles Bon-Sutpen affair. Quentin and Shreve sit in a cold dormitory room in Cambridge and imagine the conversations and events which might have occurred as Charles Bon confronted Thomas Sutpen with a devastating problem. Shreve takes the lead in this vicarious emotional conflict, and he seems to grasp the implications of the legend better than Quentin. Significantly Shreve says to Quentin at the end of the novel, "Why do you hate the South?" (p. 378).

The use of such a battery of narrators is directly related to the complexity of the story. This multiple-narrator scheme allows Faulkner to repeat the account several times, each time giving a bit of additional information; it also allows him to delay giving the complete plot, because each character-narrator is limited by his own knowledge. Quentin, of course, knows the complete story, but in his recounting of it he has to follow a limited progression so that Shreve can comprehend what is happening. The constant repetition of the tale by several character-narrators tends to become monotonous and sometimes even oppressive, but such a technique gives the story verisimilitude with the manner in which a Southerner might have learned the myth. By the end of the novel, the reader has absorbed the story, has almost breathed it in from the air. Quentin describes the process as occurring from having been born and having lived in the region of the activity, "so that what your father was saying did not tell you anything so much as it struck, word by word, the resonant strings of remembering" (p. 213).

Even though four narrators are used, the three men seem to speak with one voice. When Shreve begins to discuss the problem, Quentin thinks, "He sounds just like father" (p. 181). Later the omniscient narrator points out that the voice recounting the story "might have been either of them [Quentin or Shreve] and was in a sense both: both think as one, the voice which happened to be speaking the thought only the thinking become audible" (p. 303). Consequently the various speakers present a unified narrative.

Absalom, Absalom! is the story of Thomas Sutpen's struggle to rise from the poor white caste in which he was born to a position in the white aristocracy. Because of a snub by a plantation owner's Negro in Virginia, Sutpen determines to build himself a large plantation and to gather about him the proper accouterments of a plantation owner. He goes to the West Indies to make money, and there he marries the daughter of a sugar cane plantation owner. After the birth of their son, he discovers that his wife has some Negro blood (not Spanish as he had been told); he annuls their marriage and makes a new start in Yoknapatawpha. Finally he carves out a plantation ten miles square, builds a pretentious mansion, marries a gentlewoman, and begets a son and a daughter. But his dream is destroyed when the son by his first wife appears and courts Sutpen's daughter. This crisis causes Thomas Sutpen's white son to kill his miscegenated son, thus destroying the family which Sutpen hoped to establish. At the end of the novel, the only remaining descendant of Thomas Sutpen is Jim Bond, a moron, half-Negro great-grandson.

Thomas Sutpen encompassed many of the traits of the Southern tradition. He was associated with almost all levels of Southern society: by birth he was poor white trash; he begot miscegenated children, both within wedlock and without; he earned the wealth of the aristocratic class; and he suffered through the actions of all classes. But Sutpen was a perversion of the Southern tradition. He wanted the outward appearance of the Southern culture, but he did not appreciate the humanizing elements of the society. He was hardly more than a savage clothed in the external trappings of the Southern heritage. He was shrewd and brave, but he was possessed of an innate innocence compounded with a rough logic and a primitive sense of morality. He fails because he is naive enough to suppose that people act logically. Lacking an understanding of psychology, he assumes that material, logical factors determine the decisions of human beings. The achievement of his dream is voided by his failure to account for the human element in conflict with his design.

The short story "Wash," which is incorporated into this novel (pp. 280–292), epitomized Thomas Sutpen's lack of concern for other human beings. The plot of this incident describes Sutpen's last attempt to beget a son, and his insensate rejection of Milly Jones and her daughter because they do not happen to fit the requirements of his program. Wash Jones, from whose viewpoint

the short story version is told, finally recognizes the utter dis-
regard for human feelings which was an inherent weakness in
the Southern caste system, and he ascribes the loss of the Civil
War to this failing. This same defect arouses Wash Jones's indignation so that he kills Thomas Sutpen.

Though a weakness of the Southern tradition provides the
impetus for his plans, Sutpen does not complement the pattern
to which he aspires. In his indifference to the feelings of others,
he finds himself ostracized by society, and his obsession with
a dream precludes his successful confrontation of reality.

The story of Thomas Sutpen which Quentin tells causes Shreve
to remark that Quentin hates the South, and the final sentence of
the novel poses Quentin's struggle with the problem of his am-
bivalence toward the South. The conflict concerns the Quentin
preparing for and later attending Harvard, and the Quentin
"who was still too young to deserve yet to be a ghost, but nevertheless having to be one for all that, since he was born and bred in
the deep South" (p. 9). Quentin has to balance the tradition of
defeat which surrounds him in the South, with the realities of the
twentieth-century world. The romantic illusions of the South—
the wisteria, the roses, the magnolias—must be reconciled with
the "iron snow" of New England. For Quentin this becomes an
insurmountable problem.

This novel contains some of Faulkner's best writing, perhaps
because he was attempting to communicate many of the problems
and inconsistencies of the region with which he was most concerned. The florid descriptions and the ornate rhetorical complexity of the style engulf the reader so that he feels the weight of the
traditions and becomes enmeshed in the restrictions of the patterns. To read *Absalom, Absalom!* is to experience the heritage of
the Southerner at the beginning of the twentieth century.

AS I LAY DYING [1]

When William Faulkner states that he wrote *As I Lay Dying* as a *tour de force*,[2] the reader is prepared to accept his statement at face value. The very fact that the novel is composed of fifty-nine separate, though not always so very different, interior monologues is an evidence of its experimental nature. Nineteen of the statements are given to Darl Bundren who is the insane son of Addie and Anse Bundren. Ten more are given to the youngest child Vardaman, who is too young to comprehend exactly what is occurring, even if he does observe and record some vital information. Even though he has given a large proportion of the story to two minds—one aberrational and one immature—Faulkner is still able to so arrange the content that the complete story of the funereal trip reaches the reader with varying degrees of horror, irony, and absurdity.

The plot of *As I Lay Dying* concerns the attempt of Anse Bundren and his five children to transport the body of his late wife from their home to Jefferson, a distance of forty miles, for burial with her family. The action occurs in a very hot July over a period of a week, and it involves a series of catastrophes each one apparently capable of deterring less resolute folk. The horror of the situation is salient long before the stench and the trailing buzzards convulse the people along the road to Jefferson. The struggle to perform such a task, however, hinges upon more than obedience to a deathbed wish; and thereby Faulkner enriches the novel.

The device of using interior monologues seems a somewhat

[1] First published New York: Jonathan Cape and Harrison Smith, 1930. Subsequent references here are to the New Edition, New York: Random House, 1964.

[2] Gwynn, F. L. and J. L. Blotner, eds. *Faulkner in the University* (Vintage ed. New York, 1965), p. 87.

specious technique because in so many of the monologues the reader can feel the presence of the author telling the story; thus, the statements become simple monologues, not interior monologues. This is often true in the sections given by Darl, Cash, and by the various farmer-neighbors, except Cora. The story moves along with regularity except for the pause just after the Bundrens have crossed the river. During this digression the reader gets to hear Addie's story from her, as well as Cora's interpretation of Addie's story and Whitfield's confession of his affair with Addie. Almost all of the monologues contain dialogue which is remembered by the speaker, so that the effect of many of the monologues is virtually the same as if the first person narrator were presenting the plot.

Particularly do the monologues of Darl give evidence that the author is using him to fill in details and to enrich the story. Darl, the son of a poor hill farmer, speaks of Greek friezes (p. 211), and he accurately predicts the actions of various people, and he narrates scenes which occur in his absence. For instance, he narrates the details of Addie's death scene even though he and Jewel are quite some distance away hauling a load of lumber. Darl also presents in his speeches several of the key incidents in the novel. He relates the tale about Jewel's acquisition of the spotted horse, he tells most of the action involved in the river crossing, and he describes the burning of the barn.

The fact that Darl is insane does support the manner in which he seems supersensitive. His vision often focuses narrowly upon concrete details in a way in which the vision of others does not. For example:

The lantern sits on a stump. Rusted, grease-fouled, its cracked chimney smeared on one side with a soaring smudge of soot, it sheds a feeble and sultry glare upon the trestles and the boards and the adjacent earth. Upon the dark ground the chips look like random smears of soft pale paint on a black canvas. (p. 71)

The introspective digressions also seem appropriate to one who is mentally unbalanced. Consider:

> And since sleep is is-not rain and wind are *was*, it is not. Yet the wagon *is*, because when the wagon is *was*, Addie Bundren will not be. And Jewel *is*, so Addie Bundren must be. And then I must be, or I could not empty myself for sleep in a strange room. And so if I am not emptied yet, I am *is*. (p. 76)

On occasions Darl's monologues do reveal his own emotional stress, as in his description of Addie's death or his statements about his mother. In one he says, "I cannot love my mother because I have no mother. Jewel's mother is a horse." (p. 89)

The intuitive powers of Darl, supposedly accounted for by his madness, are attested to by other characters as well as by Darl himself. Vernon Tull expresses it thus, "It's like he had got into the inside of you, someway. Like somehow you was looking at yourself and your doings outen his eyes." (p. 119) Dewey Dell dislikes Darl because he can discern things with his eyes which others cannot know. She fears the encompassing power of his eyes.

> The land runs out of Darl's eyes; they swim to pinpoints. They begin at my feet and rise along my body to my face, and then my dress is gone; I sit naked on the seat above the unhurrying mules, above the travail. (p. 115)

If Darl gives the appearance of being a narrative tool of the author, Vardaman presents a good example of interior monologues used in a more conventional fashion. His sections generally have the disjointed, uncohesive nature of the thoughts of a young boy, frustrated and confused because he cannot comprehend the shocking events in which he is involved. The interior monologues given to Vardaman are distinctive in style and in content (as will be illustrated below).

Cora Tull's interior monologues at first seem too articulate for her character until one is told that she had been a school teacher too. (p. 11) The style and the use of Cora's utterances are characteristic of the manner in which Faulkner employs most of the interior monologues in *As I Lay Dying*. She speaks with a self-conscious remembrance of events in the past. Conversations are recalled verbatim; some of her own opinions are given, and in her case the opinions present a dramatic irony. When Darl comes in to take a final look at Addie, Cora interprets it as an expression of love. She remarks that it is Darl who has really loved Addie and for whom Addie has had a peculiar affection. Cora condemns Anse and Jewel for being avaricious and forcing Darl from his mother's deathbed. But the reader has just seen Darl arguing in favor of the lumber trip because he wants to get Jewel away before Addie dies. Cora's excessive religiosity serves as an ironic contrast to the more basic religious feelings of Addie. The religious fervor of Cora is a subject for comedy, as Vernon says:

I reckon it does take a powerful trust in the Lord to guard a fellow, though sometimes I think that Cora's a mite over-cautious, like she was trying to crowd the other folks away and get in closer than anybody else. (p. 67)

And later he says:

I reckon she's right. I reckon if there's ere a man or woman anywhere that He could turn it all over to and go away with His mind at rest, it would be Cora. And I reckon she would make a few changes. (p. 70)

Cora, and most of the other speakers, are used conventionally as first person narrators; they are conscious speakers rather than thinkers. The focus is on the details of the story which they are remembering rather than on the psychic experience of the monologuist.

Dewey Dell's monologues are often concerned with her internal emotional experience, particularly the sequence (p. 114 ff.) in which she debates whether or not to tell her father to bury Addie at New Hope. This debate has powerful personal conflict because if Anse were to bury his wife at New Hope, as Dewey Dell is confident she could persuade him to do, then Dewey Dell would miss the trip to Jefferson, where she hopes to have an abortion.

Generally the speakers are not the narrators of actions seriously important to them. It is Darl who relates the story of Jewel and his horse, the most important action for Jewel. It is Cash who narrates the capture of Darl by the officers who will escort him to the state mental institution at Jackson. Dewey Dell's attempts to purchase abortive drugs, actions in which she plays a central role, are related by the druggist and the clerk. The story of Anse's acquisition of a new wife, is narrated by Cash. Occasionally, as with Dewey Dell's account of her affair with Lafe, and Addie's account of her affair with the Rev. Whitfield, the characters do narrate an action in which they play a primary emotional role. Characters like Peabody, Tull, and Armstid narrate sequences in which they play supporting roles, but they present information about events crucial to the Bundrens. Peabody describes Addie's approaching death, Tull gives background information and recounts part of the river crossing, and Armstid explains the mule trade.

As an experimenter with the interior monologue, Faulkner has utilized in *As I Lay Dying* forms of the interior monologue varying in manner from the first person narrator type given to such characters as Tull, to the more revealing type given to Darl, Dewey Dell, and Vardaman.

An important theme in *As I Lay Dying* is the distinction between the word and the deed; this is a theme Faulkner had concerned himself with in *Mosquitoes,* before he had mastered the fictional techniques.

Addie is the most articulate character who expresses herself on the topic of words versus actions. When she discovered that she was pregnant with Cash, she learned "that words are no good; that words dont ever fit even what they are trying to say at." (p. 163) She considers Anse to be a person living by words, "He had a word, too. Love, he called it." (p. 164). And in the province of religion Addie disliked words heartily. About Cora Tull's didacticism, Addie says, "I would think how words go straight up in a thin line, quick and harmless, and how terribly *doing* [italics added] goes along the earth, clinging to it, so that after a while the two lines are too far apart for the same person to straddle from one to the other" (p. 165). And later she also comments on Cora's attempt to get her to repent her sins, "because people to whom sin is just a matter of words, to them salvation is just words too." (p. 168)

Addie distrusts words, but her daughter fears them. To Dewey Dell, words represent a truth which she wishes were not a fact. Darl says of her, "The reason you will not say it is, when you say it, even to yourself, you will know it is true" (p. 38–39).

One irony about the theme of words versus action is the fact that the purpose of going to Jefferson in the first place hangs, ostensibly, upon Anse's word, a word for which Addie seemed to have little respect. Dewey Dell makes Anse continue the trip because he had given his word.

The other children seem roughly positioned between the polarities of Anse and Addie in relation to their attitudes toward words or actions. Cash, whose first monologue consists of a rather mathematically concise list of reasons for his construction of the coffin, seems to be only slightly concerned with words but quite concerned with action. By the end of the novel, however, Cash has gradually expanded and matured until he assumes a rather philosophical role and is able to enunciate his feelings and ideas quite clearly. Concerning the sanity of Darl, he remarks:

> Sometimes I aint so sho who's got ere a right to say when a man is crazy and when he aint. Sometimes I think it aint none of us pure crazy and aint none of us pure sane until the balance of us talks him that-a way. (p. 223)

And he regrets the loss of his phonograph money in these words: "I dont know if a little music aint about the nicest thing a fellow can have" (p. 248).

Jewel, the cherished son of Addie, seems all action. Most of his statements are punctuated with violent vulgarities. He is exasperated by the plodding, wordy discussions of Anse and Darl; he is quick to make a decision and to act upon it. Dewey Dell dislikes words and wishes they were ineffective. Vardaman, the young child, has difficulty in differentiating the word and the deed. One of his monologues is, "My mother is a fish" (p. 79). But he continues to try to understand the situations in which he finds himself. Once he reasons to himself, "Then it [the fish] wasn't and she [his mother] was, and now it is and she wasn't" (p. 63). He tries to interpret his experiences but sometimes the words get confused. For example:

> He [Darl] went to Jackson. He went crazy and went to Jackson both. Lots of people didn't go crazy. Pa and Cash and Jewel and Dewey Dell and me didn't go crazy. We never did go crazy. We didn't go to Jackson either. Darl. (p. 241)

For Darl words are just one mode of communication: they are a tool. He uses them to persuade his father to send him and Jewel to haul a load of lumber; because he is jealous of the relationship between Addie and Jewel, he irritates Jewel with words; and he employs them to describe what he perceives in other people.

Anse is virtually all word. He knows that if he talks long

enough, someone will solve his problems for him. He is superiorly skilled at wheedling his neighbors in an offhanded way. Tull quite early in the novel remarks about Anse, "Like most folks around here, I done holp him so much already I cant quit now" (p. 32). But once Anse is coerced into an action, he will not easily give up. Samson says about him,

> I notice how it takes a lazy man, a man that hates moving, to get set on moving once he does get started off, the same as he was set on staying still, like it aint the moving he hates so much as the starting and the stopping. (p. 108)

And Anse does persevere in the trip to Jefferson not only because he gave Addie his word, but because he wants to get his store-bought teeth and a new wife. The actual motives for the trip contrast ironically with the espoused motive and with what the neighbors say about the actions of the Bundrens.

In *The Sound and the Fury*, which immediately preceded *As I Lay Dying*, Faulkner had created two superb interior monologues. In the latter novel, Faulkner has tested the bounds of the interior monologue. With Benjy and Quentin, he worked with the interior monologues similar to the Molly Bloom section of *Ulysses*. But in *As I Lay Dying*, Faulkner has used some monologues similar to those employed in a Virginia Woolf novel. Some of the monologues reveal almost nothing about the speaker, making him virtually a first person observer narrator; other monologues illumine the inner struggle of the speaker.

Faulkner is a writer more skilled at creating memorable characters than in portraying profound philosophical principles, and in *As I Lay Dying*, he has given life to a poor white family composed of unforgettable individuals. No transcending philosophic principle seems central in the novel, though one sees obvious allusions to the Christian religion. But the characters, in the context of the novel, do not seem imbued with significant symbolism or mythic values. *As I Lay Dying* is a horrific, grimly humorous story about realistically depicted characters.

A FABLE [1]

Rising from the same philosophical vein that produced the affirmative statements of the Nobel Prize Address, *A Fable* is a rhetorical expansion of the idea that man will not only endure, he will prevail. Begun in the early 1940's and published in the middle fifties, this work presents in an allegorical mold a secularized recapitulation of the Christ mythos. It utilizes a false armistice during World War I, to dramatize a second coming of Christ and his ineluctable second rejection by the world. For this novel, Faulkner received the Pulitzer Prize in 1955.

Structured along the pattern of the Passion Week, this novel covers, in its primary action, the activities of one week, though the biographical backgrounds span sixty or seventy years. The units composing the work do not present a strict chronological arrangement, because the author is concerned with the influence of the events on four principals: Gerald David Levine, the Corporal (Stefan), the General (Commander-in-chief of all the allied forces in Europe), and the Runner. In true accord with *in medias res* the story begins on Wednesday. The final section, "Tomorrow," lies outside the scope of the one week, but it emphasizes the influence of the theme around which that week centered.

A Fable employs an allegorical style that is rich with allusions and digressions. The Christ story is the basic metaphor of the work, but the correspondencies between characters in this work and figures in the Christian myth often involve unreligious or

---

[1] First published New York: Random House, Inc., 1954. All quotations (marked by page numbers in parentheses) are from the fifth printing of this edition.

altered details. The Corporal is the illegitimate son of the old General; he was born in a cow-byre at Christmas time thirty-three years ago; he performs miracles (of a sort); he is betrayed by one of his twelve closest followers; a final feast is served to the Corporal and his friends; he is tempted; and at his execution between two thieves, his head is accidentally pierced by a strand of barbed wire. Ironically his body becomes disinterred by a barrage of artillery as the false armistice ends, and his body is accidentally placed in the tomb of the Unknown Soldier in Paris. The old General occupies a position not so easily fitted into a niche. Because he is the Commander-in-chief and refers to everyone as "my child," he seems to represent a God-judge figure as he condemns the Corporal for mutiny. In the flight of his youth from power and riches into the desert of Africa, he tends to symbolize either Christ's departure into the wilderness or Lucifer's expulsion from heaven. When he is tempting the Corporal with liberty, power, and life, the old General seems to represent Satan. Magda and Marya, the Corporal's half-sisters are associated with Mary and Martha; the young girl of the street is associated with Mary Magdalene; other characters play roles with varying correlation to the Christian story.

The expansive digressions of the works stress its philosophical nature and comprise much of its poetic imagery. The embellishment may present a statement on the courage necessary to pity (p. 45), on man's adjustment to war (p. 124), on truth, "not even *the* truth, 'but truth,' because truth was truth" (p. 159), on politicians (p. 195), on the British lack of affinity for war, "Getting out in front armed with nothing but walking sticks, saying, 'Come along lads. That seems to be the enemy yonder and there appear to be a goodish number of them but I dare say not too many'" (p. 305), and naturally on the military "which learns nothing and forgets nothing and loses nothing at all whatever and forever—no scrap of paper, no unfinished record or uncompleted memorandum no matter how inconsequential or trivial"

(p. 240). Some of the most eloquent writing of the novel occurs in the purple patches of description which help to create the mood of timeless universality dominating the Passion Week sections of the novel. The flowing movements of masses of people receive much of Faulkner's attention, (cf. pp. 239, 186–7, and 212.) as he focuses on the power of man in action. The close of day is aptly captured in these words:

> Then the sunset gun went from the old citadel, deliberate and profound, as if a single muffled drumstick had been dropped once against the inverted bowl of hollow and resonant air, the sound fading slowly and deliberately, until at last, with no suture to mark its close, it was lost in the murmur of bunting with which the flags, bright blooms of glory myriad across the embattled continent, sank, windless again, down (p. 138)

As Faulkner describes the cavalry's dispersal of a crowd, he develops virtually a Homeric simile, so convoluted and so long continued is this particular description (p. 243). This constant use of digressions retards the progress of the story and creates a mosaic effect which diffuses the impact of the work.

The most impassioned writing of the novel, however, is reserved for the philosophical discussions in which the central theme of the novel is propounded. *A Fable* is a panegyric to Man, the mass of humanity, and it counterpoises the mass of common man against the hierarchy which forces man to follow patterns of order conceived by the ruling group. The attitudes of the four chief characters toward Man, and their varying abilities to understand Man differentiate the facets of this theme.

Gerald David Levine, is an eighteen-year-old British pilot fired by the young man's desire for glory. The false armistice occurs before David has flown his first combat mission, and he fears that the war is over; consequently, he feels that his opportunity to prove himself and to perform that for which he has been trained has been voided. His disappointment at having lost his potential military glory is compounded when he realizes the duplicity of the generals—American, British, French, and German—in deceiving the fighting men concerning the conference occurring at Chaulnesmont. But Levine does not understand the deeper implications; he does not recognize the larger issues generated by the mutiny of the French regiment; he is concerned with the surface problems, with his personal disillusionment. Because he cannot adjust to the peace he thinks the false armistice has engendered, he commits suicide.

The Corporal who perpetrated the action labeled as a mutiny understood fully the seriousness of the action he was leading. He recognized that the issue was not the mutiny of three thousand men, but the prevention of "naked and weaponless hand touching opposite naked and weaponless hand" (p. 327). The generals could do nothing except try to prevent the confederation of soldiers with opposing soldiers into a warless brotherhood of Man, which would destroy the precarious position of the generals. The Corporal perceived the need of recognizing Man's common humanity, and he saw the power that such a union might represent. He knew also that such a compassionate federation would not, could not, be permitted by the authorities of order and civilization. He did not, however, flinch to accept the gambit nor cringe before the consequence. The Corporal, though providing the impetus for almost all of the novel's action, does not participate in the moral discussions of the novel except during his temptation scene (pp. 340–354), where he does little more than reply to the extended comments of the old General.

The most eloquent spokesman in the novel is the old General, the Commander-in-chief of all the allied forces in Europe. He is the scion of a wealthy, influential family, the last male heir to a complex of powerful affiliations. Perhaps better than any other character he understands the implications of the situation in which he finds himself opposing the Corporal. He says that he is the "champion of this mundane earth" (p. 348), the advocate of fact and reality, and that the corporal is the "champion of an esoteric realm of man's baseless hopes and his infinite capacity— no: passion—for unfact" (p. 348). The old General says further "we are two articulations, self-elected possibly, anyway elected, anyway postulated, not so much to defend as to test two inimical conditions" (p. 347). He does not deprecate the Corporal's dedication to the brotherhood of man, and he recognizes that by ordering the Corporal's death, he (the General) "will establish forever that he [the Corporal] didn't even live in vain, let alone die so" (p. 332).

Of several characters who believe in the immortality of man, the old General is the one who states his faith most trenchantly. He says, "I know that he [Man] has that in him which will enable him to outlast even his wars" (p. 352). And in a passage reminiscent in wording of the Nobel Prize Acceptance Speech, the old General states his pride and respect for man "Because man and his folly. . . . They will prevail" (p. 354).

The final character of chief importance to the novel is the Runner, a British military courier, who resigned his officer's commission to become again a common soldier so that he could cure himself of "having to perform forever at inescapable intervals that sort of masturbation about the human race people call hoping" (p. 62). But he is unsuccessful. His optimism carries him into a relationship with Rev. Sutterfield of the *Les Amis Myriades et Anonymes à la France de Tout le Monde,* a relationship by which Sutterfield and the British sentry (Mistairy) meet their death as they and the Runner attempt to lead a peace movement from the British trenches. The Runner appreciates the problem posed for the authorities by the French mutiny. He recognizes that "If they ever let us find out that we can stop a war as simply as men tired of digging a ditch decide calmly and quietly to stop digging the ditch" (p. 311), then "the whole theory of arbitration, the whole tried and proven step-by-step edifice of politics and economy on which the civilised concord of nations is based be-

comes so much wind" (p. 79–80). But the Runner cannot conquer his faith in the ultimate victory of the brotherhood of man
over nationalism. The final scene depicts his disruption of the
old General's funeral near the tomb of the Unknown Soldier by
shouting that faith at the body of the man who had opposed it.

The story of the three-legged race horse (pp. 151–189), published separately as *Notes on a Horsethief* in 1950, has little to do
with the story of the peace mutiny in France in 1918, but it has a
great deal to do with the tribute to Man which constitutes the
major theme of the novel. Rev. Tobe Sutterfield who aided Harry
(Mistairy), the English groom, in his theft of the crippled racehorse, is a potent advocate of man's endurance. He bears witness
to man; he acknowledges the evil inherent in man, but he adds,
"Some day something might beat him, but it wont be Satan"
(p. 180). This background sketch also stresses the power of man.
The New Orleans lawyer meditates upon the peaceful Missouri
mob and thinks that "on his own feet and in motion, he [man]
is terrible" (p. 186) and that the giant leaders of men, Caesar,
Christ, Bonaparte, et al., had been motivated by man himself and
by the thought of just "putting some of him in one motion in one
direction" (p. 181). Particularly does the confederation of silence
have a similarity to the concerted, voluntary peace movement
among the soldiers in the trenches. The common people in the
rural areas in which the horse ran its races joined in a tacit agree-
ment to protect the horse thieves. Perhaps because the people
believed that the purpose of the theft, to keep the horse pure for
running as long as it lived, was a worthwhile motive; no one in
the regions of the races had ever heard of or seen a three-legged
racehorse or an English groom or his two Negro companions, a
fact that frustrated local and state police, the vaunted F.B.I., and
even private investigators, a fact which demonstrates Man's capacity for mutual action unforced by higher authority.

A Fable reveals an artistic vitality comparable to some of Faulkner's early and best works, *The Sound and the Fury,* and *Light*

in August; the skillful manipulation of several points of view, the rich poetic descriptions, the prose reflecting in complexity the thought it conveys, all of these are typical of Faulkner's better work. The work suffers, however, from the innate potency of the metaphor on which it is based. The Christ myth is yet too powerful in its own right to be very successfully employed as a supporting device. The story of Christ is still so potent a factor in the imagination of literate man that it tends to dominate and overshadow that piece of literature which attempts to use it. The literary work tends to conform to the myth rather than to find the myth a pliant tool. Another weakness of the novel is that the inclusion of digressions on minute details tends to obscure, at any given moment, the overall pattern of the work. Nevertheless, this novel ranks with the best of Faulkner's work.

GO DOWN, MOSES [1]

Go Down, Moses is being treated as a novel in this work because William Faulkner considered it a novel.[2] Admittedly six of the seven parts were published separately, usually in quite different versions from their *Go Down, Moses* forms. Each part is rather self-contained, generally being filled with adequate genealogical references to sketch the background for a person reading only a single story. But none of the chapters gives Faulkner's complete statement; none alone adequately develops the broad themes with which Faulkner is working. *Go Down, Moses* is a chronicle covering five generations of the McCaslin family. It is also a rather explicit statement on race relations and misce-

---

[1] New York: Random House Inc., 1942. All *Go Down, Moses* quotations are from this edition and are hereafter noted in the text by page numbers in parentheses immediately following the quotations.

[2] Frederick L. Gwynn and Joseph L. Blotner, eds. *Faulkner in the University* (New York: Vintage Books Division of Random House, 1965), p. 4.

genation. Isaac McCaslin, representing the white male line of the McCaslin family, is one of Faulkner's most emphatic spokesmen, and though Ike, as he philosophically struggles with attitudes toward God, race, and tradition, has difficulty understanding himself in "The Bear," he becomes much more lucid in "Delta Autumn." Lucas Beauchamp, representing the miscegenated McCaslin line, is a character personifying independence, courage, and personal dignity, though he also personifies the Negro's evasiveness plus an uncanny shrewdness. The Edmonds family, which rather apologetically traces its McCaslin lineage through L. Q. C. McCaslin's unnamed daughter, seems representative of the paternalistic, conventional Southern aristocracy. The leaders of this family line (Cass, Zack, and Roth Edmonds) do not make difficult moral decisions; they maintain the status quo, keep the McCaslin estate solvent, and make material progress.

As the title and the dedication imply, this novel is a tribute to the Southern Negro, to his innate virtues, and to his latent strength. This panorama is presented against the Yoknapatawpha backdrop and the action covers over one hundred years. The style is varied to suit the people and incidents of a given chapter. Pronouncements, ironies, and depictions assume an added richness when viewed within the scope of the entire work. Although there is not a contrapuntal balancing of part against part, each chapter reflects facets of those which have preceded and leads the reader into deeper involvement with the central concerns.

Was[3] The first chapter of *Go Down, Moses* begins with a description of Isaac McCaslin near the end of his life: "Isaac McCaslin, 'Uncle Ike,' past seventy and nearer eighty than he ever corroborated any more, a widower now and uncle to half a county and father to no one" (p. 3). Then the scene shifts imme-

---

[3] First published in *Go Down, Moses* (1942).

diately to 1859, before Ike was born and focuses on Theophilus (Ike's father) and Amodeus McCaslin, and Carothers McCaslin Edmonds, their nine-year-old orphaned nephew.

Though "the boy" (Cass) does not actually narrate the story, the omniscient narrator presents the experience as it appeared to Cass. His observations and reactions provide a more immediate point of view and offer opportunities for the insertion of humorous comments. The title seems appropriate because this action, a part of Ike's past, is related to him by Cass.

The story is structured along the pattern of a fox hunt. The quarry, in this instance Tomey's Turl, has run away from the McCaslin plantation to Warwick, the Beauchamp plantation, to court a young Negress, Tennie Beauchamp. Using hounds and horses, Theophilus (Uncle Buck) and Cass give chase. Though Tomey's Turl is nearly white and half McCaslin, he is not free and the McCaslin twins, over sixty, offer to sell him to Hubert Beauchamp to end the periodic chases. Apparently what the brothers wish to end is the danger that one of them may be tricked into marrying Miss Sophonsiba Beauchamp about whom Cass's grandmother (sister to Buck and Buddy) had remarked, "Miss Sophonsiba had matured into a fine-looking woman once" (p. 10). Before the capture of Tomey's Turl, Uncle Buck's accident in Miss Sophonsiba's bedroom precipitates a crisis. Only Uncle Buddy's poker skill against Hubert Beauchamp rescues Uncle Buck, and in the process Buddy also wins Tennie Beauchamp, thus ending the chase permanently.

"Was" presents a portrait of plantation life in which the owners are kindly disposed toward the slaves, but certainly both the owners and the Negroes exist in a state of moral primitivism. The clever humor, deriving from the situation and the young observer, dominates the scene, diverting the reader from more serious considerations. But the drama has begun.

The Fire and the Hearth[4]   Composed of three separate but
related incidents which occur in 1941 when Lucas Beauchamp is
sixty-seven, "The Fire and the Hearth" continues the family saga
and fills in the background with some information not before
given. This long narrative focuses on Lucas, grandson of L. Q. C.
McCaslin, and presents his relationships with Zachary (Zack)
Edmonds and Carothers (Roth) Edmonds. Told by an omniscient narrator, the story's three incidents each contribute something different to the characterization of Lucas and provide additional information about the miscegenated family ties.

Chapter One describes Lucas's shrewdness at operating an
illegal whisky still and his unsuccessful attempt to eliminate
George Wilkins, his competitor. But sandwiched into one of
Lucas's recollections is the story of Zack Edmonds's loss of his
wife and his appropriating Lucas's wife Molly as nurse for his
child, and perhaps as mistress. After almost six months, Lucas
demands his wife back. All of this digression bears upon the
story at hand because it is to Roth Edmonds, the child Molly
delivered of Mrs. Zack Edmonds forty-three years earlier, that
Lucas goes for help in removing George Wilkins. This section
stresses the sense of personal dignity, the right to independence,
and the lack of deference which stem from the McCaslin blood
Lucas had inherited from his grandfather.

Chapter Two is basically a humorous story of Lucas Beauchamp's ability to outwit a smart salesman. The plot revolves
around a money-finding machine. Humor derives from Lucas's
manipulations of other people's resources. The story reveals the
equanimity with which Lucas meets seemingly insurmountable
problems.

The final chapter of "The Fire and the Hearth" firmly unifies

---

[4] First published in *Go Down, Moses* (1942). Includes "Gold Is Not Always"
from *Atlantic*, CLXVI (November 1940), 563–70; and "A Point of Law" from
Collier's, CV (June 22, 1940), 20 ff.

the history of the white McCaslin relatives and their black kin. This incident focuses ostensibly on Aunt Molly Beauchamp's desire for a divorce from Lucas after a happy marriage of forty-five years. Roth's tender concern for Aunt Molly is explained by the fact that she was the only mother he ever knew. She was the one who tried to teach him "to be gentle with his inferiors, honorable with his equals, generous to the weak and considerate of the aged, courteous, truthful and brave to all" (p. 117). As Roth Edmonds frets over the divorce question, the omniscient narrator digresses into the history of the problem, posed partially by Lucas Beauchamp's rather insolent flouting of paternalistic authority. The story of Lucius Quintus Carothers McCaslin's begetting miscegenated children is mentioned, as are the accounts of the settlements made to the three miscegenated grandchildren. Allusions are made to the relinquishment of the family estate by Isaac McCaslin, an action which Ike seems to regret slightly as he settles Lucas's inheritance.

But the emotional peak of the chapter occurs as "the old haughty ancestral pride based not on any value but on an accident of geography, stemmed not from courage and honor but from wrong and shame, descended to [Roth Edmonds]" (p. 111). Henry Beauchamp, son of Lucas and Molly born immediately before Roth, was the constant childhood companion of Carothers Edmonds. But ultimately Roth realized that a line must be drawn between them, and this sequence concerns the anguish Roth suffers in asserting the boundary. Zachary tries to explain the situation to Roth, but neither fully understands. After this important statement on race relations and family associations, the narrative moves into the court scene where Lucas's independent spirit and misunderstanding cause the spectators to consider him insolent. The story closes as Lucas reaffirms his love for Molly with a symbolic action.

The title for this section of *Go Down, Moses* is taken from the fire which Lucas lighted on the hearth the night he and Molly married, a fire that was kept burning for the duration of their lives, a fire that symbolized their viable love. This part of the novel reveals a little more of the injustice between races, with which the book is greatly concerned, and depicts the strength of character in Lucas and Molly.

Pantaloon in Black[5] This chapter is not as closely related to the primary concerns of the novel as the other chapters are, and thus it weakens the unity of the novel. But it does provide a study in ironic contrasts which reflect favorably upon some characters in the other parts of the novel. The title is an allusion to a comic figure of the *commedia dell'arte,* Pantalone, who was active in burlesques of young couples in love. That point of reference makes the sorrow of the central character even more poignant.

The plot recounts the self-destructive actions of Rider, a grief-crazed twenty-four-year-old Negro. The opening scene is the funeral of Mannie, Rider's wife of six months. After the funeral, Rider returns to the cabin rented from Carothers Edmonds, where he beholds her silent apparition. He expresses a death wish, which he unconsciously proceeds to execute as he finds no satisfaction in work, in liquor, or in gambling. His problem, as he states it, is "Hit look lack Ah just cant quit thinking. Look lack Ah just cant quit" (p. 159). But his thinking is stopped for him when he is lynched by the relatives of the crooked gambler he has killed.

The final part of the story is related by a deputy sheriff who, for political considerations, justifies permitting the lynching. This chapter is a portrait of the love between Mannie and Rider (who had followed Lucas Beauchamp's example by lighting a fire on his own hearth), and it is a condemnation of the unjust members of a white society which fails to recognize the humanity of a Negro.

---

[5] First published in *Harper's,* CLXXXI (October 1940), 503–13.

The Old People[6]   The Old People are the ancestors of Sam Fathers, the Chickasaw chiefs who hunted the land. Out of an awareness of the harmony existing between the Old People and the land, young Isaac McCaslin came to feel that he was the guest and "Sam Fathers's voice the mouthpiece of the host" (p. 171).

This chapter of *Go Down, Moses* presents the initiation of Ike McCaslin into the world of adult hunters, and it begins the explanation of the process which causes him to make the moral choice he does on his twenty-first birthday.

As Ike, age twelve, kills his first deer, Sam Fathers who has sponsored him and taught him woodcraft, performs the rites which symbolize his physical maturity, the rites which resemble the puberty initiation rites common in primitive cultures. "The boy did that—drew the head back and the throat taut and drew Sam Fathers' knife across the throat and Sam stooped and dipped his hands in the hot smoking blood and wiped them back and forth across the boy's face" (p. 164).

This narrative sequence gives prime attention to Sam Fathers and his background. The story of Ikkemotubbe, who is here named as Sam Fathers's father,[7] is presented. When Ike is nine, Sam Fathers moves to the big woods to live. Ike understands that "the exigencies of his maturing, of that for which Sam had been training him all his life some day to dedicate himself, required it" (p. 173).

After Ike has earned his place as a hunter, Sam takes him into a dense stretch of woods where they observe a buck so large, so magnificent that it seems the spirit of the wilderness. Sam Fathers greets it with the words, "Oleh, Chief, . . . Grandfather" (p. 184). McCaslin Edmonds, the cousin who manages the McCaslin estate, also advises Ike that the only thing worse than

---

[6] First published *Harper's*, CLXXXI (September 1940), 418–25. Also included in *Big Woods* (1955).

[7] Cf. Ikkemotubbe in Dictionary of Characters.

death is shame. Ike is a young boy in this story, yet his keenness and perception already exceed those of a foil, Boon Hogganbeck, a hunter-buffoon whose grandmother had been a Chickasaw woman.

This chapter of the work explicitly discusses the theme of the primitive and the civilized. Sam representing the primitive life is juxtaposed with McCaslin Edmonds representing the conventionalized society. Cass says of Sam, "When he was born, all his blood on both sides, except the little white part, knew things that had been tamed out of our blood so long ago that we have not only forgotten them, we have to live together in herds to protect ourselves from our own sources" (p. 167). These are the two traditions which meet in Isaac McCaslin and from which he must attempt to meld a viable code of life.

The Bear[8]   "The Bear" is a story of a boy becoming a man; the story of a man making a difficult moral decision; the story of a hunt; the story of a doomed and vanishing wilderness; and it is a statement, clothed in an agonized bombast and fustian, of philosophical attitudes toward God, the Civil War, the South, and the Negro race. It is an affirmation of the virtues: pride, humility, compassion, pity. It is a criticism of the modern world and its society. It is a proclamation that the universal truths which underlie the civilized world are the primitive values.

The story is divided into five rather self-contained sections, each concluding an important chapter in Isaac McCaslin's life and each neatly closing with a peak of emotional intensity. Section one ends dramatically with Ike's meeting the bear. "It did not emerge, appear: it was just there, immobile, fixed in the green and windless noon's hot dappling, not as big as he had dreamed it but as

[8] First published *The Saturday Evening Post*, CCXIV (May 9, 1942), 30 ff. Also included in *Big Woods* (1955).

big as he had expected, bigger, dimensionless against the dappled obscurity, looking at him" (p. 209). Section two concludes with thoughts about the culmination of an era. "It was the beginning of the end of something, he didn't know what except that he would not grieve. He would be *humble and proud* that he had been found worthy to be a part of it too or even just to see it too" (p. 226. Italics added). Immediately following the magnificent scene in which Old Ben dies, section three ends as McCaslin questions Boon Hogganbeck about the death of Sam Fathers, and Ike exclaims, "Leave him alone . . . . Goddamn it! Leave him alone!" (p. 254).

Section four, the crucial philosophical section, closes as Ike, a Christ figure, resists the sexual temptation his wife offers hoping to entice him to take back his patrimony. She says, 'And that's all. That's all from me. If this dont get you that son you talk about, it wont be mine:' lying on her side, her back to the empty rented room, laughing and laughing" (p. 315). Reflecting ironically on the ideas Ike struggles with in section four, the final section concludes with Boon Hogganbeck's petty shout, "Get out of here! Dont touch them [squirrels trapped in a gum tree]! Dont touch a one of them! They're mine!" (p. 331).

Beginning with Ike at the age of ten, the action moves in a roughly chronological pattern through the story, except that section five which occurs when Ike is eighteen follows section four which occurs when he is twenty-one (and older). No section is completely apportioned by the chronology of the action because the omniscient narrator is continually inserting comments about incidents which occurred before or after the action which he is describing at the moment. This is a reflection of the author's attitude toward time. He seems to consider that all time is present, that one is the accumulation of all that is in his past, and that an author is justified in referring to any past action or to any future action which may be influenced by what he is at the moment narrating. The principal concern of the final section is the

destruction of the wilderness and man's petty attempt to circum-
scribe it and to possess it. The statements of the concluding section reflect appropriately on the pronouncements of Ike in section
four.

"The Bear" is a story of initiation, but it is not an initiation of
the same sort performed in "The Old People." This initiation has
the trappings of an introduction into problems more complicated,
more difficult to solve than those of just being an honorable
hunter. The earlier rite denoted physical skill and maturity, but
this experience is an extension of responsibility to include psychological and mental maturity.

As a maturing experience, this bear story is rife with Christian
symbolism, less inverted than that which often occurs in Faulkner's work. The very name of the central figure alludes to Judaic-
Christian history, to sacrifice, and to an early Christ-figure. Ike
"entered his novitiate to the true wilderness with Sam beside
him" (p. 195), and Sam (Samuel) anoints Ike with the blood
of his first deer. Isaac McCaslin goes into the wilderness to gain
strength and to acquire bravery, patience, humility, and pride.
Sam explains that, like people, the bitch who is severely clawed
by Old Ben knew that she would have to be brave once so that
she could continue to call herself a dog, even though she knew
that she would suffer for her bravery. He also cautions Ike, "Be
scared. You cant help that. But dont be afraid" (p. 207). Ike
strives to patiently await the approval of the wilderness, and he
considers "the long life which he had already dedicated to the
wilderness with patience and humility" (p. 199). Ike wishes to
learn "humility and pride in order to become skillful and worthy
in the woods" (p. 295), and the fyce becomes for him a symbol of
these two paradoxical virtues joined.

The fourth section, which Faulkner said should be deleted
when "The Bear" is published as a short story,[9] depends heavily

[9] Gwynn and Blotner, *Faulkner in the University*, p. 4.

upon the Christian symbolism of the wilderness experience. Not only does Ike refer to himself as chosen (p. 299), but he says that "Sam Fathers set me free" (p. 300). And Ike becomes a carpenter in emulation of Christ (p. 309).

Perhaps the richest passages of the entire novel appear in section four of "The Bear." The themes are all bound tightly together here, and Isaac becomes a spokesman enunciating wide-ranging philosophical statements which have importance for this novel as well as for the Faulkner canon. The full story of Lucius Quintus Carothers McCaslin's affair with his Negro mistress, Eunice, and his incestuous relationship with the daughter Eunice bore him are recorded here. The problems of slavery and race relations as Theophilus and Amodeus McCaslin, Ike's father and his father's twin, tried to solve them are posed. It is against these burdens, curses as Ike calls them, that he partially rebels.

In an abstruse prose, Ike tries to explain to McCaslin Edmonds all that is involved in Isaac's repudiation of the patrimony. Ike feels that the land cannot be possessed and held for a single man or a single family. He states that God [Ike calls God He] intended for man "to hold the earth mutual and intact in the communal anonymity of brotherhood" (p. 257). He explains that God had given man a second chance in the New World on the condition that man evince pity and humility and sufferance and endurance. But man failed, or at least the white Southerner failed. "Apparently they can learn nothing save through suffering, remember nothing save when underlined in blood" (p. 286). He thinks that God aroused the North and used the Civil War as a punishment to quicken the Southerners whom he says believed "that all necessary to conduct a successful war was not acumen nor shrewdness nor politics nor diplomacy nor money nor even integrity and simple arithmetic but just love of land and courage" (p. 289). And McCaslin adds "And an unblemished and gallant ancestry and the ability to ride a horse" (p. 289). Isaac goes on to condemn the Negroes, irresponsible in their freedom, and the carpetbag reconstruction which engendered hatred and ill will more virulent than the evil it presumed to cure.

Hubert Fitz-Hubert Beauchamp, Isaac McCaslin's maternal uncle, is presented as a portrait of the decaying Southern aristocracy. For a legacy to Ike, Hubert Beauchamp had filled a silver cup with gold pieces and sealed its burlap container with his ring. Changes in financial conditions, however, overpowered Hubert so that when Ike upon his twenty-first birthday opened the burlap bag, he discovered a tin coffee pot filled with I. O. U.'s and a few copper coins. This is a powerful image of the moral bankruptcy which Ike had to battle.

Luckily the heritage from his father had been more valuable. Theophilus and Amodeus had begun freeing slaves in the 1830's; but neither they nor the former slaves could solve the problem of race relations. Ike felt that the land was cursed because of its misuse and because of the social injustice perpetrated by his predecessors. Consequently he rejects his patrimony, "repudiating immolation" (p. 283), seeking to disavow himself of any conscious part in further oppression, until perhaps the curse will be lifted.

Ike's renunciation of his patrimony is an attempt to transcend that portion of his tradition which offends his moral sensitivity, to seek an earlier set of values from an undefiled time. The conscience which leads him to such a decision also brings him to a recognition which Ike himself describes as a heresy: "They [Negroes] are better than we are. Stronger than we are. Their vices are vices aped from white men" (p. 294). He continues to list their virtues: endurance, pity, tolerance, forbearance, fidelity, love of children. He seems to conceive of them as better because they are more primitive, more innately *human*, nearer to the sources of creation. Isaac associates the Negro with Sam Fathers and Old Ben as being more free than the white man (p. 295), precisely through their primitivism. But Ike is not rejecting his contemporary world while seeking the past. He is rather saying that the valuable traits of man are those which are so basic that even the primitive has them, and he decries the fact that the facade of civilization sometimes obscures them.

But the wilderness which gave Ike an opportunity to develop a code of ethics is rapidly vanishing. The narrator describes it as "that doomed wilderness whose edges were being constantly and punily gnawed at by men with plows and axes" (p. 193). The bear, Old Ben, becomes an "apotheosis of the old wild life" (p. 193), and at the end of an era the bear is killed. A few pages before the death scene, the narrator relates, "It would have to be Lion, or somebody. It would not be Boon" (p. 235), who could hit nothing except an occasional squirrel with his gun. But it is Boon who kills Old Ben with a knife and with the aid of Lion. Boon seems to have been a fitting character for the task because he too, like Old Ben and Lion, that great, indifferent blue dog, is a primitive figure. His Indian blood, small amount as it is, gives him an affinity to Sam Fathers and the wilderness; his naivete and lack of mental development also contribute to his primitive characterization. The knife itself is an instrument more primitive than the gun. In section five, Ike and Boon make a final hunting trip to the big woods. Already, however, the logging crews are moving in, and no longer is the life there epitomized by a bear or even a deer, but it is to a six-foot rattle snake that Isaac now says, "Chief . . . Grandfather" (p. 330). Boon's useless gun and his greedy attempt to keep the tree full of squirrels for himself demonstrate the futility of trying to preserve the wilderness from the path of progress and the unworthiness of trying to possess it.

By the end of "The Bear" the reader has been made aware of the full history of the McCaslin-Edmonds-Beauchamp family and has observed the struggles to maintain equilibrium in a society of changing standards. Ike has rationalized an unexpected and unconventional decision with ideas and words which he is not

quite sure he himself understands (p. 288). He is, however, acting with courage and humility, and later chapters of *Go Down,
Moses* offer clarifications of these ideas.

Delta Autumn[10]   After a long journey, the blood of L. Q. C.
McCaslin comes full circle in "Delta Autumn" as James Beauchamp's granddaughter bears Carothers (Roth) Edmonds a son.
This chapter of *Go Down, Moses* neatly balances Isaac McCaslin's positive attitude with the continuing cycle of social injustices.

Uncle Ike, now nearly eighty years old, speaks very plainly
about the philosophy which has sustained him through most of
his life, the philosophy that he tried to explain on his twenty-first
birthday. The brutalities of World War II are imminent though
the U. S. does not yet seem to be involved. Concerning America,
Ike says, "This country is a little mite stronger than any one man
or group of men, outside of it or even inside of it either" (p.
338). The war talk is used partially as a sham for the rankling
personal dissatisfaction Roth feels as a result of his relationship
with the nearly-white Negro girl. As Ike muses on the contrast
between the wilderness of his younger days and the woods in
which they now hunt, he says, "There are good men everywhere,
at all times. Most men are. Some are just unlucky, because most
men are a little better than their circumstances give them a
chance to be" (p. 345). Though Ike has personally seen much
of the weakness of man and even has had to struggle against an
inheritance of injustice, he affirms, "I still believe. I see proof
everywhere. I grant that man made a heap of his circumstances,
him and his living neighbors between them. He even inherited
some of them already made, already almost ruined even" (p. 347).
As Ike lies meditating during the night, he suddenly realizes
why he has never desired to own any of the wilderness, never
wanted to "arrest at least that much of what people called prog-

---

[10] First published *Story*, XX (May–June, 1942), 46–55. Also included in *Big
Woods* (1955).

ress" (p. 354). It is because he conceives of himself and the wilderness as coevals whose spans are simultaneously running together, "not toward oblivion, nothingness, but into a dimension free of both time and space" (p. 354).

But Isaac receives a disconcerting shock when he realizes that the woman with whom Roth has had an affair and on whom he has gotten a son has Negro blood and some of old L. Q. C. McCaslin's blood. He recognizes that no marriage between two such persons can yet be accepted in America. As an acknowledgement of their common heritage, Ike gives the girl the silver bound hunting horn he had inherited from General Compson. He thinks that the people who destroyed the woods will achieve the woods' revenge upon themselves and mankind. Although both Roth and the Negress are victims of their society, the Negress will endure sustained by her love, while Roth will suffer alone. The family chronicle and the theme of race relations fuse boldly as Ike tells the Negress that she will have to wait a while, maybe a long while yet, but he hopes such injustices will be overcome in the future.

Go Down, Moses[11] The final chapter of *Go Down, Moses,* the chapter from which the novel takes its name, recounts the story of Samuel Worsham (Butch) Beauchamp's execution and burial. The omniscient narrator focuses on Mollie Worsham Beauchamp, wife of Lucas Beauchamp and grandmother of the executed criminal. Mollie's abiding love for the grandson impels her to approach Gavin Stevens, County Attorney, and request that he find her Benjamin, whom she considers sold into slavery.

Although Mollie's love is the central concern of the story, the author also stresses the paternalistic Gavin Stevens' ability to cajole the members of the conventional society, the men around the square, into giving financial aid toward bringing the body

---

[11] First published *Collier's,* CVII (January 25, 1941), 19–20 ff.

of an executed murderer home for burial to please an old Negress. Importantly his appeal is also based on the idea that the gesture is for Miss Belle Worsham. The close relationship between white owners and former slaves is emphasized in the concern of Miss Belle for Mollie's feelings. The two of them are the same age and actually "grew up together as sisters would" (p. 375). When Mollie took Butch, she named him after Miss Belle's father.

Samuel W. Beauchamp himself seems to imply that the Negro, shut out of the acceptable society will develop an affinity for crime and the underworld where he can be accepted for his skill and lack of moral impediments. Mollie's affection for Butch demonstrates the Negro's enduring love which is not shaken by the attitudes of society.

Though Gavin Stevens is described as a highly-educated, sensitive, intelligent person, he lacks credibility. Compared with other characters in the work, especially characters (like Roth Edmonds) who have closer ties to Mollie Beauchamp, Gavin seems unrealistically excessive and adolescently altruistic in his sympathy.

The title of this chapter alludes to the freeing of an oppressed people from bondage, and that is the primary concern of the entire novel.

The complete novel is a mosaic and some of the bits glitter more brightly than others. "The Bear" reflects the most brilliant highlights. The final chapter, unfortunately, emits a dull utilitarian glow because it comprises less intense drama than other sections as it rounds out the cyclic story and brings the reader back to mundane events contemporaneous with the composition of the work.

The injustice of the white man's treatment of the Negro is the primary concern of the novel. In forcefully stating the Negroes' case, the author has glorified their position (as he glorified Col. Sartoris's activities in some of the earlier short stories). The Negro characters are depicted as being more compassionate, more self-confidently humble, and more enduring—in short, more noble than their white counterparts (except Ike). The Negroes are consistently more admirable than any other group of characters in the novel. In *Go Down, Moses* Faulkner has employed his fictional artistry to portray realistic characters struggling dramatically with the tremendous problems of human relationships.

THE HAMLET[1]

For the first time, Faulkner, in *The Hamlet,* devotes an entire book to the depiction of the Snopes family and snopesism in practice. References to the Snopeses and their chicanery occurred earlier in *Sartoris* (1929) and *The Unvanquished* (1938). This novel contrasts snopesism with a leitmotif of sexuality. Because it lacks the technical complexity of some earlier Faulkner fiction, *The Hamlet* appears deceptively simple, though it comprises some of Faulkner's most skillful writing.

The central figure of *The Hamlet* is Flem Snopes; the novel recounts his rise from the ranks of the poor white trash, even from the position as the son of a barn burner, to a place of relative affluence. His name becomes, by the end of the work, synonymous with shrewd business dealings. Snopesism takes its name principally from Flem's clever manipulations. One infers from *The Hamlet* that snopesism is the practice of meticulous adroitness in financial dealings of all types; it often involves actions which are unethical though just within the limits of the law. To successfully perpetrate snopesism, one must be close-mouthed, tight-fisted, and unsusceptible to emotional appeal of any sort. A practitioner of snopesism does not hesitate to employ

[1] First published New York: Random House, Inc., 1940. A second edition was published in 1956. Quotations in this discussion are from the third edition, published in 1964, and are marked by page numbers in parentheses.

any means to gain a profit so long as that tactic does not expose him to legal action. The snopesist preys upon the greed of his fellow men, and while his schemes work well upon the innocently unsuspecting individual, they work even better upon the avaricious person who believes that he is himself about to outwit the snopesist and make a large financial gain.

Flem was not, however, the first person to practice the economic policy which he represents. V. K. Ratliff, who is an important commentator upon much of the action and a prime participant in the remainder, says of Will Varner, "Snopes can come and Snopes can go, but Will Varner looks like he is fixing to snopes forever. Or Varner will Snopes forever—take your pick" (p. 162). Will Varner has become the owner of almost everything in Frenchman's Bend by being an ardent snopesist. Even V. K. Ratliff, the genial sewing machine salesman, is no amateur at the game. But Flem is simply better at the maneuver than anyone who matches wits with him. Flem supersedes Jody Varner in the process with only half an effort. Will Varner, who has had forty or fifty years of experience is more difficult to surpass, but because Flem is willing to marry Eula when she is pregnant with an illegitimate child, he gains an advantage over Varner. His superiority over both Will Varner and V. K. Ratliff is demonstrated finally by his management of the Frenchman's Place. Will Varner claimed that it was the only thing he ever bought that he could not sell. But after Will deeded it to Flem and Eula as a wedding gift, Flem turned it to financial gain by playing one of the oldest swindling tricks in the history of man. He utilized the salted gold mine ploy on Ratliff, who should have known better, and on Odum Bookwright, who followed Ratliff's lead, and on Henry Armstid, who was mentally deranged. Following such a successful coup, Flem moved on to Jefferson and greener fields via Ratliff's traded partnership in a side-street restaurant.

If non-Snopeses were in danger from Flem's maneuvers,

Snopeses themselves were no safer. None of the Snopeses except Flem seems able to prosper by himself, and those who cross Flem are destined for some undesirable fate as Mink Snopes was to learn. Eck who does not react with the conscienceless candor of a true Snopes is spurned by other Snopeses. Though the basic story of "Barn Burning" is repeated in Book One of the novel, the character who was named Col. Sartoris Snopes in the short story is no longer a part of the Ab Snopes family, ostensibly because he was too truthful to be a good Snopes.

Physically Flem Snopes is rather nondescript—he has stagnant watercolored eyes, a broad still face which reveals slight tobacco stains at the corners of his mouth, and a hawk-like nose which might have served as a warning to his intended victims. Although he was between twenty and thirty when he began his career as a merchant, Flem does not take the young man's pleasure in anything physical. He does occasionally chew a nickel's worth of tobacco. He seems to be nourished by the growth of his financial status rather than by food. Flem's non-human characterization is enhanced by his reputation for errorless business transactions. Though the reader of *The Hamlet* can only suspect that Flem is sexually impotent, he may observe that Flem is indifferent to women, as he is to everything except making money.

Flem Snopes's very lack of emotion is doubly emphasized by his union with Eula Varner, who is sexuality personified. Indeed Eula and sexuality serve as foils for Flem and snopesism. Eula is described as a Venus, "the drowsing maidenhead symbol's self" (p. 114), the queen, the matrix of all sex impulses; she dominated by her very presence all the males from the age of puberty to death. She seems to exist in a state of feeling without consciousness. She is presented as an organism designed specifically to arouse sexual desire and to accomplish the consummation of the sexual act. When she becomes illegitimately pregnant, she is married to Flem Snopes, a man she ignores and a man impervious to her appeal and incapable of enjoying her love.

If the marriage between Eula and Flem is without emotion, the relation between Ike Snopes and the cow, fraught as it is with sodomy, is described as filled with tender emotion. The affair of Ike and Jack Houston's cow immediately follows the departure of Flem and Eula for their Texas honeymoon, and provides an ironic parallel to their situation. The cow is saliently feminine as Eula is; the effect which the sight of the cow perpetrates on Ike is quite similar to the impact Eula has on males in her proximity. The descriptions of the cow's animal warmth and fecundity parallel the descriptions of Eula's indolent sexuality. But an ironic difference exists between Ike and Flem. Once when Labove, in his madness was contemplating the sort of husband Eula would have, he thought that Eula's husband "would be a dwarf, a gnome, without glands or desire, who would be no more a physical factor in her life than the owner's name on the flyleaf of a book" (p. 118). Flem seems to fit that role perfectly. Ike, however, has "been given the wordless passions but not the specious words" (p. 196), and the omniscient narrator describes his affair for him in a beautifully poetic diction which ameliorates the meanness of the situation and reflects ironically upon the farcical nature of the marriage between Flem and Eula.

The theme of sexuality is given a different tack in the marriage of Mink Snopes and his wife, the daughter of a white sawmill operator and a quadroon. Mink meets her at a logging camp where she summons to her bed whatever man she happens to choose from among the workers, mostly convicts, who labor for her father. She thus reverses the role of the traditional white plantation owner with respect to his practice of sexual indulgence with the Negro slaves. Mink is able to earn her love through his sexual prowess. Though Eula and Mrs. Mink Snopes both possess immense sexual capacity, each employs her attributes in a contrasting manner. Flem and Mink, though they are cousins, serve as foils to one another; Mink is sexually potent, emotionally vigorous, able to love and to hate deeply; Flem is void of sexuality, indifferent to love, capable of feeling only desire for money and apprehension over the threat to his success. Because of their conflict, Flem declines to aid Mink who is then sentenced to life imprisonment for the murder of Jack Houston.

In tone *The Hamlet* is witty, light, and genial, even amused. The work focuses on an action in which the characters, for the most part, seem to engage for the sake of good-natured competition. The loose, episodic structure, roughly following Flem Snopes's conquest of Frenchman's Bend, permitted the author to fill in the background and entertain the reader with such stories as might appropriately be told on the gallery of Will Varner's store. The work is divided into four books with the titles "Flem," "Eula," "The Long Summer," and "The Peasants." Each book includes two chapters, except the first book, which contains three chapters. Four short stories have been incorporated into the novel and the skeleton of a fifth one is recounted as background material. Book One contains the outline of "Barn Burning" and the story "Fool About a Horse." Book Three includes a greatly revised version of "The Hound." Book Four comprises "Spotted Horses" and "Lizards in Jamshyd's Courtyard." Some of the stories contribute directly to the Flem Snopes myth, e.g., "Spotted Horses," and "Lizards in Jamshyd's Courtyard." "The Hound," concerning Mink Snopes's conflict with Jack Houston, and "Fool About a Horse," concerning Ab Snopes prior to the birth of Flem, contribute little to the unity of the work.

Some of William Faulkner's most skillful humorous writing occurs in *The Hamlet* where the author exploits to the fullest his keen comic perception. The situation in which Ab Snopes tries to outsmart Pat Stamper, the super horse-trader, is inherently funny. Naturally Ab gets tricked himself, and his wife's determination to possess a milk separator compounds the comedy. The descriptions of the rampant spotted horses and the ensuing chaos presents broad farcical comedy, but in this sketch Faulkner has blended a touch of the pathetic with the comic. Mrs. Henry Armstid evokes a feeling of genuine sympathy as she pleads for the money which she had earned and saved to buy shoes for her children. Ironic comedy occurs when Jody Varner's indignation upon learning that Eula is pregnant contrasts with the pragmatic reactions of Will and Mrs. Varner. The concern of the parents for peaceful naps instead of revenge only infuriates Jody further. But the humor is not limited to specific incidents of broad comic nature; it is often found in the wry comments of V. K. Ratliff or Will Varner, or the omniscient narrator. The entire work exudes a comic tone at the fallibility of man which makes him a fit victim for a snopesist.

The poetic sensibility of William Faulkner appears in the Ike Snopes-cow section in an unusual degree. The entire sequence is overcast with a heightened imagery reminiscent of Spenser's poetry. He describes dawn in this passage which is the beginning of a virtual aubade:

> it wakes, upseeping, attritive in uncountable creeping channels: first, root; then frond by frond, from whose escaping tips like gas it rises and disseminates and stains the sleepfast earth with drowsy insect-murmur; then, still upward-seeking, creeps the knitted bark of trunk and limb where, suddenly louder leaf by leaf and dispersive in diffusive sudden speed, melodious with the winged and jeweled throats, it upward bursts and fills night's globed negation with jonquil thunder (p. 181).

The constant tender attention which Ike gives to the cow, and his plaiting chains of flowers for her, reflect the duties of a medieval or renaissance lover would perform for his lady. The artistic development here rivals the skillful work of the Benjy section in *The Sound and the Fury*.

The Hamlet involves little of the chronological complexity that often occurs in Faulkner's work. It rather begins at the beginning and moves forward. Occasional flashbacks occur as

Ratliff recounts a story from his youth, or the omniscient narrator returns to the earlier life of a character as he does in the Eula section or in the story of Mink Snopes. During the Ike Snopes-cow affair, time even seems to stand still.

Lack of technical difficulty for the reader should not, however, cause one to overlook the artistic merit of the rich comedy and the magnificent poetic imagery which designate *The Hamlet* as a superior work.

INTRUDER IN THE DUST [1]

Intruder in the Dust is a book about race relations. The most powerful focus of the novel, however, is not on race relations as a topic, though Gavin Stevens spends many pages providing philosophical explanations of them, but the central concern of the work is the mental change occasioned within the psyche of Charles Mallison as Lucas Beauchamp's insistence on independence and equality forces Charles to personally confront the problem. This work is a polemic on the South's ability to cope with its own problems, and it is a dramatization of a young man's attempt to understand and assimilate the incongruities of his Southern tradition; both these themes develop within the framework of the murder mystery.

The story begins at a crucial point with the news that Lucas Beauchamp, miscegenated descendant of L. Q. C. McCaslin, has shot a white man, Vinson Gowrie, member of a family of violent men. This incident poses an immediate problem for sixteen-year-old Chick Mallison because of a personal debt of honor which he feels toward Lucas. Four years earlier Chick had been aided by Lucas after having fallen into an icy creek. Chick tried to pay Lucas for his courtesy but was rebuffed by Lucas's attitude that

---

[1] First published New York: Random House, Inc., 1948. All quotations (marked by page numbers in parentheses) are from this edition.

the act was a matter of kindness extended by one human to another, discounting the difference in race entirely. Because of his Southern background, Chick has difficulty accepting Lucas as an equal. When he tries to repay Lucas by sending him gifts, Lucas complicates the problem by reciprocating. For the past four years Chick has been trying to discharge the debt as a "re-affirmation of his masculinity and his white blood" (p. 26). Through the experience he gradually comes to realize that Negroes have feelings just as white people do. Once after the death of Molly, Lucas's wife, Chick realized "You dont have to not be a nigger in order to grieve" (p. 25). At the time that Lucas is accused of having committed the murder, Chick believes that he is without obligation to the insolent, inflexible, composed old Negro. But he discovers that he is going to do exactly whatever Lucas requests not only because of the personal obligation but also because Lucas is relying on an old Negro saying that if one wants anything out of the ordinary done, he should get the women and the children working on it. In this case the woman is a seventy-year-old spinster Miss Eunice Habersham, who had been a childhood companion and friend of Molly Beauchamp; the children are Charles Mallison, and his coeval Negro companion Alec Sander. Men like Gavin Stevens and Sheriff Hope Hampton would not cooperate with Lucas because he does not play the game according to the rules which they feel necessary to an orderly conduct of the business at hand.

Once Chick, Aleck, and Miss Habersham discover that the grave of Vinson Gowrie contains Jake Montgomery, the novel becomes a murder mystery. At that point Gavin Stevens and Sheriff Hampton become the dominant figures, and the suspense inherent in seeking the murderer and preventing a lynching of Lucas Beauchamp whom the entire county seems determined to make admit that he is a "nigger," pervades the story. After the identity of the murderer has been clearly established, the apprehension of the culprit is accepted as a foregone conclusion, and the novel devolves into a rather wordy analysis of the actions of the Yoknapatawphans in the near-lynching of an innocent man, primarily because his skin was black.

Chick Mallison realizes that "he was responsible for having brought into the light and glare of day something shocking and shameful out of the whole white foundation of the county which he himself must partake of too since he too was bred of it" (p. 138). Since Chick accepts his own liability for a portion of the Southern injustice, he is shocked by the cowardly flight of his fellow citizens when they discover their mistake in assuming Lucas Beauchamp's guilt. They make no overt attempt to admit their guilt, and Charles says repeatedly in disgust, "They ran."

The discussions in which Gavin tries to explain to his young nephew that the Yoknapatawphans will show Lucas innumerable courtesies because of their mistake and that the injustice is principally a Southern problem seem to Charles to be simply a way to excuse the people for a gross error. Chick comes however to realize that he expects perfection of the people because they are his people and he is a part of them.

These introversions become a long defense of the South by Gavin Stevens. He insists that the Southerner is defending his homogeneity from the federal government and the rest of the country which has lost all mutual concern save "a frantic greed for money and a basic fear of a failure of national character" (p. 156). Gavin says that "Only a few of us know that only from homogeneity comes anything of a people or for a people of durable and lasting value—the literature, the art, the science, that minimum of government and police which is the meaning of freedom and liberty" (p. 154). He states that the homogeneity of the Southern Negro is even stronger than that of the white Southerner.

In a vehement tone, Gavin denounces the "outlanders" who attempt "by using federal laws and federal police to abolish Lucas' shameful condition" (p. 215). He states that the freedom of the

Lucases must be provided by the Southerner, because the Civil War could not do it, and the legislation of the years since has not accomplished it. He expresses confidence that such a day of freedom will come; then he says, "But it wont be next Tuesday" (p. 155).

Gavin never seems quite aware of the personal commitment which originated Chick's action that led him to violate a white grave to save a Negro, and he exhorts Charles by saying, "Some things you must never stop refusing to bear. Injustice and outrage and dishonor and shame. No matter how young you are or how old you have got" (p. 206).

By the end of the novel the reader has observed Charles Mallison's attitude move from a point of highly localized personal debt toward a Negro to an affirmation, greatly influenced by his uncle's altruistic arguments, that he wants to defend "Sambo" and the South from the meddling of outlanders, to insist upon the Southerner's power and potentiality for obliterating his tradition of injustice.

The author is concerned primarily with Charles Mallison, and the reader is permitted to overhear his thoughts and meditations alone of all the characters. In the early portions of the novel while Charles is contemplating his action and his response to the demand he believes Lucas will make of him, Faulkner is able to create an impression of a mirage-vacuum, as if Chick has been acting under hypnosis. Later in the novel, when the Yoknapatawphans discover their error, Faulkner successfully takes the reader into Charles's sleeplessness-induced phantasmagoric perception of their flight. The only flashbacks which occur are presented through the memory of Chick Mallison, though Gavin reconstructs part of the murder story and Lucas recounts other details of it.

The novel contains a powerful exposure of the inequity in the Southern society, even as it jealously claims that very fault and its solution as Southern prerogatives. The long expostulations of

Southern conscience tend to divide the novel into two distinct elements which though they share common characters retain a rather disjointed aspect, weakening the total impact of the novel.

The influence of Lucas Beauchamp dominates the entire novel though he himself remains for the most part in the background. He originates the actions of the other characters by his life-long habit of refusing to be either Negro or white; he peremptorily requires recognition of his inherent dignity as a human being.

The title of the work seems to stem from the opening of Vinson Gowrie's grave, but the discussions about resisting outlanders adds an element of ambiguity implying that the title also refers to non-Southerners who would dictate the moral actions of the Southerners. The philosophical attitude which Gavin espouses is an accurate description of the more moderate Southern traditionalist. The efficacy of such a philosophico-moral stance cannot be evaluated because the problem for which it is the remedy is yet too contemporaneous. Artistically the novel suffers from the inclusion of a loquacious preachment which tends to overshadow a tense murder mystery and a powerful psychological conflict.

LIGHT IN AUGUST [1]

Light in August is not one story but three. It is the account of Lena Grove, the Alabama girl, pregnant and unwed, who is looking for Lucas Burch, the father of her child. It is the fictional biography of Gail Hightower, D.D., the minister rejected by his congregation and living with his phantoms as an observer of life. And most important it is the story of Joe Christmas's search for an identity and an association which he can never find because he wants to reject what he believes to be true about himself. Lena

[1] First published New York: Harrison Smith and Robert Haas, 1932. All quotations are from this edition.

provides the continuity for the novel; Joe, the dramatic focus; and Hightower, the commentary. This novel is set principally in Jefferson, Yoknapatawpha, in the 1920's, and the current action occurs during a period of approximately two weeks. In the historical biographies included in character revelations, however, over thirty years are accounted for in the lives of some primary characters. The title, with symbolic reference to recognition, is taken from the physical description of the peculiar qualities of streaming sunlight in Mississippi in August.

Religion is an important theme of this novel, and Faulkner gives some justifiably sharp criticism of organized religion. Gail Hightower is the principal enunciator of the novel and except for a brief interpretation of the Hines-Christmas story by Gavin Stevens, he is the only literate articulator for the meaning of the story. It is for him that the light in August glows, and it is through the meditations of this character that the reader's attention is called to the physical reality of the clear brilliance of light which in Mississippi in August seems to transfix time and give a pristine glow to the environs. Rev. Hightower's name is indeed representative of the strength which the church or Christianity ought to provide for man. But Hightower has failed because he has perverted religion for his own selfish purposes. He has retreated from life and lived as a spectator so long that at the moment when he might have saved Joe Christmas, he is totally ineffective. On the insistence of Byron Bunch, Hightower is forced again to participate in life, and in his final meditation he reviews his past and recognizes his failing. But at least he has been somewhat quickened.

Other figures have religious representativeness. Mr. Simon McEachern, with his severe Presbyterian code of ethics and his simple, clear distinction of what is orderly and proper, represents a Puritanical religious attitude that is too clear-cut, too inflexible. Eupheus Hines typifies an unthinking, emotive outlet of Christianity based upon an eclectic communication between the Divine

Monster and the follower. His fanaticism is allied to the idea meditated by Hightower that the townspeople are praising God harshly as if to get revenge on Him. Byron Bunch gives a portrait of the uncowardly selflessness of Christianity. He voluntarily leads singing in a country church on Sundays. Not only is he willing to sacrifice himself for Lena, but he is willing to provoke his friend Hightower to sacrifice himself further in an attempt to rescue a stranger's grandson, Joe Christmas. Even Joanna Burden, whose very name signifies the "white man's burden" with which she is primarily concerned, is given religious overtones when she attempts, in the third phase, the final phase, of her relationship with Joe, to get him to pray with her.

The function of Joe Christmas in the novel, apart from the facile parallels between his age and his initials and the age and initials of Jesus Christ, seems not to be particularly representative of religion. His purpose seems rather to be the exemplification of a tragic situation. Because of his illegitimacy, he can never be sure of his origin. As the Negro yard man at the Memphis orphanage says to him, "You dont know what you are. And more than that, you wont never know. You'll live and you'll die and you wont never know" (p. 363). Joe's search for an identity which he can never find because though he thinks he is a Negro, he cannot bear to long identify himself with Negroes, poses Joe as a truly tragic figure. The pathos which may have been lurking in the background, becomes poignantly real in the narration of Joe's parentage during the discussion between Hightower and Mrs. Hines. The reader becomes aware that Joe may have had no Negro blood at all and that his life of self-destruction may have been in vain. Faulkner is pointing up the tragedy of a miscegenated human who cannot identify with either of the segregated groups in his society. The actions of Joe in the Negro church on Tuesday night highlight his feelings of frustration as he curses God and thumbs his nose at the Negroes and at Watt Kennedy, the white sheriff. Unfortunately the tragedy is all the more real if the miscegenation is a mental apparition. One does not know whether such realization ever comes to Joe, because after this disclosure, one never views Joe from his own point of view again. Only the perceptive commentary of Gavin Stevens provided any insight into the hope Joe Christmas might have gained from his interview with Mrs. Hines, and Stevens emphasized the indecision which is ultimately responsible for the destruction of Joe. The scene in which Joe Christmas is overcome by Percy Grimm (whose name is almost unpardonably allegorical) follows the explanation by Stevens, and it closes with an appropriately violent description of Joe Christmas in the triumphant serenity of death.

The placid submissiveness, the overpowering illogicality of the female is aptly captured in the figure of Lena Grove. She begins the story and she ends it. It is her story which provides the frame for the Joe Christmas and the Gail Hightower expansions. She comes into Jefferson quite by coincidence at the very time that the primary action of the novel begins, and after that adventure is completed, she takes Byron Bunch and moves on, providing the subject of the epilogue (which is the final chapter).

In *Light in August* Faulkner manipulates time to enmesh the reader in the lives of his characters and to stress the cumulative effect of time. Continually in the novel, Faulkner quite simply states a fact of great importance for the narrative, and then he utilizes flashbacks to explain the importance to the reader. For example, the fire from the Burden house is seen by Byron Bunch and Lena Grove, and all the townspeople. In the following chapters the background of the house and its importance for the novel are given. Or consider the Percy Grimm story. The last sentence of chapter eighteen informs Byron Bunch, "That nigger, Christmas. They killed him" (p. 418). Though the reader has anticipated the end of Joe for some time, the bare statement prods his imagination and curiosity to its peak. Then in chapter nineteen Faulkner gives the psychological biography of Percy

Grimm which explains his grisly part in the death of Christmas. This caterpillar device, this taking a giant step forward and then flashing back to tell the story in chronological order is utilized in the Christmas-Burden affair, the McEachern story (partially), and in many of the incidents of Joe's flight following the murder. By stopping his characters or his story in mid-action, Faulkner is stressing the idea that at any given moment a person is the cumulation of all that has happened in his life. Gavin Stevens states this idea lucidly as he explains the jail break and the death of Joe. He says "Not pursuers: but himself: years, acts, deeds omitted and committed, keeping pace with him, stride for stride, breath for breath, thud for thud of the heart, using a single heart" (p. 424).

The conspicuous characteristics of Faulkner's style—the long involved sentence and the telescoped words—are present in *Light in August*. Consider the following from the first page of chapter six:

> Knows remembers believes a corridor in a big long garbled cold echoing building of dark red brick sootbleakened by more chimneys than its own, set in a grassless cinderstrewnpacked compound surrounded by smoking factory purlieus and enclosed by a ten-foot steel-and-wire fence like a penitentiary or a zoo, where in random erratic surges, with sparrowlike, childtrebling orphans in identical and uniform blue denim in and out of remembering but in knowing constant as the bleak walls, the bleak windows where in rain soot from the yearly adjacenting chimneys streaked like black tears (p. 111).

But these elements rarely overshadow the importance of the story. Rather they are subordinated and transcended so that the telling makes of this story a great novel. In chapter seventeen, dealing with the birth of Lena's baby, one finds epitomized the superior craftsmanship which characterized the novel. The flashback is here, the interior monologue is here, the excellent use of a

variety of dialect dialogue is here. And most important a peak of
emotional intensity is here as Hightower tries to "save" Byron
Bunch from Lena Grove. All three threads of the story are firmly
united here and some indication is given of the direction in which
the novel will move. Artistically, *Light in August* is one of Faulkner's best novels.

THE MANSION [1]

Throughout the canon of William Faulkner's work, one finds
him using the same story several times, never in exactly the same
way, and almost never in the same length or form. In *The Mansion,* Faulkner employs this tendency to good advantage, for not
only does he successfully bring to a close his chronicle of the
Snopes family, but he utilizes a story he had used three times
before to provide the dramatic unity of the novel.

In the author's headnote to the work, Faulkner writes that
this book is "the final chapter of, and the summation of, a work
conceived and begun in 1925." The struggle carried on by Gavin
Stevens and V. K. Ratliff against snopesism is concluded in this
work, with the defeat of Senator Clarence Egglestone Snopes by
means of the "dog thicket" (p. 316), with the outmaneuvering
of Orestes and Flem Snopes, and with the mutually eliminating
feud between Flem and Mink Snopes, in which vendetta Linda
Snopes Kohl plays an important part.

Sen. C. Egglestone Snopes, who has risen from the simple ward
handyman for Will Varner to the position of state legislator and
on to the office of state senator, reaches the peak of his career
when he decides to run for the national House of Representatives.
Having already proved himself a shrewd politician of the Bilbo-

---

[1] Published New York: Random House, Inc., 1959. All quotations from the
novel are from this edition and are marked with page numbers in parentheses.

Long ilk, though not so smart as either of these, Sen. Snopes appears unbeatable to Gavin who moans in despair that he and his generation are too old to thwart the corruption of Clarence. V. K. Ratliff, however, with his attitude that "there must be a pure and simple answer to it" (p. 313), finds an effective solution which *is* so simple that Gavin gasps in dismay. But the wile ends the Snopes political threat.

Orestes Snopes has not appeared in other novels of the Snopes saga, and his altercation with Mr. Meadowfill seems not especially related to the primary plot of the novel. He is just another Snopes to be combatted, and this time Gavin is successful in opposing snopesism. This digression also adds a well-done touch of comedy to the novel which has so many dark overtones.

Flem Snopes, the progenitor, the original sponsor of the Snopes flood, has gained a large measure of respectability for himself by the time that this novel begins. He has even helped to eliminate irrespectable Snopeses from Jefferson. The dramatic action of the novel focuses on Flem positioned at the apogee of his success; he is a successful banker, owner of a fine home, and a well-recognized member of his church, Baptist naturally. But the threat to his continued enjoyment of his gains is Mink Snopes, a cousin whom he had refused to aid in a murder trial thirty-eight years earlier and whom he had deliberately plotted against by getting M. W. Snopes to help add twenty years to Mink's sentence. With the death of Flem and the banishment of Mink, Gavin feels that Jefferson has gained some surcease from the imminent threat of snopesism, even though he recognizes some strange Snopes faces at Flem's funeral.

The end of the struggle does not come, of course, for the Snopeses alone. Gavin, after he is fifty years old, marries Mrs. Melisandre Harriss, and that action helps to settle Gavin. Near the end of the work he relinquishes the dream which has sustained him through other trying times, the task of translating the Bible back into classical Greek and ultimately back into Hebrew;

he gives up this plan because "he was too old now and the real tragedy of age is that no anguish is any longer grievous enough to demand, justify, any sacrifice" (p. 392).

For Linda Snopes Kohl, life has almost reached a rounding out, a balancing point. She has always loved Gavin Stevens, as she says to him, "because every time you lie to me I can always know you will stick to it" (p. 175). He has been lying to her all her life to protect her from the knowledge of her own birth and the state of affairs between Flem and Eula; that is, he has been trying to save her from snopesism. Linda marries Barton Kohl and goes with him to fight in the Spanish Civil War, where she is deafened by a bomb blast and he dies in a plane crash. After she returns to Jefferson, isolated from life and humanity by her physical injury which is symbolic of the psychic wound the knowledge of her situation within the Snopesistic milieu might have caused, she learns from Gavin that they can love without the necessity of having sexual relations. Linda, perhaps for revenge against Flem for having created the circumstances which caused Eula's suicide, gets Mink out of Parchman Penitentiary, knowing that the first thing he will do is to kill Flem. After Flem's funeral Linda leaves Jefferson and Gavin's life apparently forever.

The final scene focuses on the old men, Ratliff and Gavin Stevens, nearly sixty, performing a final duty for the daughter of Eula Varner. The book closes on the image of an old man, seeking sleep and rest, being absorbed back into the earth.

The novel is structured by its emphasis on three pivotal characters: Mink, Linda, and Flem. The first five chapters, which compose the section titled "Mink," are presented variously by the omniscient narrator and by the limited narrators V. K. Ratliff and Montgomery Ward Snopes. This section presents for the fourth time the story of Mink's disagreement with Jack Houston, for which Mink ultimately kills Mr. Houston. This version portrays Jack as arrogant, intolerant, and proud; his harsh nature forces Mink to the point at which only murder could assuage Mink's desire for relief. The author stresses in *The Mansion* that Mink was not a contentious man but one simply dogged by misfortune which crowded him into a desperate defense of some semblance of human right and dignity. Mink has been greatly humanized from the outright meanness which was his characteristic in *The Town*. The omniscient narrator presides over most of the section dealing with Mink, though occasionally Mink's thoughts are given in italics. The sexual allusions of the Mink Snopes section and those found in the M. W. Snopes monologue are considerably more gross than those found in other sections or monologues. This tendency underscores the more basic, more animalistic natures of Mink and M. W. Snopes.

The second division of the novel is entitled "Linda." The six chapters which compose this section are all narrations from a limited point of view; V. K. Ratliff in the first two sections reviews the story of Eula Varner and her conflux of young men; then he recounts the history of Linda Snopes Kohl since she left Jefferson following her mother's funeral. Charles narrates three of the chapters, continuing the story of Linda and Gavin, and describing the approaching Second World War. Gavin narrates one chapter which is extremely tense as Linda and he discuss the nature of the love they share.

The final section is titled "Flem" and all the chapters are presented by the omniscient narrator, though at times one of the limited narrators presents a specific incident. In this section, the threads of story are all brought together as Mink, aided by Linda, achieves his vengeance, and then Gavin and Ratliff help Mink escape.

The variety of vantage points employed contributes to the technical complexity of the novel, as Faulkner shifts frequently from Mink's story to Linda's and back again, and the constant use of flashbacks further complicates the structure of the novel. The shifting point of view, both of speaker and of chronology, weaves the complete Snopes story into the background so that *The Mansion* becomes a complete work in itself.

Just as the revenge motif of Mink Snopes provides a dramatic tension which helps to unify this rather dichotomous work, another element also works toward synthesizing the impact of this novel; it is the theme of compassion for man's common plight, a sympathetic recognition of man's common humanity. This theme was central to *A Fable* where it was treated with dignity and eloquence. In *The Mansion* it is contained in the vernacular expression "the pore sons of bitches." Reba Rivers, madam of a Memphis house of prostitution, first introduces it when she says, "All of us. Every one of us. The poor son of a bitches" (p. 82). Mink later meets the same sentiment from Rev. Joe Goodyhay, a former-Marine preacher-of-sorts, who prays for his congregation with these words, "Save us, Christ. The poor sons of bitches" (p. 282). And finally at the end of the novel, Gavin says, "There aren't any morals, ... People just do the best they can" (p. 429). To which Ratliff replies, "The pore sons of bitches" (p. 429); and Gavin echoes his words. The humanizing of the character Mink Snopes strongly supports the theme of man's common plight, of man doing the best he can in the circumstances in which he finds himself.

V. K. Ratliff, who has been in the preceding volumes of the Snopes saga, a shrewd, alert, even bemused observer of life, is portrayed in *The Mansion* as a man of unusual sensitivity. He understands Gavin and Gavin's relationship to Eula Varner's daughter better than even Gavin himself. V. K., because of his deep understanding of human nature, strikes up an immediate friendship with Myra Allanovna, famous New York tie designer. His pristine sensitivity permits an instantaneous rapport with the sculpture of Barton Kohl, sculpture which even sophisticated Gavin Stevens could not fathom. Ratliff with his insistence upon the simplicity of life serves as Gavin's continual reminder of the basic human facets, foibles, and potentialities of each man.

With a touch of sympathy, William Faulkner in *The Mansion* has rounded out his chronicle of the Snopeses; a chronicle portraying success built on human weakness; a chronicle placing in opposition not Good and Bad but amalgams of both; a chronicle juxtaposing idealism with pragmatism, complexity with simplicity; a chronicle of one family: Man.

MOSQUITOES [1]

New Orleans and Lake Pontchartrain, that expanse of bay forty miles long and twenty-four miles wide north of New Orleans, provide the setting for *Mosquitoes*. Partially because the entire production, (from the prefatory note, ". . . they were bigger, vicious; ubiquitous as undertakers, cunning as pawnbrokers, confident and unavoidable as politicians." to the last syllable), avoids the use of the word *mosquito,* this novel presents the appearance of a carefully contrived piece of literature. Unfortunately, the saliency of the artifice alone could not give life to the creation.

The novel is structured very carefully in chronological fashion, the sections, except "Prologue," and "Epilogue," assuming the labels of the day of the cruise, i.e., "The First Day," etc. The voyage takes four days, though the action of the novel covers the space of six days. The activities of each day are delineated by labels noting the time, e.g., seven o'clock, eight o'clock, etc. Such constant reference to time allows the author to shift scenes and points of view simply, though somewhat mechanically; it also creates in the reader an attitude of "and then"—an attitude reflecting the weakness of plot. "The Prologue" is a rather con-

---

[1] First published New York: Boni and Liveright, 1927. Subsequent references are to this edition.

ventional introductory section, but the epilogue reaches a peak of artistic excellence which demonstrates the uneven quality of the novel.

Within the simply ordered chronology of *Mosquitoes,* the author assembles thirteen characters, places them on a yacht, *The Nausikaa,* and expects them to create through their conversations a sparkling novel. Most of the characters, highly pseudo-sophisticated, are portrayed in a realistic mode, though they tend to become stylized, almost type characters.

Mrs. Maurier, the hostess for the group, is presented as a figure of the society matron who patronized the arts and artists though she is incapable of empathic response to them or to their mediums. Mr. Julius Kauffman, characterized as "the Semitic man," is a figure of sophisticated realism. Mr. Talliafero is a businessman who is relatively sensitive even though he submerges his sensitivity in an attempt to seduce women. Gordon is the sculptor, the genuine artist, who experiences life, and creates; he participates almost not at all in the verbosity of the novel. Mark Frost (whose name alludes to his lack of warmth) is a character who has some platitudinous insights into the truths of life but who is too apathetic to create poetry or to have an affair when a woman offers herself to him. Major Ayers is a blustry, credulous Englishman who wants to make his fortune by selling salts for the biological preoccupation of the American public. Dorothy Jameson is a frustrated woman as well as a frustrated painter. And Mrs. Eva Wiseman, (her name is almost allegorical) is the author of a book of verse and the sister to J. Kauffman; she is a rather sophisticated woman.

The younger members of the yachting party represent various facets of youth. Jenny Steinbauer is the sexual arouser, Patricia Robyn is the ingenue, Pete Ginotta is the insouciant one, and Theodore Robyn, twin to Pat, is the pre-occupied young man. Patricia provides a certain amount of humor and realistic sympathy, because she seems to have a natural independence of mind which allows her to ignore sham and discern truth.

Dawson Fairchild is of special interest because he is modeled on Sherwood Anderson, of whose clique Faulkner was a member at the time this novel was written. The comments of the characters in the novel often coincide clearly with statements Faulkner himself made about Anderson. For example consider what three of *Mosquitoes*'s characters say about Fairchild:

> "There's a man of undoubted talent, despite his fumbling bewilderment in the presence of sophisticated emotions" [Julius Kauffman said].
> "Despite his lack of self-assurance, you mean," Mark Frost corrected.
> "No it isn't that," Mrs. Wiseman put in. . . . "having been born an American of a provincial midwestern lower middle class family, he has inherited all the lower middle class's awe of Education with a capital E" (pp. 241–242).

Then consider what Faulkner himself said about Anderson: "Anderson didn't quite have that confidence in his own capacity to pick and choose." [2] "Yes, he [Anderson] had the unlettered man's boundless and almost baseless respect for literacy, for education." [3] Furthermore the story that Dawson told Major Ayers about Andrew Jackson's descendants with the fish ranch (with its overtones of the Old Southwest humorists) is one that Sherwood Anderson and Faulkner told for fun. Faulkner later said the story was unpublished. [4]

Even though the portrait is sometimes uncomplimentary, the characters generally respect Fairchild as an effective artist.

---

[2] F. L. Gwynn and J. L. Blotner, *Faulkner in the University* (Vintage Books ed., 1965), p. 229.

[3] Ibid., p. 230.

[4] Ibid., p. 232.

They point out that he is too much concerned with being American, but then they acknowledge that he is in the direct line of a good American tradition, the tradition of the Emersons and the Lowells.[5]

Faulkner's almost characteristic treatment of time with movement from the present into the past contrasts with the continuous plodding of the more obvious structural time markers he has utilized. Sometimes the flashback is very skillfully done as when Mrs. Wiseman observes Jenny Steinbauer repel Mr. Talliafero. Time almost stands still during the narration of this humorous incident. At other times, however, the flashback is more mechanically employed. Consider the beginning of the epilogue in which Faulkner takes each of the characters in turn and reports on his activities immediately upon leaving the cruise. When he has completed the action involving one character, he returns to the morning of the docking and follows another character into the future.

Another technical consideration is the deficiency of unity. Apart from the spatial unity of the story, which at best is artificial, the theme of words vs. action serves as a unifying device for *Mosquitoes*. This theme is applied to two ideas: sex and art. Sex, or the pursuit and/or contemplation of copulation, is the instrument of humor and the embodiment of the inefficacy of the characters. Art, the creative impulse and its expression whether in writing, painting, sculpting, etc., is the subject of long discussions, but little action.

Mr. Ernest Talliafero (born Tarver), a widower, spends most of his time and energy planning seductions. He is never able to bring one of his plans to fruition because he plots in a dream world which is shattered the moment it comes in contact with the real world. He is easily foiled by the woman who does not respond as he has anticipated, and he irritates the other characters by his constant babble concerning his infallible plans. The recur-

---

[5] Ibid., p. 242.

ring leitmotif of the thwarted Mr. Talliafero is broadly comic. The novel begins and ends with Talliafero, and the reader comes to anticipate the next bit of inanity from this bumbling person. The ego-disintegrating climax of his pursuit of Jenny Steinbauer destroys his confidence for the moment, and he pours out his troubles to a writer who lives in the apartment beneath Fairchild's. In exasperation the writer tells Talliafero, "Do? Do? Go to a brothel, if you want a girl" (p. 345). When this exhortation is rejected by Talliafero, the focal point of Talliafero's problem is cited. He wants the idea of pursuit and conquest more than he wants coition—almost as if he were proving his masculinity to his friends by constantly talking about making a seduction. After this final defeat, Talliafero realizes that he will soon be married again. Marriage would provide him with the safe opportunities to indulge in his fantasies.

Major Ayers, Dawson Fairchild, and the Semitic man present a middle ground between the extremes of Talliafero and Gordon. Mark Frost is phlegmatically situated in the central region also. These men, mostly older, are quite concerned with the implications of sex in the story. They leer at Jenny and Patricia, jest at the machinations of Talliafero, and condone the healthy impulses of the younger characters. But these men, plus Mrs. Wiseman and Miss Jameson, are the principal figures in the art discussions of the novel. Though Mrs. Wiseman is quite aware of the sexual interests of the others, viz., *Satyricon in Starlight,* and though Dorothy Jameson unsuccessfully attempts to seduce both Mark Frost and Pete Ginotta, these two women and these four men spend most of their time discussing art and literature. Their quite extended conversations often have to do with the confusion between words and deeds. Fairchild admits, "You begin to substitute words for things and deeds" (p. 210).

Then the Semitic man asks, "If you just talk long enough, you're bound to say the right thing some day. Is that what you mean?" (p. 210) Julius Kauffman constantly attacks Fairchild for his belief in the effects of words and for talking and shouting until he, the artist, has made the non-artist citizen of the world nervous. It is important to note that none of the people participating in these long discussions accomplish anything concrete. All they do is engage in talk—inactivity.

Mrs. Maurier hardly fits in either of these categories for two reasons: 1) she doesn't engage in the conversations because she has nothing to say, and 2) she had rejected love in her youth to marry for position and finance. She has become a lonely, sterile personality.

Gordon, the sculptor, is the antithesis of inactivity and tautology. He vents his creative impulse in the production of arresting statuary. He dislikes the dilettantism of the yachting party, but he is attracted by the ingenuousness of Patricia. He rejects the "literary discussion" violently as he contemplates, "Talk, talk, talk: the utter and heartbreaking stupidity of words. . . . Ideas, thoughts, became mere sounds to be bandied about until they were dead" (p. 186). He smolders quietly in his desire for Patricia and when that feeling is not gratified, he turns, in a vigorous action to a prostitute for the satisfaction of his physical need. Gordon's direct action immediately precedes and contrasts with the hesitant inefficiency of Talliafero. It is significant that among the artistic group of characters, Gordon is the only one who is engaged in performing the deeds rather than simply spouting words.

The words which create so much tedium in the novel do seem to be important from one point of view. The discussion of literature and life seems to reflect the views of Faulkner himself rather than just the ideas of the characters. It is as if Faulkner took the opportunity of having four different personae through whom he could enunciate his own views. Possibly it was an attempt by the author to verbalize and thus free himself from the ideas and the influence of Sherwood Anderson. Two considerations support this contention. First, when Fairchild, Julius Kauffman, Mark Frost,

Mrs. Wiseman, Dorothy Jameson, and only incidentally Major
Ayers, discuss literature, they agree. The disagreements which
would normally arise in discussions with literary people are
singularly lacking. The ideas in the discussions expand and develop as if they were all of a piece, as if one person were speaking.
This movement suggests a propagandistic purpose.

Secondly, the ideas expressed often agree remarkably with those
pronounced by the writer William Faulkner. Fairchild comments
about the artistic compulsion "we have to do it, they don't. They
[the consumers of art] can take it or leave it" (p. 321). Faulkner
said, "He's [the writer has] got to have to write, he don't know
why, and sometimes he will wish that he didn't have to, but he
does." [6] Later Julius Kauffman says,

> Life everywhere is the same, you know. Manners of living it may
> different. . . . but man's old compulsions, duty and inclination:
> the axis and the circumference of his squirrel cage, they do not
> change (p. 243).

Faulkner, in answer to a question about whether his characters
were Mississippians or not said,

> I don't think that people are that different. . . . I'm simply using
> the background, the color, the smells, the sounds that I am familiar
> with, but the people. . . . would have the same anguishes, the
> same hopes.[7]

Though William Faulkner liked to pose as an unlearned country
man, a "veteran sixth-grader," [8] these long expostulations on the
art of writing reveal unequivocably that he was a writer well

---

[6] Ibid., p. 19.

[7] Ibid., p. 87.

[8] Ibid., p. 53.

aware of the theories and technical problems of his craft. Certainly a more detailed study than is possible here could profitably be done on the relationship between the artistic discussions of *Mosquitoes* and the artistic philosophy of William Faulkner.

Mosquitoes is a dull novel because the ideas enunciated in the work are not brilliant or clever enough to compensate for the lack of action. A great tedium of inactivity becalms *Mosquitoes* just as the sand of Lake Pontchartrain arrests the motion of *The Nausikaa*. The technical considerations of time-manipulation, characterization, and theoretical exposition overcome the story line and destroy the plot.

One problem which weakens the novel is that the author cannot seem to decide which character or which two or three characters are central. Rather indiscriminately he treats any one of a dozen characters as fully as he does any other one. A lack of dramatic unity results. When the novel ends, the reader has no sense of completeness. On the contrary, the novel has described the actions of a group of people for six days; some of the people are successful; some are not. It really seems to have made little difference. The tracing of the post-yachting activities of each of the characters into his own life leaves one with a sense of just that many dangling stories.

The one section of the novel which deserves particular attention because of its excellence is the "Epilogue." Though it begins with a rather methodical examination of each character, the "Epilogue" demonstrates flashes of brilliance in the treatment of Miss Jameson's frustration by Mark Frost, and in the odious desperation of Talliafero's un-passionate pursuit. The interspersing of the story of the dead beggar with the activities of Fairchild, Kauffman, and Gordon gives an extension to their activities. A reminiscence of Eliot is felt in the manner of juxtaposing death and life. The fantasy quality of the beggar's story with its overtones of religion, sex, and initiation, helps Faulkner to achieve "that instant of timeless beatitude. . . . that passive state of the heart

... in which the hackneyed accidents which make up this world
—love and life and death and sex and sorrow—brought together
by chance in perfect proportions, take on a kind of splendid and
timeless beauty" (p. 339).

Perhaps Faulkner's own comment about the work evaluates it
best: "I'm not ashamed of it [*Mosquitoes*], because that was the
chips the badly sawn planks that the carpenter produces while
he's learning to be a first-rate carpenter, but it's not a—not an
important book in my list." [9] *Mosquitoes* is not a first-rate piece
of work, but it does show the writer struggling with his art.
Though he gives attention to theme, idea, and characterization
to the detriment of plot, he is working out his own ideas concerning the novel, and he is endeavoring to produce a piece of writing
with literary merit.

PYLON [1]

Pylon is William Faulkner's attempt to write a Waste Land
novel, but the type is no more suited to his mature gifts than it
was when he published his first novel, *Soldiers' Pay,* in 1926. The
product is a novel marred by inconsistencies, flat characters, and
mechanical techniques. The work is virtually an exercise in putting words together. An omniscient narrator presents the story of
the unusual affair between two aviators and a woman; the scene
is New Valois which corresponds closely to New Orleans.

Faulkner apparently put so much energy into developing the
mood of apathy and indifference that the background overpowers
the characters. Such a situation is quite unusual in a writer who

---

[9] Ibid., p. 257.

[1] New York: Random House, Inc., 1935. Quotations (marked by page numbers in parentheses) are from the photographically reproduced edition of the
first printing.

is as adept at characterization as Faulkner is. The story occurs against the backdrop of Mardi Gras and the opening of the new Feinman Airport. But none of the gayety intrudes upon the somber story of the Shumanns. Jack Holmes (the parachutist), Laverne Shumann, and Roger Shumann (the racing pilot) exist in the fringes of the spotlight; they are constantly seen at oblique angles so that they never develop the depth of character necessary to support the dramatic tension of the story.

Perhaps the most important inconsistency is that the narrator cannot at first decide whether the unnamed reporter or Jiggs (the Shumann mechanic) is to be the point of reference. The novel begins as Jiggs purchases a pair of boots which reappear continually through the novel. Most of the information about the Shumanns comes to the reporter, and thus to the reader, through Jiggs. He relates the history of Roger Shumann's career as an aviator and the story of Laverne's past. In many of the scenes with Laverne, Jack Holmes, and Roger Shumann, the emphasis is on Jiggs, so that the others who should be the focal characters appear only in a peripheral light. In the early part of the novel the reader identifies with Jiggs because he is the most clearly presented character.

But the narrator gradually comes to employ the reporter as the pivotal character, until at the end of the work the reporter stands as the central figure. He is presented as a cadaverous person, over six feet tall and weighing about ninety-five pounds, who exists in a dreamy, semi-conscious state. The reporter is a shadowy figure, with almost no past and virtually no personality. It is hinted that his mother may be a prostitute or a party girl, but even that is ambiguous. The clear light of characterization never falls on him; consequently he is so vaguely drawn as to be ineffective.

Another inconsistency occurs in the development of Laverne Shumann's role as a sex symbol. Certainly the sordid experiences of her youth, the titillating account of her first parachute jump, and her polyandrous situation delineate her as a figure with great physical appeal. The reporter is virtually overcome by desire for her, and apparently his concern for the Shumanns is predicated upon his captivation by her sensuality. But she is specifically described as wearing men's under shorts, as wearing the overalls so that she looks like a man; as contriving "to wear the skirt beneath the sexless trenchcoat as any one of the three men would" (p. 79); she is mechanically inclined, working on the airplane engine just as another fellow might. She lacks the tender feelings that a mother should have for her son. She first teases the boy about the uncertainty of his paternity, and she expresses only convenience at leaving him with his grandparents. Altogether she seems quite androgynous.

Though Laverne is supposed to have powerful sex appeal, her relations with Jack Holmes and Roger Shumann, her husband, are of an explicitly unconventional nature. The reporter says of them, "they aint human. . . . you can't anymore imagine two of them making love than you can two of them airplanes" (p. 231). He also implies that the partner is unimportant to Laverne when he says to Roger, "how it's you and him and how maybe sometimes she dont even know the difference, one from another, and I would think how maybe if it was me too she wouldn't even know I was there at all" (p. 175). Perhaps it is the physical act which is unimportant to her or to them, no more intimate to them than sleep or food or shelter. She is almost not a sexual figure but a machine used for convenience. In a drunken stupor the reporter describes their love-making in these mechanical images: "And the ground they plow from Iowa; yair, two farmers' boys downbanked; yair two buried pylons in the one Iowadrowsing, womandrowsing, pylondrowsing" (p. 110). But such a view contradicts her influence on the reporter and the man earlier associated with her.

Although the peculiar constitution of the Holmes-Shumann triangle marks these characters as unconventional, it does little to distinguish them as individuals. They lack realism, warmth, and credibility. These three, who provide impetus for the story, seem interested in nothing except flying. The reporter says that "they aint human like us; . . . . Burn them like this one tonight and they don't even holler in the fire; crash one and it aint even blood when you haul him out; it's cylinder oil the same as in the crank-case" (p. 45). In this respect Jiggs' boots serve as a differentiating factor, separating him from his three associates by his concern with something material, tangible, and personal. These three central characters are unconvincing, not because they are depicted as mechanical, but because the reader can never get a clear view of them. They wander through the experiences of the reporter or Jiggs. Only in the flashback recounting Laverne's first parachute jump do any of them occur in scenes which do not give top priority to some other character. The problem is not that they are inhuman, but that they are ephemeral cardboard figures who lack clarity.

These aviators are not Waste Land characters, because they have found a meaning in life; admittedly they are not concerned with ordinary social values, but their flying activities are important to them. The money earned from the competition is not the primary incentive for them. As one reporter says, "They were trying to do what they had to do, with what they had to do it with, the same as all of us only maybe a little better than us" (p. 290).

The reporter, however, does have attributes of a Waste Land figure. In the chapter entitled "Love Song of J. A. Prufrock," he is Prufrock. He has been rejected by Laverne without his even seriously attempting to approach her. He has dared to risk his boss's anger to get money for the Shumanns, he has made decisions which aided Roger in getting the second airplane, but he is generally ineffective; his endeavors come to nothing. Finally after the fatal crash, the reporter realizes that his situation is virtually hopeless. He meditates, "tomorrow and tomorrow and tomorrow; not only not to hope, not even to wait: just to endure" (p. 284).

A final weakness, which should not have been a problem to the writer who had created *The Sound and the Fury* or who would create *Absalom, Absalom!*, is that the technique is often mechanically obvious. The most salient characteristic of Faulkner's style in this novel is his monotonous use of telescoped words, e.g., *downfunnelled, cadaverface, corpseglare, stilldamp* (which all occur in the first paragraph of page 41). Occasionally the combination of words is particularly effective, as in *lightlyclattering* (p. 235) or *pavilionglitter* (p. 139). But the device is employed so frequently that most of the impact is lost; often the combination is not even specially apt, e.g., *fiercelyburning* (p. 185), or *parkinglots* (p. 139). Another recurring mechanical weakness is that the shift from one situation or geographical location to another is not smoothly accomplished. Two such instances are the shift from the reporter's obtaining a jug of absinth to the editor's leaving the newspaper building (p. 85), and the movement from the Myron, Ohio, home of Dr. Carl Shumann back to the city news room (p. 313). Allowing the art to manifest itself too obtrusively is not the mark of the best artistic endeavor. Because Faulkner did exercise his authorial abilities to efface the artifice in works before and after this novel, one concludes that *Pylon* is not an example of Faulkner's careful effort.

THE REIVERS[1]

The last novel of Faulkner's career, *The Reivers,* a novel which he could conceivably have written with his left hand, is a novel of initiation. It concerns the loss of innocence by an eleven-year-old boy, and it contains a rather incompatible admixture of comedy and didacticism and employs themes and relationships that are common ones in the Faulkner canon.

---

[1] Published New York: Random House, Inc., 1962. All quotations from the novel are from this edition and are marked by page numbers in parentheses.

One of the simplest of all Faulkner novels, this work is set in the framework of a grandfather reminiscing about his own introduction into the world of personal moral responsibility for the hearing of his own grandson. The frame occurs in 1961, but the primary action occurred in 1905. The continual shifting between the two chronological moments is perhaps the most complex technical consideration of the novel because the voice of the narrator seems at times to be the voice of a grandfather, and at other times it seems to have the tone of the eleven-year-old.

The Reivers is a comic work. Some of Faulkner's most obviously humorous characters are found in this novel. Particularly noteworthy are Boon Hogganbeck, who is quite prominent in "The Bear," Miss Reba Rivers, who is significant in *Sanctuary,* and Ned William McCaslin Jefferson Missisipi, who occurs only in this novel. Otis, the nephew of Miss Everbe Corinthia, with his excessive worldliness seems an older form of Uncle Bud from *Sanctuary*; he is a good foil for the mannerliness and morality of Lucius Priest.

The humorous aspect of the novel is supported by comic situations included almost as set pieces for that very purpose. The shooting incident between Boon and Ludus,[2] the crossing of Hell Creek bottom, and the scene at Miss Rivers's house in which Otis betrays Mr. Binford are of this sort. The gently comic tone of the early description of Boon's psychological battle with Boss Priest over the car is a more effective use of comedy than the specifically comic situations. The comic scenes lack the fine turn of phrase and the subtly moving descriptions which are so much a part of the superb comedy of *The Hamlet* or "My Grandmother Millard."

The impact of the actions of the plot on Lucius Priest is the most important focus of the novel. This is basically the story of

---

[2] In "The Bear" section of *Go Down, Moses,* this incident occurs in 1878; here it occurs in 1905.

his being thrown into situations which he would normally not have had to face at such an early age, perhaps even never have had to face, and of his discovery that he had lost forever the innocence and the ignorance of childhood, concerning which Grandfather Lucius Priest, the narrator, does say at one point, "His [a boy's] only innocence is, he may not yet be old enough to desire the fruits of it, which is not innocence but appetite; his ignorance is, he does not know how to commit it, which is not ignorance but size" (p. 46). Nevertheless the novel emphasizes the anguish of soul which Lucius Priest experiences as he participates, through commission or acquiescence, in lying and deception. The moral instruction which one generation of Priests receives from the preceding one as a matter of course receives continual emphasis. The contrast between Lucius Priest and the other occupants of the Memphis house of prostitution is similar to the dichotomy of "quality" versus "unquality" in "There Was a Queen" though the result of such an emphasis is more conventionally instructive in *The Reivers*. The sermon which Boss Priest gives Lucius at the end of the novel, on the attributes of a gentleman, as he tries to help Lucius realize that he, Lucius, must now, in incipient maturity, learn to live with the stains of his sin upon his soul brings to a manifest climax the didacticism which has recurred throughout the novel. Grandfather makes his point unfeignedly.

The plot is structured, as the title implies, upon the theft of an automobile and a horse, and the tension depends upon Ned's ability to race the horse successfully so that all three offenders might return to Jefferson with a minimum of retribution to face. Minor elements, such as the conflict between Boon and Butch Lovemaiden over Miss Everbe Corinthia or Otis and his desire for money, help to complicate the story line and strengthen the tension. Though the plot moves in relative chronological simplicity from the moment that the narrator, Grandfather Lucius Priest, begins his reminiscence, some actions which were omitted at the beginning, ostensibly because Lucius, the eleven-year-old, did not participate in them, are recapitulated in Ned's explanation of the sequence of events.

In addition to the carry-over of characters from Faulkner's other work, certain themes also reappear in *The Reivers*. The importance of the grandfather-grandson relationship occurs here. Father is a relative nonentity; the dominant personality is that of the patriarch. Such a relationship is stressed in *Sartoris* and in the Charles Mallison-Gavin Stevens associations of *Knight's Gambit* and *The Town* and *The Mansion*. Another theme, common in the work of Faulkner which occurs in *The Reivers*, is that of the gentlemanly agreements not to embarrass one another which abound in the paternalistic Negro-Caucasian relations. It appears here in the John Powell-Maury Priest tacit assumption concerning John's pistol, and in the Ned McCaslin-Boss Priest restraint over the bets on the horse race. Such arrangements allow the white man to pronounce edicts restricting the freedom of the lower economic group and allow the lower economic group to ignore the edicts so long as neither party brings the issue to a confrontation, disadvantageous to both. Such arrangements are personified by Simon Strother in *Sartoris* or almost any other Negro in Faulkner's novels and short stories, except Lucas Beauchamp, who considers himself outside the pale of such an arrangement.

The Priests with whom the novel is primarily concerned are a branch of the McCaslin-Edmonds family; they have occurred in no other novel, and since they are a full-blown family, drawn with a dominant grandfather and aspects of five generations, they might have provided Faulkner with the opportunity for an entirely new family cycle. One disadvantage of such a potential, however, is that they seem to fit a familial pattern representing an amalgam of Faulkner's own family with various elements of families earlier utilized.

The Reivers falls short of Faulkner's better work because it lacks the technical complexity, the artistic vitality, the artistic fiber which characterize Faulkner's best efforts.

REQUIEM FOR A NUN [1]

The historical cycles of a people alternate with the baring of a human soul in *Requiem for a Nun*. The people are the Mississippians; the soul belongs to Temple Drake. Faulkner employs contrapuntal arrangement of historical narrative-expositions and purely dramatic sequences to place in balanced juxtaposition the cyclical development of a society with the "petty pace" of an individual life.

The historical narratives are used as preludes to the three acts of the dramatic sections, and ostensibly they take their names from the three buildings in which the most important actions of the dramatic sequences occur. "The Courthouse: A Name for a City" relates the history of the Courthouse at Jefferson, Yoknapatawpha, from its inception to the present. The legends surrounding the reason for its construction, one of which ascribes its origin to the exigency of paying for a lost lock, are presented in a narrative style typical of Faulkner's Yoknapatawpha stories. It is in this courthouse that Nancy Mannigoe is tried and sentenced for the murder of Gowan and Temple Drake Stevens's infant daughter. "The Golden Dome: Beginning was the Word" is a recounting of the history of Jackson as the capital of Mississippi. Gavin, and Temple, and secretly Gowan, travel to Jackson so that Temple can confess her corruption to the Governor. "The Jail" is an eloquent exposition of the history of Jefferson and its sur-

---

[1] Published New York: Random House, Inc., 1951. All quotations from the novel are from this edition and are marked by page numbers in parentheses.

rounding area, utilizing the jail as a point of reference. This discussion is actually a recapitulation of the South's history; in addition it recounts a legend of the sort which gives the Southerner personal identification with a heritage which says, "Listen, stranger; this was myself: this was I" (p. 262). Nancy Mannigoe is confined in this same jail, and Temple Drake Stevens last visits her here.

These narrative-expositions pose the historical sequences which constitute the past of Southerners, Mississippians, and Yoknapatawphans. Various stages in the societal development of the milieu in which Temple Drake Stevens lives are presented, and the incidents recorded stress that the continuum of motion which man calls progress proceeds despite the limitations of individuals, despite the yieldings to exigencies, even despite the inanities of human beings. These sections transport the reader into the powerful realm of imagination where "the rubble-dross of fact and probability" are burned away, "leaving only truth and dream," emphasizing that "there is no time: no space: no distance" (p. 261). Significantly the drama of *Requiem for a Nun* concerns truth on a personal level, as Temple seeks expiation for her wickedness.

The story of Mrs. Temple Drake Stevens's attempt to work out her own soul's salvation is presented in the form of a play, with division into acts and scenes and with appropriate stage directions. These dramatic sequences concern Temple Drake Stevens's struggle with the truth about herself, which results in a Calvinistic confession that she has an inherent affinity for evil.

By the end of *Sanctuary,* for which this work is a sequel, the reader is quite aware of Temple's inner corruption. But at the beginning of *Requiem for a Nun,* Temple Drake has been Mrs. Gowan Stevens for eight years and is the mother of two children, a son Bucky and an infant daughter. The throes of admitting the truth are the more intense because Temple must tear down the facade of Mrs. Gowan Stevens and rip clear through to Temple

Drake, about whom confession must be made before any hope can exist for redemption. The whited sepulchre of corruption must be removed by Temple herself, and for this reason Gavin insists that the appeal to the Governor must be made by Temple Drake, not Mrs. Gowan Stevens.

This religious drama pivots on the contrast between Temple and Nancy Mannigoe. Temple was the daughter of a wealthy judge, a descendant of statesmen and soldiers, "the all-Mississippi debutante whose finishing school was the Memphis sporting house" (p. 116). She is held as a willing captive by Popeye Vitelli, a murderer for whom she later committed perjury and sent an innocent man to his death. She is the young Jeffersonian socialite who is now seeking absolution for her past by asking clemency for the murderess of her daughter. Conversely, Negro Nancy Mannigoe (a corruption of Maingault) is a "Whore, dopefiend; hopeless, already damned before she was ever born, whose only reason for living was to get the chance to die a murderess on the gallows" (p. 120–1). In her ignorance Nancy, having tried everything else she knew, suffocated Temple's infant to save the marriage of Gowan and Temple, and to secure the home of Bucky. This death, this murder, is the moral act of love which motivates Temple's desire to save Nancy's life. Ironically, Nancy understood from the beginning the import of her act and did not shrink from its consequence, but Temple must writhe through the agony of a public confession before she recognizes the moral implications of her own actions.

Under the guise of procuring pardon for Nancy, Temple Drake Stevens, accompanied by Gavin Stevens, goes to Jackson to confess her past crimes to the Governor, hoping that he too will realize Temple's ultimate responsibility for the death of her child and free Nancy. After Gavin has forced Temple to realize that "The past is never dead. It's not even past" (p. 92), she is able to confess that she liked the evil of the Memphis experience, that she had loved Alabama Red, and that her intended elopement with Red's brother Pete occasioned Nancy's drastic action. Rising, still tearless, from her kneeling position before the Governor's desk, Temple finds Gowan in the Governor's chair and understands that he now knows all of the past she had kept from him. Temple also recognizes that Nancy's sacrifice is requisite and that the trip to Jackson was not for Nancy but for her own soul.

An important distinction between Nancy and Temple is that Temple is still, even at the end of the work, basically concerned with herself, while Nancy's thoughts are of others. When Nancy tries desperately to prevent Temple's elopement with Pete, her concern is with the welfare of the children. She says, "I aint talking about any household or happiness neither— . . . I'm talking about two little children" (p. 188-9). In the final interview also, Nancy is not anxious about her death; she is trying to tell Temple that the answer to her problems is to "Believe" (p. 283). The tension in the earlier dramatic sequences arises not from whether or not Nancy will be saved but from how much of her past Temple must reveal to the Governor. Temple's ultimate concern is "What about me? Even if there is one and somebody waiting in it to forgive me, there's still tomorrow and tomorrow. And suppose tomorrow and tomorrow, and then nobody there, nobody waiting to forgive me—" (p. 283). The difference in religious attitudes is represented, whether Faulkner intended it or not, by the distinction between Nancy's "Yes, Lord" (p. 51), and Temple's excessive use of the catch phrase "Oh, God." The title refers to Nancy, the devout religious figure about whom Gavin says, "In the eyes of the law, she is already dead" (p. 82).

Furthermore, Nancy Mannigoe is the only believable character in the drama; the others, and this is particularly true of Temple, seem wooden or type characters lacking vitality, mouthing unconvincing lines which sound more like an author writing than a character speaking. *Requiem for a Nun* is a quite uneven work. The historical narrative-expositions for the most part far exceed in quality the dramatic sequences, which simply illustrates that Faulkner was a novelist, not a dramatist.

SANCTUARY[1]

Sanctuary is the ill-conceived product of a master artist. Faulkner prominently proclaimed that it was planned as a horrifying tale for the purpose of making money. Recognizing Faulkner's penchant for irony, one might be tempted to look for other purposes in the novel. Such an activity would be treacherous and would likely better reveal the aptitude for analogy in the examiner's mind than any inherent excellence in the work.[2] *Sanctuary* did two things for Faulkner: it made money for him and it made him notorious. It is an invective against society, and partially against women. It is Faulkner's most angry novel and one of his least satisfactory esthetically. It is a work filled with artifice, but a most important trick in the novel—the ironic death of Popeye —is too artificial. *Sanctuary* is set in Jefferson and some characters who have appeared in earlier work are given major roles. An attitude of despair and distaste pervade this novel and distinguish it from other Faulkner novels except *Requiem for a Nun,* its sequel.

Stylistically the hand of Faulkner is to be seen in *Sanctuary.* The lush prose verbiage, the interest in parallels, the furtive symbolic allusions, and the excellently narrated comic scenes all

---

[1] First published New York: Jonathan Cape and Harrison Smith, 1931. Subsequent references here are to the Modern Library Edition, 1932, which has the same pagination as the Cape and Smith publication.

[2] One of the most lucid and reasonable discussions of *Sanctuary* is to be found in Lawrance Thompson's *William Faulkner* (New York: Barnes & Noble, Inc., 1963).

reveal the hand of the mature artist working through the material.

The sham that is conventional society is the object of ridicule and tirade in this work. Horace Benbow represents an attempt to get away from the destructive classification of men into neat little boxes of conformity. His story of the shrimp and his distaste for the rut in which he found himself give notice at the very beginning of the novel that the stultifying facade of society will be assaulted. Horace is a man kindly disposed, highly idealistic, and totally ineffective. His opponent, with whom he is contrasted from their very first meeting at the spring, is not representative of the civilization from which Horace is revolting. Popeye is himself a departure from the mores and codes of the majority. But Popeye has enough practicality to perceive the weaknesses of conventional society and turn them to his own advantage. He is engaged in a highly lucrative liquor traffic, which while indubitably illegal, panders to a vice in society. Thus Popeye finds within the framework of his environment a niche for his nefarious life; he accommodates the realities of society to himself. Horace, significantly, does not choose to cooperate with his environment; he laments its deficiencies and illogicalities, but he does not understand how to manipulate them to advantage. Perhaps more importantly he lacks resolution, as he himself says, "I lack courage: that was left out of me" (p. 18).

Horace considers women as the root of his problem, and they do dominate him quite easily. Ruby Lamar infers immediately that he is a man to be manipulated by women. She says, "He better get on to where he's going, where his women folks can take care of him" (p. 13). His women folks, in the person of Mrs. Narcissa B. Sartoris, master him completely. Narcissa ruins his case by collaborating with the District Attorney, she sends him back to Belle, the selfish woman he stole from Harry Mitchell, and all Belle says when he returns is "Lock the back door" (p. 360).

Horace curses the suspicion of women which implies that his relations with Ruby Lamar are improper, and he rails against women whom he imagines to be the moving force responsible for Ruby Lamar's having been thrown out of the hotel. He objects to his sister's antipathy toward Ruby and toward his participation in the Goodwin case. But even while he verbally rejects the interference of women in his affairs and disavows any concern for their opinions, he

> knew he was just talking. He knew that she [Ruby] knew it too, out of that feminine reserve of unflagging suspicion of all peoples' actions which seems at first to be mere affinity for evil but which is in reality practical wisdom. (p. 241)

The invectives uttered by Horace are, however, neither so bitter nor so pertinent to the central theme of the novel as those pronounced by Ruby Lamar. Ruby has a clear insight into the moral weakness of Temple Drake and she does not mince words in exposing it. She condemns the love of sham in which Temple glories. Temple has no respect for the truth so long as she can keep up appearances; that she is in reality a slattern (as Ruby labels her) is inconsequential if she can pretend to be a lady. Ruby Lamar, former prostitute and at the time of the novel living with Lee Goodwin without benefit of clergy, has a clearer moral insight. Ruby's life is guided by her selfless love for Lee Goodwin for whom she dares the social ostracism of an uncharitable society. She does not plead ignorance of actualities or of the consequences of her actions as Temple through youth would seek an excuse. Ruby understands the rules and she is willing to take the risks without cringing at the punishment. Because she loses Lee, she suffers the only genuine loss in the novel. The injustice which society and its court deal to Ruby gives tragic overtones to her actions.

Temple Drake's suffering is not tragedy, because she is deceitful at the beginning of the novel and she is deceitful at the end. The only change in her condition is that she herself recognizes just how deep the corruption goes. Temple's attitude toward her degradation prevents empathy. Ruby describes her actions at the Old Frenchman's place as more in the nature of coquetry than in the nature of fearful flight. Popeye apprehends the tremendous vanity in Temple, and though he is the agent of her horrendous violation, he is able to maneuver her easily with appeals to her egoism. That she has been brutally attacked and is being kidnapped is less important to Temple than the possibility that someone who knows her in the respectable role of Judge Drake's daughter will see her, her make-up awry, riding in Popeye's Packard.

The scene between Temple and Red at the Grotto night club reveals the intensity of her nymphomaniacal moral destitution. In this meeting of emotional frenzy, Temple reveals completely the corruption which has been latent in her all the time. The total admission of the coarse nature which Temple has tried to hide behind a facade of apparent conformity to the conventions of society reveals what has been being made clearer and clearer as the novel progressed: that Temple enjoys the degradation.

With the revelation of Temple's inner grossness, Faulkner damns the society which praises appearance above honesty, the environment which values the facade of respectability more than justice and truth. The story of Temple Drake is a superbly ironic mockery of hypocrisy. The symbolic use of Temple as a painted woman representing the falsities of unwholesome society is epitomized in the court scene. Temple, her naturally black hair dyed red, carrying the platinum bag Popeye had bought her, perjures herself to condemn an innocent man and protect her sensual escapade from the scandal it would create if exposed. Faulkner not only symbolizes the discrepancy between the appearance and the reality of society, but also vividly portrays the violence which such a society will condone to protect that inconsistency. The lynching of Lee Goodwin is the final comment upon the depravities of society, and this statement is repulsively caustic. The return of a defeated Horace Benbow to his obsequious position in Kinston is an appropriate image; this Prufrock too admits his weakness, his subservience to appearance.

A parallel of depressing implications also centers on Horace Benbow. At the beginning of the novel he is berating little Belle because she has picked up a boy on the train. Sen. Clarence Snopes refers to Horace's father as a judge and expresses the hope, feigned or otherwise, that Horace will someday attain that position. After he returns to Kinston, Horace calls little Belle at a house party to discover her deeply involved with another young man. The parallel implies that little Belle is another Temple, that she is morally corrupt though she has the appearance of being a proper young lady from an upper-class family. Perhaps she is following the example of adultery set by Horace and her mother. The implications of this parallel are a scathing rebuke to the artificiality of society.

Irony is perhaps most forcefully met in the personal story of Popeye and the account of his execution for a murder he did not commit. This entire sequence calls attention to the needlessness of Popeye's death. His familial background is a pitiable one, from his syphilitic birth on December 25, to his suicidally insane grandmother, to the annual visits with his incapacitated mother in Pensacola. Though the reader might feel some pity because of the background from which he comes, the irony of his death is so great that it not only puzzles his lawyer, but it also distracts the reader with inexplicable questions. One wonders if Popeye is virtually committing suicide because he has lost Temple, why he has so suddenly lost interest in life, and if Popeye's own baseness has shamed him into seeking escape in death. The injustice of his case, the deliberation of the jury for eight minutes, and his calm acceptance of death all parallel Lee Goodwin's case. Popeye, however, is not a victim of society; he dies by his own will. But the perplexing manner of his death voids the sympathy created by his biography and presents a disconcerting ambiguity.

Along with all of the gross actions of the novel, Faulkner does manage to include a few humorous touches throughout the work. Miss Jenny's comments are piquant, as they were in *Sartoris*. Miss Reba Rivers is herself a fine comic character. She conducts the affairs of her bordel with a high sense of merriment, and she seems to be amused with the comic arrangement of Virgil Snopes and Fonzo [Winbush] as boarders in her house. Uncle Bud, Miss Myrtle's beer-drinking child visitor, provides some clever scenes, and Red's funeral provides some excellent farcical moments. The levity of Miss Reba Rivers offsets the sordid nature of the relationship between Popeye and Temple, just as Faulkner's technique of revealing very gradually and in retrospect the account of Temple's experience in the crib prevents the incident from becoming pornographic.

Sanctuary resolves itself with a particular neatness. Lee Goodwin and Popeye have both been executed. Gowan Stevens and Temple Drake have both fled to Europe. Horace Benbow has resumed his servile position with Belle. Narcissa is no longer vexed by the unconventional actions of her brother, and she can pursue her narcissistic pleasures. The novel, however, seems to suffer from a defect seen in Faulkner's earliest novels. The idea behind the novel seems to overpower the characters. Ruby Lamar, Lee Goodwin, Mrs. Genevieve Du Pre, and Miss Reba Rivers are notable exceptions. It is significant that most of the major characters suffer a lack of reality which may be induced by Faulkner's employing some sort of inverse religious symbolism, the exact delineation of which has yet to be explained. One recognizes such obvious references as *sanctuary, temple,* and the statement "My father's a judge." Popeye was born on Christmas day, he was illegitimate, and in his death section he constantly says, "For Christ's sake." Thus Temple may be the Sanctuary and this may be the story of the ravaging of the sanctuary. Horace leaves Belle ostensibly because she insists on eating shrimp every Friday. This is a matter too ambiguous and too detailed to be fully examined here.

SARTORIS[1]

When Roland was finally prevailed upon to sound his thirty league horn at Rouncevaux, glorious death in battle was already assured. Help could not arrive in time to save him, and the story of his bravery, albeit fraught with juvenile enthusiasm and temerity, was destined for legendary immortality. Such action is the subject of Sartoris; the novel closes with these thoughts:

> But perhaps Sartoris is the game itself—a game outmoded and played with pawns shaped too late and to an old dead pattern, and of which the Player Himself is a little wearied. For there is death in the sound of it, and a glamorous fatality, like silver pennons downrushing at sunset, or a dying fall of horns along the road to Rouncevaux. (p. 380)

A *sartoris* then is a man deeply concerned with the death wish, a man seeking an exit from this life, not just a departure but a departure like a shooting star or like "another rocket to glare for a moment in the sky, then die away" (p. 358). Suicide will not suffice; but a glorious death—in battle, in a duel, in a speeding car, or face to face at the hands of an enemy—lends the touch of glamour to a life of heady recklessness. *Sartoris* recounts the glories of a family of forceful if sometimes incautious men and the strong-willed women who supported them. This novel is based upon the history of William Faulkner's own family. Col-

---

[1] First published New York: Harcourt, Brace and Company, 1929. Reissued 1951. Subsequent references to *Sartoris* are from that edition. Other editions have the same pagination.

onel William Cuthbert Falkner (the great-grandfather for whom the author is named) fought colorfully in the Civil War, returned to Mississippi to build a railroad, to run for a seat in the legislature against his erstwhile partner, and finally to be shot by that partner. These activities correspond to those of Col. John Sartoris. J. W. T. Falkner, the author's grandfather was a banker, corresponding to Bayard (old). The author himself was an R.A.F. aviator in World War I, though he did not actually engage in the war. A younger brother Murry C. Falkner served in World War I in Europe and was wounded in France. A third brother Dean Swift Falkner also an aviator died in an airplane crash in Mississippi. A composite of these activities provide the experiences of Bayard and John, the Sartoris twins. *Sartoris* is a lively portrait of the audacious impetuosity that was *sartorisism*.

Young Bayard is the Sartoris with whom the novel is most concerned. He has returned from World War I, physically well, but psychically injured because his younger twin, Johnny, has been killed in the war. The novel follows his activities from the spring of 1919 to the summer of 1920 as he tries to adjust to the unexciting life of a small town and to compensate for the loss of a part of his twinship. Ultimately the dissatisfaction with himself leads him to abandon his family and his pregnant wife and to find death testing a new aircraft he knows to be unsafe.

The relationship of the twins, who flew in the same R.A.F. squadron, is an extremely potent one. Quite unintentionally friends continually bring the difference in personality to Bayard's attention. Since he fares ill in such comparisons, his guilt feelings are naturally increased. John is drawn as the twin who was dominated by a spirit of amity toward other people. He made a parachute jump because the regular parachutist became ill, and John did not want the country people to be disappointed. (p. 72) He always remembered to take a few trinkets to Mandy, the MacCallum cook, because he knew the thought behind the trinkets meant more to her than money (p. 332). Everyone, except sour Aunt Sally Wyatt, who could never keep the twins straight, recalled John as warm, generous, and spontaneous (p. 356). Jackson MacCallum sums up the general impression of Johnny "Gittin' a whoppin' big time outen ever'thing that come up" (p. 333). And patriarchal Virginius MacCallum echoed, "He was a fine boy" (p. 333). By contrast Bayard is characterized as unfeeling, filled with bleak arrogance, and enjoying nothing. At one point he thinks, "Three score and ten years to drag a stubborn body about the world and cozen its insistent demands. . . . And he was only twenty-six. Not much more than a third through it. Hell" (p. 160). He never reveals remorse for his first wife and infant son who die while he is in England with the R.A.F. Narcissa Benbow Sartoris, his second wife, says of him, "He doesn't love anybody. He won't even love the baby. He doesn't seem to be glad, or sorry, or anything" (p. 298). Bayard seems never to have forgiven Johnny for dying in the war and leaving him behind. Every mention of any exploit of Johnny's adds to the anguish Bayard feels. Bayard feels guilty because he was unable to prevent John's death. Once he thinks, "You did it! You caused it all; you killed Johnny" (p. 311). Any comparison between himself and John aggravates the feeling of guilt. The irony is that the dead twin most enjoyed life and was appreciated by other people. Aunt Sally comments, "It was a judgment on 'em, taking John instead of that other one. John at least tipped his hat to a lady on the street, but that other boy . . ." (p. 74).

The violent spirit of their young twinship presses upon Bayard until he exorcises it somewhat by burning John's bear-trophy, his New Testament, his hunting coat, and a picture of his Princeton eating-club group. John is representative of life lived with a flair for the spectacular and with complete enjoyment. Bayard, conversely, presents not a tendency to pleasure or enjoyment but a compulsion to recklessly dare death to remove him. Though John never appears in the novel, his spirit is a powerful impetus to the actions of his twin.

Almost as soon as he returns to Jefferson, Bayard purchases a racing auto in which he carelessly speeds over Yoknapatawpha. After recovering from serious injuries gained in a major accident, Bayard marries Narcissa Benbow and settles down for a time to the conventional activities of a country gentleman. But when he scares his grandfather literally to death with his reckless driving shortly before Christmas 1919, he abandons the family. First he visits for several days with the MacCallum's; he contemplates suicide, but he rejects it. On Christmas day he leaves Mississippi and pursues a peripatetic existence. Finally in Dayton, he dies in the one way that a Sartoris can approve.

Old Bayard's position is somewhat peculiar. He was too young to be a hero in the Civil War (in which his father gloried) and too old for the Spanish American war (to which his sons went), and certainly too old for WWI (to which his grandsons went). He was not a man of blood and action as the other Sartorises had been. He has lived a long life, and perhaps as he says, "I am the first of my name to see sixty years that I know of. I reckon Old Marster is keeping me for a reliable witness to the extinction of it" (p. 104). Even his death is a departure from *sartorisism*. He dies of a heart attack, which, despite Virginia Du Pre's prediction that no Sartoris ever died from natural causes, is a quite natural cause, predicted by Dr. L. Q. Peabody. He does have one thing in common with young Bayard though. Dr. Peabody states it succinctly: "You'd be about as well off dead, anyhow. I don't know anybody that gets less fun out of living than you do" (pp. 99-100). Both Bayards pursue their lives with a joyless determination, seeking the few opportunities for a glorious death which present themselves.

But Bayard's position as witness is more suitably filled by Mrs. Virginia Sartoris Du Pre (b. 1839), youngest sister of Col. John Sartoris, and great-aunt to young Bayard Sartoris. In 1869, when she had been "two years a wife and seven years a widow at thirty" (p. 8), Jenny Du Pre came to Col. John Sartoris' Mississippi home and she had remained ever since. At the time of *Sartoris* she has watched Sartorises come and go for eighty years. She rants against the headstrong, heedless actions of the Sartoris men and yet she is herself a goad to that action. She regales her family with the story of her brother Bayard and his gallantly foolish death escapade. She says that wars just give Sartorises an excuse to get killed, but she glories in opportunities for women to evince strong endurance, opportunities which come by the deaths of their men. She twits Bayard (young) by saying that her Bayard achieved more with a horse in his two-bit war than Bayard (young) had been able to accomplish with his fancy airplane; at least he got himself decently killed. Narcissa felt that Miss Jenny was trying to make "me one of them" and that she would try to do the same thing to Narcissa's child. Consequently Narcissa named her son Benbow Sartoris. But persistently Miss Jenny replies, "Do you think . . . that because his name is Benbow, he'll be any less a Sartoris and a scoundrel and a fool?" (p. 380)

Faulkner seems to applaud Miss Jenny as a representative of the strong-willed women left in the South after the Civil War, women faced with the problem of strengthening and supporting men disheartened by a cruel war, women for whom *will* became a powerful tool for implementing order and meaning in a disrupted society. But these women were too often retrospective and sentimental. To compensate these tendencies in Miss Jenny, Faulkner has endowed her with a willingness to accept some aspects of the new and has given her a comic position as a sharp-witted, sharp-tongued commentator. Miss Jenny immediately accepts Bayard's car, goes for a long, speeding ride in it, and alights saying, "I wish I smoked cigarettes," and "Is that as fast as it'll go?" (p. 78) She forces old Bayard who has a wen on his cheek to visit a blood and glandular disease specialist in Memphis; and she never forgives Dr. Peabody because Will Falls' salve cured the wen. Miss Jenny continues her maternalistic domination of the Negroes as if slavery were still in vogue.

Miss Jenny's comic highlights, which prevent an effusive display of mawkish sentiment that might easily have engulfed the novel, focus principally on her resolute expression of unconventional attitudes. She tells scandalous stories, traditionally unsuited to one of her social status. She remarks at the end of a bridge party, "I think we are all tired of your party. I know I am" (p. 29). She is noted for her irate eloquence which soars when she reprimands Simon for telling old Bayard that young Bayard has returned. (p. 38) She is characterized by the author thus, "Miss Jenny, being a true optimist—that is, expecting the worst at all times and so being daily agreeably surprised—" (p. 204). About a gossipy woman Miss Jenny says "I admire strong character, even if it is bad" (p. 202). The fact that she rules the Sartoris household with a will only slightly less determined than that of a genuine martinet also gives added force to her comic quipping. Only at the end of the novel when she has outlived all the Sartorises except Benbow does her unrealistic determinism show traces of senility.

Narcissa Benbow Sartoris is a much less interesting character than Mrs. Du Pre, but she is certainly just as functional. She is the twenty-six-year-old sister of Horace Benbow and a member of one of the older, wealthier families in Jefferson. The letters which Byron Snopes writes anonymously to Narcissa and which Narcissa enjoys receiving, are an element of structural unity. The continual recurrence of the letters and the machinations of their perpetrator have the value of a subplot. Narcissa's connection with Horace is also an aid to the structural unity of the novel because it joins the Horace Benbow-Belle Mitchell affair to the Sartoris story. The marriage of Narcissa and Bayard and the birth of their son contributes to the continuity of the Sartoris family. The narcissism to which her name alludes is not strongly developed in this work. Indeed she is one of the more unselfish characters in the novel: she loves her brother dearly; she visits Miss Jenny frequently; she visits Bayard often while he is ill.

But her love for Bayard, springing up so suddenly is somewhat like the attraction of the moth for the light. She is frail, and he is destructive. Though his indifference is matched to some degree by her apathetic acceptance of events, Narcissa's connection with Aunt Sally also gives Faulkner an opportunity to present the attitude which the more conventional citizens of Jefferson had toward the rambunctious Sartoris twins. Aunt Sally rails on their ungentlemanly conduct and concludes, "Pride, false pride" (p. 74). It is Aunt Sally also who provides an opportunity for the insertion of the Snopes history into this story. Through the character Narcissa, Faulkner is able to weave various additional threads into the Sartoris tapestry.

Sartoris is the first novel in which the full range of Faulkner's literary powers can be felt. Early novels are marred by ineptitudes of various sorts, but here he has attained an early stage of mastery. The narrative moves forward primarily in the simple chronological order; the history of Col. John Sartoris is presented skillfully through the conscious reminiscences of old Will Falls; the background of Mrs. Virginia Sartoris Du Pre is brought in cleverly through an association with the colored glass which she brought from North Carolina. At one point—the day that Miss Jenny, Bayard (old), and Dr. Alford go to Memphis and Narcissa sits with Bayard (younger)—the time is halted and two different sections of the story begin at the same time and move forward toward a single point in time. And within the Bayard-Narcissa account of the day, the receipt of another Snopes' letter earlier in the time is revealed. The artistry of the narrative technique in Sartoris is remarkably clear, uncomplicated, and self-effacing.

A delightful element of this novel is the use of humor. Faulkner is a master of comic technique, and Sartoris exhibits some good examples of that fine craftsmanship. Much of the humor, as previously stated, centers on Mrs. Virginia Du Pre. With a flair for words she displays a zest which belies her eighty years. She is a master (or mistress) of repartee which she uses to dominate everyone from old Bayard to the Negroes. It is in her relations, too, with Simon and Isom and other lesser figures that her acid tongue spicily flavors the novel.

The Negroes themselves are the second major focal point for comedy. Elnora, Simon's daughter, is frequently depicted as singing. At the end of one section she sings "[the sinner] Say, 'Preacher got de women jes' de same ez I.' Oh Lawd, oh Lawd! Dat's whut de matter wid de church today" (p. 24). At the beginning of the next section Simon (Deacon in Proposed Second Baptist Church) goes into Belle Mitchell's kitchen to flirt with Meloney Harris. Another instance of effective humor derives from Caspey, Simon's son, who returns from World War I the day after Bayard does. He sits in the kitchen and tells about his experiences in France, both his military and his amatory experiences. The reader may relish the serious discrepancy between what he did and what he says he has done. The words in one part of Caspey's story are reminiscent of Rudyard Kipling's satiric poem "Tommy." [2] Simon in his loquacious pomp is the comic character in several scenes but in none is he funnier than when involved in getting old Bayard to repay funds of the Proposed Second Baptist Church, funds which Simon has "put out" for certain favors from Meloney Harris who uses the money to open a beauty salon.

In addition to a comic function, the Negroes exemplify another of William Faulkner's skills, that of dialectician. With great care and precision, Faulkner accurately depicts the language of the Negroes. He reproduces, in the intractable English spelling, the r-less speech, the use of d for th, and other phonetic distinctives of their speech, but more importantly he captures the rhythm of their sentences, their idioms. The Negro dialect is also scrupulously differentiated from the speech of the lower white classes typified by old Will Falls, or the MacCallums. The lower white

---

[2] A two page dissertation on the mule is well done, but it relies too heavily on the tradition of the literary comedian. Cf. p. 278.

class dialect is also *r*-less, but it is marked principally by the irregular verb forms and apocope characteristic of good seventeenth century English. Both of these dialects are nicely distinct from the speech of the well-educated Southerner represented by Aunt Jenny or old Bayard. Horace Benbow, Oxford trained, has a speech still different though in a less important and more pedantic manner. And there are even a few lines of Scottish dialect in the novel. These variations in dialect are not the result of superimposing a preconceived pattern upon the material, but the result of accurate observation of the speech in his region by William Faulkner.

Sartoris is a rather digressive novel despite the more obvious unifying factors. If young Bayard Sartoris is the central character (and the general focus of the novel as well as the sheer quantity of space devoted to him would indicate that he is) then the relationship of certain digressions to him is of primary importance.

The stories of Col. John Sartoris, told through Will Falls and the story of Col. John's brother Bayard, narrated by Virginia Du Pre, have the purpose of delineating the character and scope of *sartorisism,* of which Bayard (young) is the prime example among the living characters of the novel. The several digressions in their relation to *sartorisism* describe the tradition from which young Bayard comes and depict the forceful predecessors with whom he is compared.

Byron Snopes's letters to Narcissa Benbow, previously mentioned in the nature of a subplot, constitute the subject of the longest recurring digression. This series of actions contributes a great deal more than an insight into the selfish aspect of Narcissa's character. The reader could get the same intimation about Narcissa without knowing the identity of the person writing the anonymous letters. A substantial contrast is made by calling the reader's attention to the perpetrator of letters. In direct contradistinction to the indifference of Bayard toward Narcissa, Byron Snopes is consumed with physical desire for her. As a character he represents emotion; yet because he is drawn so vividly and realistically, he transcends the type character classification. Not only is he depicted as a sanguinary person in his letters and in his angry reaction to Virgil Beard, but also the fact that he cuts his knee and bleeds profusely (the only character in *Sartoris* who bleeds) implies symbolically the purpose for him in the novel. He is also named for a quite sanguinary literary figure. In addition to Bayard's indifference, Byron also contrasts appropriately with the rather academic interest which Dr. Alford displays in Narcissa. Because class distinctions make it impossible for Byron to vie openly for Narcissa's attention and because Narcissa's failure to respond to his anonymous letters precludes a secret liaison, Byron in a display of violent, if culpable, emotion leaves the scene. But not before his digression has strengthened the primary action of the novel.

The story of Horace Benbow and Belle Mitchell provides a digression which lends an entirely different kind of contrast to Bayard. Horace is on a par with Bayard socially and economically. Each has "plenty of money"; and each has participated in World War I (though in differing capacities). Mrs. Virginia Du Pre says, "They [Bayard (young) and other Sartoris men] ain't my Sartorises; . . . I just inherited 'em. But you just wait: you'll have one of your own to bother with soon; you just wait until Horace gets home, then see how long it takes him to get over it." (p. 53). Perhaps it is in this reaction to the war that Bayard (young) and Horace differ most. Bayard lost a part of himself (John) in the excursion and cannot find solace in anything; thus he chooses to pursue the glorious death of other sartorises. The war, however, seems to have affected Horace very little beyond giving him a dislike for Montgomery Ward Snopes and an interest in glass blowing. Horace falls dutifully into the family tradition of practicing law and continues an affair with Belle Mitchell which had apparently begun before he left for the war. Bayard also settles for a time into the family tradition of planta-

Mahon on the Cincinnati train, he gives a capsule statement of the plot:

> But he [Lt. Donald Mahon] was asleep. They looked at his face, young, yet old as the world, beneath the dreadful scar. Even Gilligan's levity left him. "My God, it makes you sick at the stomach, don't it? I wonder if he knows how he looks? *What do you reckon his folks will say when they see him? or his girl— if he has got one. And I'll bet he has (p. 29).* [Italics added]

Once he has set forth his intention, Faulkner moves directly into a review of the problems confronting returning soldiers. Though the pivotal figure is Lieutenant Donald Mahon of the RAF, the novel is chiefly concerned with the actions and reactions of the people who surround him.

Cadet Julian Lowe's problem is one of resentment at having been denied the opportunity of proving himself in the war. The nineteen-year-old cadet did not complete his training in time to engage in the actual conflict of the war. William Faulkner could himself sympathize with one in such a position since he had completed his preparation with the Canadian branch of the RAF only in time for the armistice. Cadet Lowe also serves a structural purpose to be discussed below.

Private Joe Gilligan (also called Yaphank) is a representative of a great many soldiers whose time on the fringe of the war was spent more in drinking and playing poker than in fighting. He has been discharged from the military but has not yet accommodated himself to the civilian world. His life is given an immediate directive when he finds and adopts Donald Mahon as a ward. He is joined in the adventure of caring for Lt. Mahon by Mrs. Margaret Powers.

The widow of Lieutenant Richard Powers, Margaret is suffering from a feeling of guilt because her husband had died believing that she loved him. They had met and married while she was working with the Red Cross in New York. After they had been married for three days, he was shipped to Europe. She thought that they had both realized that they did not love each other for "always." She made up her mind that she should write him and cancel their marriage on a friendly note. Before he received her letter, however, he was killed. Knowing that he had died with the situation unresolved made Margaret feel that she had been dishonest to him. The attention and later marriage to Donald is an attempt to absolve herself of the guilt feeling.

The Reverend Dr. Joseph Mahon, rector of the Episcopal church in Charlestown, faces the problems of a father whose son, once considered killed in battle, has suddenly come home. That the badly scarred body of Donald Mahon has simply come home to die is a reality which is most difficult for the minister to accept. Until the very latest moment he exhibits a frenetic hope shored up with platitudes.

The very fragile, sunlight-and-honey character, Cecily Saunders, is literally jolted from the lips of one suitor by the announcement that her erstwhile fiance is returning home that very day. Confronted by the prospect of marriage to a hideously scarred and slowly dying Donald Mahon, Cecily seeks an escape in a whirl of social activities and the attention of several suitors, finally eloping with George Farr, a suitor whom she has already taken as lover.

The problems of the above mentioned characters are the crucial ones for the novel, but there are other facets of the soldier-returned theme which are given relevant play in the story. First Sergeant Rufus Madden, who served under Captain Green and later under Lt. Powers, has returned to Charlestown, but he must keep silent about his memories of the war, particularly those memories pertinent to Mrs. Margaret Powers whom he meets at a dance. James Dough symbolizes the soldier who comes home with a physical injury—in this case a wounded leg. He must deal with the excess

of attention and sympathy which his role as war hero attracts.
A rather bitterly humorous aspect of this theme is portrayed
through Mrs. Burney, mother of Dewey Burney. Though Dewey
was under indictment for stealing sugar at the time that he was
permitted to enlist and though he shot Lt. Powers in a moment
of frenzy, his mother and his hometown never knew the real
story of his death. Madden, who did know, kept silent and
humored Mrs. Burney, who took great pride in the fact that her
son had died a hero's death on the battlefield. His death caused
people on socio-economic strata above her to pay some attention
to her.

When all of these problems and facets of the soldiers' return
have been examined, and when resolutions of one sort or another
have been achieved, the novel ends.

The structure of the novel is supported not only by the consideration of the adjustments of the returning soldiers, but also
by two other devices. A rather obvious horizontal chronology is
maintained, and a continual emphasis upon sexual attraction
helps to unify the novel.

The function of Julian Lowe is associated with both of these
devices. In Cincinnati he proposes to Mrs. Powers who postpones
him and sends him home to San Francisco, to mother and to activities more in keeping with his age. He is drawn to her partially by her beauty but perhaps more so by her emotional
maturity; she has known more of life. By allying himself with
her he would obviate some of his disappointment and gain a rich
personal relationship. His letters to her serve a double purpose.
They prominently call attention to the passing of time, dating the
whole sequence of the action, and they reveal changes in Julian's
attitude toward Mrs. Powers and toward himself. When he is in
San Francisco and she is in Charlestown, his interest in her is
weakened by the girls he dates and the impetus toward school
which his mother provides. Since he is younger than the other
soldiers presented in this novel, he is more easily acclimated to

the civilian world. By the time Mrs. Powers writes to tell him that she has married Donald Mahon and that Donald has died, her letter is returned by the Post Office department stamped "Removed. Present address unknown." The dissolution of the artificial ties between Julian Lowe and Mrs. Margaret Powers Mahon coincides neatly with the end of the novel, but those ties have served as an effective, if perhaps overly conscious unifying device.

Sexual desire is personified in *Soldiers' Pay* through the character of January (Januarius) Jones. The description of him when he first appears sets the pattern for his actions: "Jones, Januarius Jones, born of whom he knew and cared not, becoming Jones alphabetically, January through a conjunction of calendar and biology" (p. 56). By calendar and biology he is a satyr, having been born under the sign of Capricorn and having nurtured sexual desire in himself. He is lately a fellow of Latin in a small college, he talks of fauns and fornication, he greets almost every woman with his yellow look of desire, and he attempts to seduce all three of the women with whom he is associated—Cecily Saunders, Emmy, and Mrs. Powers.

From his appearance at the beginning of chapter two until the end of the novel, Jones and his machinations are utilized as a continually recurring refrain which strengthens the unity of the work. He begins as soon as he sees Emmy to plan designs upon her body, but he is diverted by the more attractive Cecily Saunders into a pursuit of her. Once he finally realizes the futility of his attentions to Cecily, he makes one patently ineffective approach to Mrs. Powers. Thereafter the primary story is interspersed with the physical clashes of Emmy and Jones. The frank licentious attitudes and actions of Mr. Jones also serve to underscore the unfulfilled desires of other characters. Julian Lowe wanted to make love to Mrs. Powers, but she easily thwarted him. Joe Gilligan too desires Mrs. Powers but only on the most respectable terms. She is unwilling to grant the permanence of such an arrangement, and consequently the spectre of physical desire is continuously present in their relationship as a mark of individual isolation. The honesty of Jones' intentions is in contrast to the hypocritical facade which Cecily builds to separate her real self from the view of other people. Jones even ridicules the imminent marriage of Donald and Cecily because of the dying man's lack of interest in sex or anything else.

Though Mr. J. Jones is smoldering with desire, he is notably unsuccessful in his pursuits. He has the potential of a good comic character—he is obese, witty, and a failure. Yet somehow in the handling of this character, Faulkner focuses on non-humorous inconsistencies rather than on the comic ones. To be sure Jones is at times comic, witness the foot-in-the-bucket-of-water, the physical repulsions he suffers as Emmy slams a door on his hand or outdistances him in a chase. But the scene in which he proposes to Cecily is a renunciation of the tenets he has held previously, and that inconsistency conflicts with the image of him as a comic figure. It prevents the smile or the guffaw which might have been evoked from the reader at Jones' every appearance.

Weaknesses occur in the treatment of other characters. Mrs. Margaret Powers Mahon is presented as a character whose sensitivity, maturity, and goodness are extremely complimentary to her twenty-four years. Yet the flatness which envelops her character most of the time is rarely broken, e.g., the conversation with Mrs. Burney in a downtown store. Perhaps it is that she is too good—too consciously good, that is. Her acceptance as an authority on people and their reactions is a rather self-conscious technical consideration. Her actions are not those of a believable character. Rather they are the actions which the author seemed to consider appropriate, in this given set of circumstances, to a character symbolizing the "good woman." Her motivation seems unconvincing and remote rather than pertinent and immediate. Her actions toward Cecily and Emmy savor too much of the condescending intrusion which she and Joe Gilligan deplore in other people. Her ridicule of Gilligan's name, while it is artistically justifiable—indeed a touch of reality—conflicts seriously with the image of kindness which the author has laboriously built up for her. She is a peculiar character who seems more the embodiment of an idea than a human figure.

At the beginning of the novel, Private Joe Gilligan, though he is drunk, is an interesting, rather witty character who shows latent excellence. But after the arrival in Charlestown, he is neglected, appearing only in the role of a somewhat slow-witted male nurse for Donald and a confidant to Mrs. Powers. Once the train bearing Mrs. Powers Mahon has left Charlestown, Yaphank again displays some of his earlier depth. It is unfortunate that so plausible and appealing a character was sacrificed.

Two minor points need to be mentioned. The vengeful response of Young Robert Saunders to the experience of having Mrs. Powers see him nude at the swimming hole seems unrealistic and unnecessarily intense. His reaction is apparently intended to complement, if not engender, Cecily's intention to marry Donald, but instead of strengthening the action, this episode detracts from it by its lack of verisimilitude. The descriptions of Cecily which are effective when first used grow somewhat monotonous with repetition. She is continually described as lithe as a sapling or bending like a tree or as wearing too thin clothes, "you can see right through her." The clothes, always too revealing, which represent an important facet of her character, receive so much attention that they tend to obscure the character. This device can be made quite effective as it is with Caddy's muddy drawers in *The Sound and the Fury*, but Cecily Saunders is the worse for it.

One of the strongest features of *Soldiers' Pay* is the descriptive writing. Most descriptions focus on nature, such as the pigeons around the spire of Rev. Mahon's church, or Rev. Mahon's garden. The descriptions of "Niggers and mules" (p. 151) are quite good and are anticipatory of the descriptions of Frenchman's Bend and Jefferson that will fill the later work. Sometimes the descriptions are well used to provide a shift in point of view—

consider the interlude (p. 115) while Mr. Saunders gets his first view of Donald. One particularly striking description is the image of Cecily in George Farr's mind—"Her body prone and naked as a narrow pool, flowing away like two silver streams from a single source."

The conscious artist is at work in this novel as evidenced by the use of snatches of interior monologue, the self-conscious erudition of Rev. Mahon and J. Jones, the clear unity of the work, and the descriptions mentioned above. *Soldiers' Pay* has its excellent moments—the early train scenes, some of the George Farr-Cecily Saunders scenes, and the touching funeral sketches. But it also has pedestrian moments—most of the Mrs. Powers scenes in Charlestown, the platitudinous chapter two, and some of the Cecily Saunders scenes. With all of the alert craftsmanship apparent in it, *Soldiers' Pay* should be an excellent novel. It is not. The intellectual interest in the problems overpowers the action and the characters, and the lack of consistent good quality weakens it. But it is a first novel which promises better things.

THE SOUND AND THE FURY [1]

On several occasions Faulkner said that *The Sound and the Fury* was his best novel because he worked hardest on it and he made the most magnificent failure in it.[2] No matter how confused one might become in reading the initial section for the first time, one cannot escape the realization that this novel is a work of sheer creative genius; the power of a master artist pervades each section and thrills the reader as he works his way from the idiot's

[1] First published Random House, Inc., 1929. References here are to the Vintage Books paperback (Random House) which has the same pagination as the Modern Library edition of 1946.

[2] Gwynn and Blotner, *Faulkner in the University*, p. 61.

section, through the contortions of an unbalanced mind, through the sarcastic irony of an egomaniac, and into the resolution given in the stately prose of an omniscient narrator.

No one can actually know what actions, what images, occur in the mind of a non-verbal idiot who has the capacities of a three-year-old (p. 36), but what William Faulkner presents in the April 7, 1928, section of *The Sound and the Fury* is remarkably feasible. For Benjy, the world is sensuous; he hears, he smells, and he sees. Taste and touch seem less important. He often relates taste in phrases like "the steam tickled into my mouth" (p. 45). Touch has most often to do with sensations of coldness, which he can also smell, and with a satin slipper which belonged to Caddy. The importance of the slipper to Benjy seems to stem more from the fact that he associates it with Caddy than from the smoothness of the fabric.

To Benjy hearing is an important sense. He hears the cows chewing in the barn, he hears the rain on the roof, and he hears what people say. He does not understand all he hears, but he can comprehend certain things, chiefly names. Roskus says, "He know lot more than folks thinks" (p. 51). He recognizes Caddy's name and after her departure from Jefferson, he begins to moan whenever anything reminds him of her. For that reason he likes to watch the golfers, and when they use the word *caddy,* he begins to moan. Faulkner says in the Appendix that Benjy cannot remember his sister but he remembers the loss of her (p. 19). Later he will remember the loss of his pasture and firelight when he goes to the state mental institution near Jackson.

More important than hearing however is sight. Benjy gives Faulkner an opportunity to tell the Compson story, or parts of it, through the eyes of one who did not comprehend what he saw. Benjy's sight is remarkable. He sees things that other Compsons do not or will not see. He observes scenes that subtly explain many secrets to the reader. Benjy watches Mr. Compson become a helpless alcoholic; he sees Caddy with her lovers; he sees the details of children at play that explain the directions the lives of the children will take when those characters reach adulthood; he sees his mother's interest only in herself; he watches Caddy climb up the pear tree to peek at the funeral of Damuddy; and he sees Miss Quentin climb down the tree to run away.

Some of the scenes Benjy is witness to have particular significance. He watches and records the scenes in which Caddy's drawers become muddy and the scene in which Dilsey says of the mudstain, "It done soaked clean through onto you" (p. 93). This image of the muddy stain soaking through becomes a central one in the explanation of Caddy's doom. Benjy watches as Luster and the carnival man with the red tie discuss the material evidence of Quentin's licentious conduct. This revealing scene becomes tinged with irony later as Jason says, "just you let me catch you doing it one time on this place, where my mother lives" (p. 258). He accompanies Caddy as she delivers a letter from Uncle Maury Bascomb to Mrs. Patterson, and he recounts the action as Mr. Patterson intercepts the letter. Thus Benjy's observances illumine his Uncle's character and clarify a later illness his uncle suffers. Through this objective, seeming indiscriminate use of Benjy's sight and hearing, Faulkner achieves a finesse and a significance that would be virtually impossible to obtain otherwise.

But it is with the sense of smell that Benjy discriminates and makes judgments, even though he himself does not understand why he reacts as he does or what he is implying with his reactions. Perhaps no one except Faulkner could fully realize the significance of Benjy's olfactory distinctions. When Caddy is in Benjy's good graces, he says, "Caddy smelled like trees." When Damuddy and Quentin (male) die, Benjy notes that he can smell it. Exactly what the *it* is Faulkner leaves to the mind of the reader. And when Miss Quentin's escape is recognized, Benjy says that he could smell *it*. He also notes that he can smell cold, and rain.

The significance of Benjy's smell-judgments seem to have to

do with morality. He dislikes the scent Caddy has when she has been with some one of her paramours, and he remarks that she no longer smells like trees. He rejects Caddy when she puts on lipstick or perfume. Benjy also applies this same measurement to Miss Quentin. But when the artificiality or the impetus to immorality has been removed, Benjy again notes that "Caddy smelled like trees." Consequently the reader comes to accept Benjy as a spokesman for what is natural and therefore good, as opposed to that which is sophisticated and disingenuous.

Benjy's moral judgments are also recorded by his moaning and whimpering. Sometimes Benjy records that he starts to cry, but most often the reaction of some other person indicates that Benjy has begun bellowing. Benjy bellows when the golfer dishonestly takes Luster's golf ball (that Luster obtained the ball dishonestly in the first place seems not to have registered on Benjy). He also moans when Caddy or Miss Quentin displeases him. In these instances, the moaning serves a negative adjunct to the positive statement about the odor of trees. These devices provide a simple, good-bad value system which one must not accept too readily nor extend too far. Benjy also wails when his toys or his flower or the view of a fire is removed, just as any young child objects to the cessation of what is pleasant or customary.

Another remarkable facet of the Benjy section is its style. It is quite different from the involved, highly complex writing which is the trademark of Faulkner. This passage is grammatically and rhetorically simple. In fact, the syntactic simplicity, dictated by the involutions of the subject matter, is a remarkable achievement. What *is* sometimes difficult is the deliberate confusion of the chronological point of reference. The use of italics to indicate that a chronological shift has been made is helpful. For Benjy, Time has no meaning; his mind ranges freely from the present to any point in the past. The events in this section of the novel are joined by association, not by chronological compartmentalization. In this manner Faulkner has used the stream-of-consciousness device to narrate important aspects of his story. Benjy's mind wanders to a dozen or more different time periods during the course of April 7, 1928, but each event has some important relevance to the story at hand. The present is thus Time Cumulative; all that has gone before is a part of the Now. This concept is central here as it is in many of Faulkner's later works.

Benjy's observations are made to seem appropriate to him by the turns of phrase in which they are expressed. When Luster closes the stove door, Benjy says, "The fire went away" (p. 77). When Luster moves Benjy's flower, the notation is that it went away. (p. 73) Sometimes humor is evoked by the manner of Benjy's statements. For example, after Uncle Maury has been given a black eye and a burst lip by Mr. Patterson, Benjy notes, "Uncle Maury was sick. His eye was sick, and his mouth" (p. 62). At other times his descriptions simply seem poetic. He says of the rustling trees, "The trees were buzzing, and the grass" (p. 57). When lights are turned on in a room at night, he says, "The windows went black" (p. 79). Benjy describes his mother's hand patting Caddy on the back, "Her rings jumped on Caddy's back" (p. 81). Fear in a person's eyes is denoted by saying, "Her eyes ran" (p. 87). During the incident for which Benjy was gelded, a touch of pathos surrounds his attempt to communicate to the girls the feeling for Caddy which the appearance of any school girl evokes in him. He says, "I was trying to say, and I caught her, trying to say, and she screamed and I was trying to say and trying . . . ." (p. 72).

Unquestionably Benjy's section of *The Sound and the Fury* is a masterwork of consummate literary skill. But when the tale of the idiot did not satisfy the story, Faulkner turned to the mentally deranged brother and gave him a chance.

Quentin was the oldest of the children of Jason and Caroline Bascomb Compson; he was even from childhood a very sensitive person. He developed a sense of honor and propriety for the acts of human beings which no amount of his father's pessimism could dampen. Because Quentin could never make his conception of life fit the realities, he drowned himself.

Whereas Benjy was relatively oblivious to time, Quentin was harassed by it. He speaks of himself as "in time," and he wants to get out. Mr. Compson presents his son with the grandfather's watch so that Quentin would not have to expend all his energy trying to conquer time. But that is exactly what Quentin does. Quentin says, "That Christ was not crucified: he was worn away by a minute clicking of little wheels" (p. 96). In his concern with getting out of time, Quentin performs the act of breaking the crystal and tearing the hands from his grandfather's watch. Significantly he sheds his blood in the act. Quentin goes into a jeweler's shop to find out if any of the watches in the windows are accurate. The horologist replies, "No. But they haven't been regulated and set yet" (p. 103). And that is Quentin's problem too. He has not been regulated to the world's chronology, to the world's pattern, to the world's standards. He seems to fit but he does not.

The association with the Blands epitomized Quentin's situation. He is, for them anyway, a representative of the proper Southern society; he has manners and breeding. He knows the proper code of conduct; he writes proper social correspondence. He can be relied upon to respond as a gentleman in all affairs. But a serious discrepancy exists between the facade which Quentin tries to live and the actualities of life. And he can never reconcile the two.

The sexual liberty which his sister practices is so heinous that Quentin will not accept it, preferring instead to claim that they have committed incest, preferring damnation for the two of them so long as they are together rather than the separation which will result from her marriage. Quentin is repelled by Herbert Head whom he knows to be a blackguard. A sense of guilt arising from his own experimentation with a neighbor girl condemns him for Caddy's fall. Because he cannot sublimate Caddy's folly and thus "isolate her out of the loud world so that it would have to flee us of necessity" (p. 195), Quentin does the next best thing. He removes himself from the world.

Though the "sin" of Caddy is the immediate impetus to Quentin's suicide, other suggestions are given in his deranged thoughts.

He recalls his mother's rejection of all her children except Jason. He remembers her offer to take Jason and go away, leaving Mr. Compson the other three children. Mrs. Compson says that Jason is the only one of her children who has any common sense. In her attempt to maintain her sense of dignity in the face of Mr. Compson's imperious remarks that his family is better than hers, Caroline B. Compson becomes excessively egocentric; she sets Quentin a pattern for ignoring reality and assuming that things are as one wants them to be.

Mr. Compson too had his influence on Quentin's inability to adjust. He was an unusually pessimistic fellow, denigrating almost any concept of honor and nobility. Man, so he implied, was little more than an animal. Such an unpleasant view of life was certain to be rejected by his highstrung, adolescent son. Mr. Compson says, "A man is the sum of his misfortunes" (p. 123), and "it was men invented virginity not women" (p. 97). He also says that virginity is just a word, a negative concept contrary to nature (p. 135). With the example of selfishness in his mother and the epitome of apathy in his father, Quentin found himself with nothing to sustain him when his sister, the one person in the world whom he loved and respected, failed him.

Because he is depicting a sensitive, sophisticated mind in the process of disintegration, Faulkner has employed a complex style filled with parataxis, interruptions, and interior monologues in the Quentin section. The unhinging event is Caddy's giving herself to Dalton Ames, an incident which continually dominates Quentin's consciousness, preventing his mind from focusing on the present reality. At one point while mentally reliving the attempt to defeat Dalton Ames and thus preserve his sister's honor, he enters a psychotic state and attacks Gerald Bland. Quentin is vanquished in both encounters.

This section is fraught with symbolic representations for Quentin's disturbing problems. Time, symbolized by the clocks, is a trapping device which limits Quentin and destroys him. The odor of honeysuckle torments Quentin and confuses him. Once he says, "Honeysuckle was the saddest odour of all, I think" (p. 187). Later he notes, "the honeysuckle got all mixed up in it the whole thing came to symbolise night and unrest" (p. 188). Perhaps honeysuckle is symbolic of his home and the psychic wound he suffered there. Quentin is also concerned with his shadow and whether he can trick it or not. He thinks, "Niggers say a drowned man's shadow was watching for him in the water all the time" (p. 109). Quentin tries desperately to get away from himself. The vignette about Quentin and Julio's sister is symbolic of the role which Quentin adopted toward Caddy. He even refers to the little Italian girl as "little sister." And he is no more successful in his attempt to help the little girl in Massachusetts than he is in aiding the younger sister in Mississippi. In the mind of Quentin, at any rate, the experience of his wallowing in the pig pen and then throwing mud on Caddy is representative of his part in her degradation. He feels that he goaded her, inspired her to engage in fouler deeds than he did. That this may be a figment of his deranged mind is partially supported by the childhood remembrances of Benjy in which Caddy is depicted as a headstrong, willful little vixen. Dilsey even refers to her once as Satan.

The Blands might be symbolically considered as a projection of Mrs. Compson and Jason. Quentin knew that Jason envied his year at Harvard; he brooded upon Mrs. Compson's preference for Jason. Mrs. Bland is doing everything for Gerald that Mrs. Compson might wish to do for Jason. The close tie between Mrs. Bland and Gerald corresponds to the special link between Jason and Mrs. Compson, a link signified earlier by Jason's special relation to Damuddy, likely the maternal grandmother. Mrs. Bland's sickening bragging on the superiority of Gerald parallels Mrs. Compson's pride in the fact that Jason is more Bascomb than Compson. If this correspondence is accepted, then Quentin would have two subconscious motives for wishing to attack Gerald.

Faulkner has constructed in section two of *The Sound and the Fury* a skillful reflection of Quentin's deranged mind with its psychological symbols, its innuendoes, and its desire for death. Through this portrait he has darkened the outlines and shadows of tragedy in the Compson family.

Section three, "April 16, 1928," is narrated in the first person by Jason, "The first sane Compson since before Culloden and (a childless bachelor) hence the last" (p. 16). This is a marvelously ironic section and Jason's sarcasm places him in the category with such wonderfully evil villains as Iago and Richard III. He is a thoroughly self-revelatory villain and as such reveals more than he realizes.

From his very first remark, "Once a bitch always a bitch, what I say" (p. 198), to his last one (which echoes the first), Jason seems intent on showing just what a resolute, clear-headed businessman he is. He presents himself as something of a wit too with his facetious, sarcastic remarks which often turn out to be rather humorous. His mother says, "I know I'm just a trouble and a burden to you," but instead of calming her feelings and reassuring her as the rest of the family has always done, he replies, " 'I ought to know it,' I says. 'You've been telling me that for thirty years. Even Ben ought to know it now' " (p. 199). Later he finds Miss Quentin in the kitchen in her kimono. " 'I reckon that's your school costume, is it?' I says" (p. 201). He enjoys talking about how hard he has to work to feed a bunch of Negroes. Of Dilsey he says, "But that's all right: we need somebody in the kitchen to eat up the grub the young ones cant tote off" (p. 203).

Jason seems to constantly deride his family. He refers to Benjy as the "Great American Gelding" (p. 280). He ridicules the pride the family has taken in the fact that famous people have arisen in the family. He says, "Blood, I says, governors and generals. It's a damn good thing we never had any kings and presidents; we'd all be down there at Jackson chasing butterflies" (p. 247). When Dilsey remarks that she is the proper one to raise Miss Quentin because she (Dilsey) has raised all the other Compsons, Jason retorts, "And a damn fine job you made of it" (p. 216). He takes pride in the fact that he is much sterner in his dealings with Candace than their father ever was. Jason insists to Miss Quentin that he *will* uphold the family position in town, but she replies, "I'm bad and I'm going to hell, and I dont care. I'd rather be in hell than anywhere where you are" (p. 207). Later after Jason has been unsuccessful in attempting to catch Miss Quentin with the red-tie fellow, he goads her with feigned kindness at the dinner table. Quentin states unequivocally the result of Jason's cruelty, " 'Whatever I do, it's your fault,' she says. 'If I'm bad, it's because I had to be. You made me. I wish I was dead. I wish we were all dead' " (p. 277).

Not only does Jason seem to take pleasure in being the unsentimental member of his family, but he also glories in his role as an aggressive businessman. He has tricked his mother out of a thousand dollars which she thinks is invested in the hardware store where he is employed. He uses as much money as he can to speculate on cotton futures, and he assumes the stance of big operator, trying to impress Doc Wright and I. O. Snopes. He constantly curses the New York "jews" (not Jews by religion he says), because they mislead the country speculators and then take their money. Jason is arrogant toward Earl, his employer, and toward the Negro who works for the store. But Uncle Job, in an excellent squelch gives just the proper evaluation to Jason's cunning,

"You's too smart fer me. Aint a man in dis town kin keep up wid you fer smartness. You fools a man whut so smart he cant even keep up wid hisself," he says, getting in the wagon and unwrapping the reins.

"Who's that?" I says.

"Dat's Mr. Jason Compson," he says. "Git up dar, Dan!" (p. 267)

It is Jason's very bumptiousness which adds a measure of dramatic irony to the verbal irony he himself employs. After having told the reader how he tricks his mother who thinks he is good, he remarks quite seriously about religious people, "If there's one thing gets under my skin, it's a damn hypocrite" (p. 246). Though he considers himself very clever as a duper of his mother and Quentin and Caddy, his niece tricks him by stealing not only some of the money he has gained by deceit from his sister, but also some of the money he has struggled so hard to save from his salary. He is constantly threatening to whip her if she does anything else to annoy him, yet she impudently flouts his wishes with no more harm than a verbal redress. The townspeople understand the machinations of Jason, so that the sheriff refuses to aid him in his search for Miss Quentin. He says, "You drove that girl into running off, Jason" (p. 320) and adds "And I have some suspicions about who that money belongs to that I dont reckon I'll ever know for certain" (p. 320). Though the other speculators think that Jason is doing well, even during a market slump, he loses more than any of them. Jason's presumption almost gets him killed when he attacks the wrong man at the carnival camp in Mottson. It is a mark of weakness too that Jason, who must confront a mechanized world, is allergic to the odor of gasoline. All things considered, Jason is rather unsuccessful in his designs and that failure contrasts ironically with the portrait he paints of himself as an intellectual, aggressive personality.

When each of the three Compson sons have tried to tell the story, Faulkner himself attempts to complete the task.[3] None of

---

[3] Jean Stein, "William Faulkner: An Interview," from *William Faulkner: Three Decades of Criticism*, ed. Frederick J. Hoffman and Olga W. Vickery. (Michigan State University Press, 1960), pp. 73–74.

the women in the family are given a chance to explain the situation, though ostensibly Dilsey is the focus of the final section. Perhaps none of the women was suited for a role as expositor. Candace was aware of the psychological, moral, and financial situations in the family, but she was ostracized from the family during a crucial period. Mrs. Compson would not serve apparently because she had perceived only those things which she pleased to see. And Caddy's daughter Quentin was so young that she was unaware of the tradition of decay into which she had been born.

The final section focuses on Dilsey in her role as enduring witness to the downward movement of the Compsons. It is she who says, "I've seed de first en de last" (p. 313). That this section occurs on Eastern Sunday and that Dilsey and Benjy attend a church service has a symbolic significance for the story. Dilsey has been able to adjust to the inequities of life (*viz.,* the inaccurate clock for which Dilsey accurately and unhesitatingly compensates). Her position as Negro is crucial to this view of realism and Faulkner's comment, "They endured" (p. 22), supports the characterization of Dilsey as representative of her race, an American group noted for patient endurance. She is, too, a prime example of selfless service, a primary exhortation of Christianity. Dilsey also has a clear moral vision; she has suffered much but she has not whimpered nor steeped her mind in self-pity. She has not blamed God for misfortune nor expected special dispensations from Him. Her calm moral stance is a clean contrast to the simpering of Mrs. Compson in lamenting the loss of Miss Quentin, "Whoever God is, He would not permit that. I'm a lady. You might not believe that from my offspring, but I am" (p. 315).

But being a lady or a descendant of generals and governors is no assurance that inward corruption will not destroy a person or a family. The closing scene is appropriately given to a young

Negro boy and a thirty-three-year-old idiot whose moral sensitivity is innate and uncorruptible, and for whom flowed "cornice and facade . . . post and tree, window and doorway, and signboard, each in its ordered place" (p. 336).

The Sound and the Fury is not an easy novel to read the first time. It is quite difficult without prior knowledge of the family situation. Most of the difficulty centers upon the first two sections, revealed through aberrational minds. One might suggest that the sections would be better ordered in some other fashion, but certain justifying arguments may be presented for the present arrangement. In regular chronology, Quentin's section (June 2, 1910) would come first, Jason's section (April 6, 1928) second, Benjy's interpretation (April 7, 1928) would be third; and the present final section would remain as it is. The contents of the sections, however, are of greater significance than any arbitrary date that might be assigned to them. Benjy's exposition ranges from the present to the earliest recollection he has; more of the scenes from the early Compson childhoods are given in his part than are given elsewhere. Consequently, despite the date, the material given there chronologically precedes that given in predated sections. Likewise in Quentin's interior monologues, the material given concerns events later than those recalled by Benjy and earlier than those with which Jason is concerned. The two final sections thus arrange themselves naturally.

The Compson family suffers disaster for reasons as diverse as the personalities of its members. Mr. Compson is oppressed by the responsibilities which he has inherited; he looks backward upon the mistakes of his predecessors and he is so appalled by them that he seeks solace in bourbon. His moral energy is sapped by a despairing contemplation which precludes the action which might have rescued him and his family. Mrs. Compson's solipsistic world is only large enough to encompass her insistence upon inherited nobility and her wallowings in self-pity. She clings to a tradition of gentility which is no longer valid, and in the process she makes herself and everyone around her miserable. Quentin is the son who never matures beyond the idealism of adolescence. His life is a study in arrested moral progress, and he would prefer death to a reduction in his delusions of honour and his own potency. Candace comes to terms with the world in a materialistic manner which damns her and alienates her from the cold, uncompassionate tradition of her family. But she is not hypocritical and she does evince certain admirable human emotional qualities. Jason accommodates himself to the world by taking as his code *snopesism* and excelling in it. He is virtually unfeeling and his damnation arises from the ignoble philosophy he espouses. Miss Quentin seems justified in blaming her moral bankruptcy on Jason. He inherited her mother's sensitive temperament which has warped through Jason's cruelties. And Benjy existed.

The Sound and the Fury is the story of a family of moral cripples, a family as surely doomed by inherent weaknesses as Poe's Ushers. It is the story of individuals attempting to find a successful pattern to life, and mostly failing. Their story might be seen as an analogy for the decline of the Southern aristocracy and Benjy can be seen as an allusion to Christ. But such symbolism can easily violate the artistry of the work itself. One should remember that Herbert Head, a wealthy Indianian, is just as corrupt as the Compsons, that other Jeffersonians (Earl and the sheriff) experiencing the same post-Civil War changes do not prostitute themselves morally, and that Faulkner generally utilizes symbols in an allusive manner rather than in an allegorical manner.

As a creative work of the first magnitude, *The Sound and the Fury* will endure!

THE TOWN [1]

The second volume of William Faulkner's trilogy on the Snopes family is *The Town,* published seventeen years after the first volume had appeared. Focusing, not as its antecedent, *The Hamlet,* had done on Flem Snopes's desire for material gain, but on Flem's need for respectability, this novel does a great deal to humanize the character Flem Snopes; similar to its predecessor, *The Town* keeps Flem in the background while it emphasizes the frantic actions of other characters who try to understand Flem and to forestall his gains.

Employing a technique earlier used in *As I Lay Dying* (1930), *The Town* is structured upon a series of limited narrations. Three characters are used as narrators: Charles Mallison, who narrates ten of the reminiscences; Gavin Stevens, who recounts eight of the sections; and V. K. Ratliff, who narrates six of the monologues. In utilizing Charles Mallison, Gavin Stevens's nephew, Faulkner economically combines two narrators, Gowan Stevens and Charles Mallison. Charles relates events that occurred before his own birth, by ascribing his knowledge of them to Gowan Stevens who was at that time living in the Mallison-Stevens home. By this device Faulkner is able always to have a young, naive observer on the scene of a continuous action which happened over a period of twenty years. The presence of a young boy—twelve years old or younger—allows the author to bring out sexual innuendoes with a touch of gentle humor or to emphasize the humorously devious actions of adults as witnessed by the clear eyes of a child. The young narrator also provides a bland point of view from which to recount the witty remarks of Maggie Mal-

---

[1] Published New York: Random House, Inc., 1957. All quotations from this novel are from this edition and are noted by page numbers in parentheses.

lison or from which to present a consensus statement about the
action under consideration. At the very beginning of the novel,
Charles Mallison says "So when I say 'we' and 'we thought' what
I mean is Jefferson and what Jefferson thought" (p. 3). Charles
serves virtually as a chorus, commenting on the basic action of the
plot.

Gavin Stevens serves also as a monologuist-narrator who does
not grasp the significance of the action in which he is involved.
But in his case the failure to understand does not arise from youth
but from his inveterate talkativeness. Gavin is a loquacious chaser
of poets' dreams; he often ignores reality as he plunges headlong
into what he conceives to be the logical cause behind an action.
He is often talking, expounding his own theories when he should
be listening and observing. Sometimes he does not even understand what it is that he wants himself, as was the case in his suit
against Manfred de Spain for malfeasance in office, when what he
really wanted was Eula Snopes. Unlike the monologues of
Charles Mallison or V. K. Ratliff which comprise mostly recounted actions, most of the monologues presented by Gavin
abound in meditations upon the actions which have occurred or
which are about to occur. Gavin does not seem to understand
women, but when Eula tells him that "Women aren't interested
in poets' dreams. They are interested in facts. It doesn't even
matter whether the facts are true or not, as long as they match
the other facts without leaving a rough seam" (p. 226), he glibly
repeats this statement several times as if it were a principle he had
formulated. Ratliff says to Gavin, "You never listened to nobody
because by that time you were already talking again" (p. 229).
Gavin's verbosity helps to maintain interest as the reader follows
Lawyer Stevens's attempt to reason through Flem's actions to his
goals. But Gavin is almost always wrong because he races on into
his own fantasies, inaccurately ascribing motives and actions to
Flem. Lawyer Stevens's ineptitude becomes a recurring *leitmotif*,

and finally Gavin says in desperation, "What more can you want of men than I have already failed to do" (p. 313).

In contrast to the naive observer characterized in Charles Mallison and the uncomprehending observer characterized in Gavin Stevens, V. K. Ratliff represents a subtly clever observer who listens carefully and perceives quickly. If he does not understand the implication of an action, he simply admits his ignorance, and he does not hypothesize himself into error. He searches for the simplest explanation for the machinations of Flem Snopes, and he is more often correct than his more learned lawyer friend. Gavin characterizes him with these words, "Ratliff with his damned smooth face and his damned shrewd bland innocent intelligent eyes, too damned innocent, too damned intelligent" (p. 33). Ratliff's perspicacity and alacrity are emphasized by his awareness that Gavin uses one speech pattern when talking with his uneducated constituents and another when he is addressing a better educated person, and by his attempt to consciously emulate Gavin's more acceptable speech habits. Ratliff calls Charles Mallison's attention to Gavin's varieties of speech. He recognizes early in the novel that Flem's motivation is his desire for respectability, a fact only discovered by Gavin late in the work. Lawyer Stevens's failure to recognize this important facet of Flem's nature is another recurring *leitmotif*, as Ratliff continually reminds the reader that Gavin has "missed it" again.

Though the story moves rather straightforwardly through the work with often a barely perceptible shift from one speaker to another, the major unifying element of the novel is the theme of respectability. Flem Snopes has learned by the beginning of the work that he can easily make money and gain material possessions. But as Ratliff says, Flem learned almost too late that the one thing which he had to have to give meaning to his life or to permit him to enjoy peace in his life was not money or power but respectability (p. 259). Consequently Flem has to have a house furnished in a decor perfectly suited to the American man who has achieved a fairly large degree of success but who will yet attain a more acceptable place in society. Flem cooperates with Gavin in ridding the town of M. W. Snopes and personally arranges I. O. Snopes's departure from Jefferson, because he (Flem) had to protect his own name for the sake of respectability. But Gavin did not apprehend Flem's meaning when he said, "I'm interested in Jefferson. . . . We got to live here" (p. 176).

Gavin Stevens even unwittingly aided Flem in his effort to gain respectability by insisting that Maggie Mallison, Gavin's twin sister, call on Eula Varner Snopes and get the Cotillion Club to put its stamp of approval on her. Gavin was at that time blinded by his passion for Eula. Public acceptance is an important theme in the discussions of the town's attitude toward Eula and Manfred's adultery (see pp. 15, 307). Gavin Stevens's desire to get Linda Snopes away from Jefferson arises from his fear that her sense of a respectable place in society will be shattered if she learns that she is the bastard daughter of Eula Varner and that Flem is not her father.

Two of the best written comic sections of the novel had previously been published as short stories: "Centaur in Brass" (pp. 3–29), and "Mule in the Yard" (pp. 231–259). These two stories have been dovetailed into the construction of the work by employing "Centaur in Brass" to stress Flem's upward struggle, and "Mule in the Yard" to emphasize Flem's desire for respectability. "Centaur in Brass" also contributes to the novel by its double plot of cuckoldry. The infidelity of Tom Tom's wife parallels Eula's unfaithfulness. But the reactions of the husbands are importantly different. Tom Tom and Turl work in amicable cuckoldry because Tom Tom is ignorant of the situation. When he does find out about the adultery, he immediately reacts first with vengeance, and later with a humorous reasonableness. Flem, on the contrary, seems aware of the Eula-Manfred situation from the beginning and employs the disreputable arrangement for personal aggrandizement. He employs the adulterous relationship as Ratliff says, "like that twenty-dollar gold piece pinned to your undershirt on your first maiden trip to what you hope is going to be a Memphis whorehouse" (p. 29). And when, after continual recurrence, Flem does unpin it, he precipitates the crisis of the novel.

The Town does much to mollify the image of Flem Snopes as a completely impersonal figure who is interested mechanically in financial gain only. By emphasizing Flem's susceptibility to the same pressures for social acceptance that play upon other people, Faulkner has made Flem less odious and more pathetic. Eula says of Flem, "You've got to be careful or you'll have to pity him" (p. 331). And Flem could not stand pity.

This novel advances the Snopes story, adds a new dimension to the characters Flem and Eula Snopes, and enhances the character of V. K. Ratliff, but it lacks the artistic vitality and excellence of Faulkner's earlier work. Perhaps because it is the middle work of a trilogy, The Town moves too evenly and steadily toward a given point in the Snopes chronicle. It is neither marred by basic ineptitudes nor distinguished by especially brilliant writing, with the exception of "Mule in the Yard."

THE UNVANQUISHED [1]

Although the first six chapters of The Unvanquished appeared originally as short stories published from 1934–36, the addition of "An Odor of Verbena" gave the completed work the character of an apprenticeship novel, because Bayard's decision in the last chapter reflected the influences of the earlier episodes. Structurally the novel is unified by narrator and chronology. Bayard Sartoris,

[1] New York: Random House, Inc., 1938. Quotations (marked by page numbers within parentheses) are from the Random House photographically reproduced 1965 edition of the first printing.

son of Col. John Sartoris, narrates all seven chapters which focus on various incidents in his life. The first six episodic accounts concern events during or immediately after the Civil War; the final chapter centers on the crucial action in which Bayard avenges the death of his father. The novel is arranged in regular chronological order: "Ambuscade" occurs when Bayard is twelve years old; "Retreat" and "Raid" happen when he is fourteen; "Riposte in Tertio," "Vendee," and "Skirmish at Sartoris" take place when he is fifteen; he is twenty-four when the crisis of "An Odor of Verbena" arises.

The final dramatic action demonstrates the influence earlier events have had on Bayard. He is depicted as a sensitive person who has assimilated a code of values from his relationships to his father, his grandmother, and his Negro companion, Ringo, and from his own adventures.

Bayard was too young to fight beside his father in the Civil War, so he remained at home with his grandmother, Rosa Millard. Yet the presence of his father was a potent factor in his life. He romanticized the military activities of Col. John Sartoris, who, when he was occasionally at home, told Ringo and Bayard tales of bold raids and clever maneuvers outwitting the Yankees. Bayard observed the courage of his father and sought to emulate it. After the war John returned with a dream and with Drusilla Hawk, cousin to Bayard's deceased mother. Drusilla had disparaged the dullness of antebellum Southern aristocratic life and gloried in the active war, riding and fighting with Col. Sartoris's troop. John and Drusilla, who were married at the insistence of Mrs. Hawk, strove to maintain a semblance of society as John thought it should be in a Mississippi struggling under the mismanagement of Reconstruction. But the Colonel's dream was powerful, stretching beyond him, and his determination to accomplish his goal made him intolerant and domineering. Brought to desperation by Col. John Sartoris's harassment, B. J. Redmond, former friend and business partner, killed him.

Bayard recognized the elements in his father's personality which demanded respect but destroyed friendships. He chose not to follow the determined, ambitious pattern of his father's life, and he elected to avenge his father's death in a manner which Drusilla could not at first comprehend.

Balancing and, in some instances, counteracting the influence of Col. Sartoris is the power of Bayard's grandmother, Mrs. Rosa Millard. The first four chapters present her as the matriarch of Sartoris plantation; no one dared risk her ire. She gives Bayard (and Ringo too) conventional instruction in Ten-Commandment-type morality and inculcates social courtesies in them. But through her devout life, she does much more. She sets Bayard an example of unselfishness and tolerance. She ascribes their good fortune with the Yankees to the hand of God and uses the illegally obtained mules and money to help those less fortunate than she. Granny's constant practice of kneeling in sincere prayer is not unnoticed by Bayard. He and Ringo both kneel with Rosa Millard in the empty church when she confesses to God her sin in tricking the Union soldiers. She says "I did not sin for gain or for greed. . . . I did not sin for revenge. . . . I sinned for the sake of food and clothes for Your own creatures who could not help themselves" (p. 167). Mrs. Millard is killed when she does practice her trick, intending personal profit. Her desire to have some money to hand to Col. John when he returned, led her to consort with the cowardly criminal Grumby who shoots her. The revenge Bayard and Ringo take on Grumby is also important in Bayard's later decision.

The constant companion to Bayard in all the activities of his youth is Marengo (Ringo), a Negro, son of Simon. He and Bayard were born at the same time, were suckled at the same breast, and had eaten and slept together, so that no difference in race was important until Bayard went away to study law. Bayard recognized unenviously that Ringo was smarter than he, and when Ringo came to Oxford to inform him of Col. John's death,

Bayard meditated on his dependability. Ringo is the companion who shares Bayard's grief over the death of the colonel, and perhaps better than any other person, he understands the sense of honor which motivated Bayard's confrontation with Redmond.

But Ringo makes his own contribution to the novel. He is the wit, the comic character. When the story of the railroad (a mark of Bayard's advantage) is about to be diverted by the pathetic progression of Negroes, Ringo exclaims, "I been having to hear about niggers all my life. . . . I got to hear about that railroad" (p. 103). Though Granny (as Ringo also addresses her) credits the hand of God with their good luck with the Yankees, Ringo takes the initiative in making further gains with the same trick; then he retorts, "Whose hand was that?" (p. 130) He expresses a clever insight into Rosa Millard when he says, "And don't yawl worry about Granny. She 'cide what she want and then she kneel down about ten seconds and tell God what she aim to do, and then she git up and do hit" (p. 105-6). And with his quick wit, Ringo best aids Granny in executing her plans.

Besides these members of his immediate family, Bayard is influenced by his experiences with the Yankee he and Ringo shot at, the McCaslin twins, and Grumby. Bayard relates that as he raised the sights on the rifle to shoot the Yankee, he thought, "He looks just like a man" (p. 28). This incident and his other associations with Union soldiers helped him to recognize that the human brotherhood included even enemies. The comments of Col. John Sartoris about Uncle Buck and Uncle Buddy McCaslin's ideas of social relationship seem to have impressed Bayard particularly. Their attitudes that the earth was held in communal possession by properly behaving citizens, that Negroes should earn their freedom (this thirty years before the Civil War), and that the poor whites and plantation owners would both profit from pooled resources, seem to have indicated to Bayard the direction of future hope in human relations.

The affair with Grumby seems to have influenced Bayard in

two ways. First, it reinforced his idea that a cowardly man is the most dangerous sort to deal with. Granny was attempting to out-bluff Grumby, but because he was a coward, he became frightened and shot her. Secondly, the violent revenge which Bayard and Ringo took on Grumby seems to have directly contributed to the lack of violence in Bayard's revenge of Col. John Sartoris's death. The brutality which Bayard and Ringo at fifteen perpetrated on Grumby apparently quenched forever any appetite Bayard might have had for ferocity. Because he had reacted against Grumby with excess, Bayard seems able to deal in deliberate restraint with Redmond.

The final chapter, "An Odor of Verbena" presents dramatically the challenge Bayard accepted in his father's death. The influences of the past are brought to bear as he is torn by the religious teachings of Granny Millard, by his own intuition that God's supreme commandment is "Thou shalt not kill," by the remembrance of the Grumby vengeance, and by Drusilla's demand for the bloody retribution of her husband's death, an ultimatum strengthened by the expectation of Col. John Sartoris's former soldiers. Bayard decided to act with a bravery beyond his father's capacity, a bravery which required allegiance to a higher code than that of Col. John Sartoris.

The Unvanquished romantically depicts the adventurous experiences of Southern women and children during the Civil War and the struggle to begin rebuilding a post-war life. It uses these incidents to poignantly portray a young man growing out of that unrealistic enchantment with the excitement of war, turning his back upon violence, and performing a difficult moral action with courage.

THE WILD PALMS[1]

The chapters of *The Wild Palms* alternate between two contrapuntally balanced stories, "Wild Palms" and "Old Man." The relationship between the two parts builds upon obvious similarities and differences. Each tale focuses on an unmarried couple forced into a binding association by a power which the couples do not understand, and both couples are confronted with the problem of impending childbirth. The omniscient narrator presents the thoughts of the central male characters but not of the female; the men have similar experiences of timelessness and failure to roll a cigarette. Though "Old Man" occurs in 1927 and "Wild Palms" in 1937–8, both men are finally assigned to Parchman Penitentiary. The differences imply an inverse parallelism. Charlotte and Harry place all of their energies on maintaining their love; the convict (hereafter called the Tall Convict) and the woman struggle for simple physical existence. Harry is quite articulate about his experiences; the Tall Convict is virtually non-verbal for most of the narrative. Strong emotion dominates the actions of Charlotte and Harry; the Tall Convict is almost emotionless. But differences in philosophies and meanings complement the more salient distinguishing features and contribute to the raddled effect which creates the powerful impact of *The Wild Palms*.

Wild Palms   The impetus for the actions of "Wild Palms" is love between a man and a woman. The man in this case is Henry Wilbourne (Harry), a medical intern who lacked only a few weeks until the successful completion of his medical training.

---

[1] First published New York: Random House, Inc., 1939. All quotations from *The Wild Palms* are from that edition and are marked with page numbers in parentheses.

The woman is Mrs. Charlotte Rittenmeyer, wife of Francis Rittenmeyer and mother of two daughters, Charlotte and Ann.

With clear honesty Harry and Charlotte insist that their affair be frank and open, and though Mr. Rittenmeyer will not grant Charlotte a divorce, he does voluntarily permit her to make the experiment in love. Charlotte, the more forceful of the couple, recognizes the inherent pain in such a love as she and Harry possess. She says that "love and suffering are the same thing and that the value of love is the sum of what you have to pay for it and any time you get it cheap you have cheated yourself" (p. 48).

Such a love is difficult to maintain because Charlotte insists that their affair has "to be all honeymoon, always. Forever and ever, until one of us dies" (p. 83). Harry and Charlotte struggle to perpetuate such a relationship that they will be good enough, worthy enough, so that love will not go away.

But all of the challenges to their love do not come from within the partnership. Society cannot resist trying to destroy their "illicit love" (p. 82) just as women, and Charlotte in particular, are drawn to such a union by the dangers it offers. Society has powerful weapons with which to demolish the love of Charlotte and Harry. It employs the intimidating lack of money and later the more subtle temptation of comfortable respectability. Although they successfully evade these two traps, Harry says, "Of course we cant beat Them; we are doomed of course; that's why I am afraid" (p. 140).

The ultimate danger to their love arises from Charlotte's accidental pregnancy. A child would force social conventions upon the vagabonds or drain away a vital portion of the love between Charlotte and Harry. At last Harry, driven by desperation and Charlotte's pleading, performs an unsuccessful abortion.

As their love draws to a disastrous conclusion, they are ironically confronted by a doctor and his wife who personify all the forces against which they have been struggling. Living in a Mississippi coastal town, the doctor, with a Baptist background, exudes a superficial morality, desiring people to conform and be respectable. He is indifferent to their not being married so long as he does not have to enunciate the fact, because he knows that once it "was said aloud between them [the doctor and his wife], he would turn the renters [Harry and Charlotte] out" (p. 9). Though his wife has an "implacable and invincible morality" (p. 15), she (Miss Martha) reacts with hard-headed pragmatism when she discovers Charlotte's fatal condition. Miss Martha suggests that her husband help the couple get away from that locality, and she rebukes his desire to send Harry to prison; she says, "You're mad because he used a scalpel without having a diploma. Or did something with it the Medical Association said he mustn't" (p. 290). Then she goes and prepares Harry a cup of coffee.

Once Charlotte dies, Harry sits in jail listening to "the threshing of the invisible palms, the wild dry sound of them" (p. 295) and meditating on his condition. He lacks the will to escape or to commit suicide, even when Francis Rittenmeyer, Charlotte's husband, tries to help him. He thinks, "I have made a bust even of that part of my life which I threw away" (p. 283), and his final thought is "between grief and nothing I will take grief" (p. 324). And so he will apparently serve his fifty-year man-slaughter sentence in Parchman Penitentiary.

"Wild Palms" is a well-written story revealing Faulkner's mastery of the narrative techniques. The flashback, the fluency of diction, the precise characterization are all fully under the artist's control. But the actions of Charlotte and Harry fail of the tragic proportions necessary to arouse the empathy of the reader. Charlotte and Harry deliberately consider the eventualities of their gamble on love. Only then do they leave their respectability and conformity to attempt the experiment. Their situation is analogous to one in which Oedipus, knowing his father's identity, might deliberately set out to murder him and then marry his own mother, recognizing beforehand that what he intended to do would only bring sorrow and unhappiness; that it would be an affront which the gods would not ignore. Charlotte and Harry are not noble figures guilty of hubris; they are weak lovers perpetrating an action that is merely foolish.

Old Man Only little more than half as long as "Wild Palms," "Old Man" is the story of a convict's attempt to rescue a pregnant woman during the severe Mississippi River flood of 1927. The Tall Convict was an ignorant hill countryman who had never seen the Mississippi River, let alone fought against one of its rampaging floods. He is a character of action rather than words, and only at the end of the story does "the inarticulateness, the innate and inherited reluctance for speech" (p. 332) dissolve so that he can easily narrate his experiences to his fellow prisoners.

The Tall Convict uncomplainingly performs the tasks set for him in life which he considers to consist "of having to get up sooner or later and then having to lie down again sooner or later" (p. 147). He glories in "his own honor in the doing of what was asked of him, his pride in being able to do it, no matter what it was" (p. 166). Though he is troubled with a tendency to hemophilia, he essays to accomplish whatever assignment is given him, without ever thinking of doing otherwise. Ingrained in his very nature is the attitude that "After all a man cant only do what he has to do, with what he has to do it with, with what he has learned, to the best of his judgment" (p. 258).

Insisting on returning the boat and the woman to Vicksburg, where he started out, the Tall Convict has to work his way up from New Orleans where he was swept by the flood (p. 332). He stops along the river at various places and does odd jobs; sometimes he kills alligators with a knife and main strength; sometimes he plows a sorghum plantation. But in all of these activities he recalls how good it is to work and make money. Though he has several opportunities to escape, his only thought is to surrender his charge, turn his back "on all pregnant and female life forever and return to that monastic existence of shot-guns and shackles where he would be secure from it" (p. 153). With litotes he remarks to the deputy sheriff at the end of his expedition, "Yonder's your boat, and here's the woman. But I never did find that bastard on the cottonhouse" (p. 278).

The descriptions of "Old Man" are magnificent landscapes of a mammoth river gone berserk. The turbulence and destruc-tion of the Mississippi's flood crest are vividly captured in images of the swirling water like the "mane of a galloping horse and, phosphorescent too, fretted and flickered like fire" (p. 156), of "entire trees leaping and diving like porpoises" (p. 157), of the skiff hovering in "weightless and airy indecision like a bird above a fleeing countryside, undecided where to light or whether to light at all" (p. 157).

The pregnant woman whom the Tall Convict is sent out to rescue remains rather quietly in the background, obedient to the Tall Convict, simply waiting for him to take her to whatever safety he had intended for her. When her baby boy is born on an Indian mound, she and the Tall Convict deliver it. Later she provides the comic element in a humorous scene as the Tall Con-vict contends with a skiff full of snakes. Though the Tall Convict has been without a woman for two years and though he does get into a fight over another man's wife, he does not approach his charge sexually because he considers her a millstone which he must take to Vicksburg to remove from his neck.

Ironically, and probably illegally, the Tall Convict has ten years added to his sentence because he returns after the Governor had pronounced him dead and posthumously dismissed him from the penitentiary. It is the fate of the Tall Convict that he must serve a longer sentence for completing the task the warden had given him; the Tall Convict is punished unjustly to excuse the inefficiency of public officials.

The complementary contrast between "Wild Palms" and "Old

Man" is the difference between the intangible and the tangible, between the abstract and the concrete. Charlotte and Harry are talkative, thinking people. They verbalize their experiences, their plans, and their ideas. The Tall Convict and the woman do not often speak; they act. Harry and Charlotte pursue love, sacrificing everything for a concept, an abstract situation which they consider bliss. The Tall Convict and woman simply want dry land, or even solid mud. Harry describes the condition in which he existed after losing his virginity, by saying that he was outside of time, that he was weightless in space, beyond the reach of realistic time (p. 137). The Tall Convict actually experienced such a feeling while he was first in the clutches of the flood (pp. 144–45). Harry's apathetic failure to obtain work and his indifference to any vocation is accentuated by the Tall Convict's pleasure in physical labor. Harry and Charlotte fail in their un-respectability as they had known they must. The Tall Convict succeeds in his unconventionality and is punished for it, though with a penalty to which he does not object.

The counterbalancing of these two stories in alternating chapters maintains reader interest at a high level. The intermeshing of the stories leads the reader to deduce that *The Wild Palms* is not about Harry Wilbourne or Charlotte Rittenmeyer or the Tall Convict but about Man attempting to succeed at life by whatever method he deems best. That he fails is not important; how he fails is.

Short Story Commentary

◆◆◆◆◆◆◆◆◆◆◆◆◆◆◆◆◆◆◆◆◆◆◆◆◆◆◆◆◆◆◆◆◆◆◆◆

Ad Astra Told by a first person narrator, "Ad Astra" (The title is from the British R.A.F. motto) is the recollection of an incident which occurred twelve years earlier near the end of the First World War. It concerns the despair felt by a group of R.A.F. pilots in France; [Bayard] Sartoris, Bland, and Monaghan are among the Americans in the story. The group also comprises an Indian subadar, who issues platitudes characteristic of the calm Oriental religions, and a captured German pilot, who has renounced his baronetcy but who hopes for great artistic development in Germany after the war. Since this is intentionally a sketch of perplexed people in a confusing time, the plot is non-existent. The fourth paragraph describes the despair and outrage better than the dramatic sequences portray it. [First published

American Caravan IV (New York: The Macaulay Co., 1931), pp. 164–181. First collected in *These 13* (1931). Included in *Collected Stories* (1950).]

Afternoon of a Cow (published under pseudonym Ernest V. Trueblood). First published in *Furioso*, II (Summer 1947), 5–17. Uncollected.

All the Dead Pilots The women died on the fourth of August, 1914, when England entered the First World War; the pilots died on the eleventh of November, 1918, when the war was over. The pilots died because they were left baffled and lost in the age of confusion; they became cogs in wheels, losing their purpose for existence. "All the Dead Pilots" centers on flyers who escaped that fate by dying earlier in a moment of glory. In this case the focal character is John Sartoris, Bayard's twin, and the plot glorifies sartorisism[1]—a blend of inanity and foolhardy bravery.

Johnny, the invincible American overcomes Spooner, the invulnerable Englishman, embarrassing him so that he leaves the continent and returns to England. The characters lack depth and reality, perhaps because the first person narrator, a military mail censor, is reminiscing about thirteen-year-old events which he knew only second hand to begin with. From this view point, the actions of Johnny Sartoris, "good-for-nothing hellion" (p. 531)[2] with a vocabulary of maybe two hundred words, seem rather flat. Expository passages at the beginning and the end carry the message of the story. For other treatments of the same theme see *Sartoris*, "Ad Astra," and "Victory." [First published in *These 13* (1931)]

---

[1] For a fuller definition of *sartorisism* cf. the discussion of *Sartoris*, the ending of the novel, and the ending of this short story.

[2] Quotation (marked by page number in parentheses) is from *Collected Stories of William Faulkner* (New York, 1950).

Ambuscade First published *Saturday Evening Post,* CCVII (September 29, 1934), 12–13 ff. See the discussion of *The Unvanquished* (1938); in which this short story is included.

Artist At Home The witty, nonchalant tone of the omniscient narrator in "Artist at Home" is so strong and pervasive that it almost has the quality of a persona. The narrator even addresses the readers at several points. The clever atmosphere of the story is felt in the expository comments, e.g., "a poet is human, it seems, just like a man" (p. 636),[3] as well as in the repartee of Roger and Anne Howes, the couple whose home is continually invaded by arty acquaintances.

The crisis of the plot occurs when John Blair, the young poet, ceases attention to Pinkie, the Negro cook, and begins pursuing Mrs. Howes. Touched by the immaturity of Blair, Anne Howes tries to establish a deep relationship with him. Part of the humor of the situation arises from Roger Howes' apparent indifference to the entire affair. Mr. Howes, a successful writer of fiction, is concerned with eliciting the latent good poetry from the young man. The affair and the effort are rewarded with the one good poem which Blair had the power and the time to compose.

The story is concerned principally with the process by which literary art is created. The recurring symbol, the pram, aids in maintaining the narrator's critical distance, which is an integral part of this short story. The excellent manipulation of the narrator's point of view makes "Artist at Home" one of Faulkner's most successful short narratives. [First published in *Story*, III (August 1933), 27–41. First collected in *Collected Stories* (1950).]

Barn Burning First published in *Harper's*, CLXXIX (June 1939), 86–96. First collected in *Collected Stories* (1950). See dis-

---

[3] Quotation (marked by page number in parentheses) is from *Collected Stories of William Faulkner* (New York, 1950).

cussion of *The Hamlet* (1940) into which this short story was incorporated.

The Bear   First published in *Saturday Evening Post,* CCXIV (May 9, 1942), 30–1 ff. Revised for inclusion in *Go Down, Moses* (1942). Included in *Collected Stories* (1950), and *Big Woods* (1955). See the discussion of *Go Down, Moses.*

A Bear Hunt   Set in Major de Spain's hunting camp, twenty miles from Jefferson, "A Bear Hunt" is a comic story about a prank and a delayed revenge. Two narrators tell the story; one begins by setting the scene and identifying the characters, especially Butch Provine. Then Ratliff, his face badly beaten, begins his narrative, which completes the story. Lucius (Butch) Provine, beset with hiccups, is the central character. Ratliff's attempt to play a joke on Butch and, incidentally, to cure his hiccups backfires. The prank involves Indians, and Ratliff utters some choice irony on the white man's treatment of Indians. The physical retribution meted out to Ratliff provides slapstick comedy; knowledge of the perpetrator of the prank and of his motivation maintains suspense and presents a subtler form of humor. The conclusion unifies the narrative because what had earlier seemed a casual digression about Provine's wild youth becomes the key to the story. [Because "A Bear Hunt" was revised to coalesce with the unity of *Big Woods* (1955), this discussion is based on the version in *Collected Stories* (1950). The primary differences between the two versions are that the character known as Lucius Provine in the *Collected Stories* is named Lucius Hogganbeck in the later account, and that in the *Big Woods* form the beginning narrator is the grandson of General Compson. First published in *Saturday Evening Post,* CCVI (February 10, 1934), 8–9 ff.]

Beyond   The theme of the phantasy "Beyond" is immortality. Set principally in Jefferson, in 1933, this sketch is told by an omniscient narrator who reveals the thought by an omniscient narrator who reveals the thought and actions of the spirit of Judge Allison, who has just died. The dramatic tension exists in the spirit's logical, forced recognition of death. In search of that "integral consistency which, whether it be right or wrong, a man must cherish because it alone will ever permit him to die" (p. 792),[4] Judge Allison's spirit visits what purports to be a literal version of the Christian heaven. Apparently seeking the soul of his dead ten-year-old son, the judge meets a man representing blind hope, but the figure only merits Allison's sardonic smile. There the spirit of the agnostic judge meets Mothershed, the violent atheist with whom Allison had often discussed the possibilities of immortality. Mothershed, representing unconscious faith clothed in outward opposition to the church, only disappoints the judge. Here also the spirit receives no certainty from the soul of the renowned agnostic Robert Ingersoll, who does not himself know the answers to Judge Allison's questions. Because he has never been able to divorce himself from reason, the Judge's spirit must reject the faith of a woman and child symbolizing Mary and Christ. At the climax of the story, Judge Allison eloquently rejects the idea of immortality and argues for death as the final end of man. He says, "But because of death, I know that I am. And that is all the immortality of which intellect is capable and flesh should desire" (p. 796). [First published *Harper's* CLXVII (September 1933), 394-403. First collected in *Doctor Martino and Other Stories* (1934) and included in *Collected Stories* (1950).]

Black Music The humorous story of a man's first, and probably only, inebriation, "Black Music" relates the broad consequences of this man's drunken actions. The frame story, told by a first person narrator to whom Wilfred Midgleston relates his story,

---

[4] Quotations (marked by page numbers in parentheses) are from *Collected Stories of William Faulkner* (New York, 1950).

is set in Rincon (in a Spanish speaking area, probably in Latin America) twenty-five years after the major incident. Two kinds of humor are employed in the narrative. Dramatic irony provides the subtle comedy of the frame, and farcical actions provide the slapstick comedy in Midgleston's tale.

Both the dramatic irony and the broad comedy depend on the personality of Wilfred Midgleston, draughtsman in a New York firm. He is a meek, superstitious, and immature man, dominated by his wife. According to his version of the wild incident, Wilfred was chosen by Pan to play the role of a faun haunting a wood in Virginia. Firmly believing that he has performed something that is not in the lot and plan of mortal man, Midgleston flees. Contemporaneous newspaper accounts strengthen Wilfred's belief. Though the details of the story pointedly imply that Mr. Midgleston, a teetotaler, was merely intoxicated and that his actions were the result of a highly imaginative mind released through weakened inhibitions, Wilfred never recognizes the truth he reveals. [First published in *Doctor Martino and Other Stories* (1934). Included in *Collected Stories* (1950).]

The Brooch Pivoting on the conflict inherent in the stratified society of a Mississippi hamlet, "The Brooch" is the story of an immature man who allows his mother to destroy his marriage and him. Between two rings of the telephone, the omniscient narrator skillfully sketches the background for the climactic incident which constitutes this narrative sequence.

The heirloom brooch is the instrument by which Mrs. Boyd defeats Amy, the daughter-in-law she disdains, and Howard, the son she has debilitated. Mrs. Boyd had earlier driven her husband away by her fastidiousness.

The desire to get beyond the reaches of time, to express a rejection of an unpleasant occurrence in time, is symbolized by two stopped clocks. One is silenced by Mrs. Boyd at the time of her stroke, another by Howard in this incident when he learns of Amy's infidelity. The ambiguity of Amy's statement, "My dear little baby" (p. 661),[5] reflects on both her dead child and the immaturity of Howard. The discussion of Howard's affinity for particular parts of *Green Mansions* also delineates his loneliness, his emotional ineptitude. The story builds to a strong conclusion culminating appropriately in Howard's suicide. [First published in *Scribner's Magazine*, XCIX (January 1936), 7–12. First collected in *Collected Stories* (1950).]

By the People   First published in *Mademoiselle*, XLI (October 1955), 86–9 ff. Uncollected. Incorporated into *The Mansion* (1959); see the discussion of *The Mansion*.

Carcassonne   In "Carcassonne" a pauper (apparently Wilfred Midgleston of "Black Music") imagines himself riding into battle against the Saracens, serving with Godfrey of Bouillon and Tancred, and performing glorious actions similar to the First Crusade. The vivid imagery describes the clash of opposing armies, the natural beauties of medieval Europe, and the squalor in which the pauper finds himself. The sketch is set in the attic of a cantina in Rincon (Cf. "Black Music"). The title seems to refer to a southern French city important to Christian crusaders. The city serves as a symbol of imaginative escape from reality into the romanticized, idealized actions of the past. The name may also be a pun on *carcasse* (skeleton) because the pauper's skeleton exists apart from his imagination and presents him with bits of trivial information, such as chamfron, a term in Medieval armory indicating the headpiece for a horse. The precise wording and the appropriate allusions of this brief sketch create a reverie effect. [First published in *These 13* (1931). Included in *Collected Stories* (1950).]

---

[5] Quotation (marked by page number in parentheses) is from *Collected Stories of William Faulkner* (New York, 1950).

Centaur in Brass   First published in *American Mercury*, XXV (February 1932), 200–10. First collected in *Collected Stories* (1950). See the discussion of *The Town* (1957) into which this short story was incorporated.

A Courtship   Built upon the old folk theme of the dark horse, "A Courtship" depicts a contest between Ikkemotubbe and David Hogganbeck for the hand of a girl referred to only as Herman Basket's sister. Ironically an unlikely third competitor wins the girl. The story is told much later by a son of one of Ikkemotubbe's friends, and it describes Ikkemotubbe as an admirable brave at a time before he went to New Orleans and came back to usurp the position of Chief. Indeed the story posits the idea that Ikkemotubbe leaves the plantation and goes to New Orleans because of his disappointment over the loss of the maiden.

The description of Herman Basket's sister is reminiscent of the description of Eula Varner in *The Hamlet*; indeed the whole story is similar to the courtship of Eula. The genealogical snobbery of Herman Basket's aunt is a slight mockery of the Southern aristocrats; she is condescending toward Ikkemotubbe because she was "the second cousin by marriage to the grand-niece of the wife of old David Colbert, the chief Man of all the Chickasaws in our section" (p. 364–5).[6]

Eating contests, races, and other competitive activities which fill the narrative, are conducted with such amiability that the story suffers a basic lack of tension. [First published in *Sewanee Review*, LVI (October 1948), 634–53. First collected in *Collected Stories* (1950).]

Crevasse   Set in Europe during the First World War, "Crevasse" is a short, intense sketch employing type characters. It is realistically narrated by the omniscient author. It concerns a party

---

[6] Quotation (marked by page number in parentheses) is from *Collected Stories of William Faulkner* (New York, 1950).

of soldiers whom a cave-in traps in a chalk cavern. In the grot bodies of Senegalese troops are seen rotting in the positions in which the gas of 1915 had surprised them. Although twelve of the soldiers are lost in the landslide, the captain and his thirteen men dig themselves out. This is a kind of brief sketch for which Faulkner had no penchant. [First published in *These* 13 (1931); included in *Collected Stories* (1950).]

Death Drag   "Death Drag" is a sketch focusing on the visit of three stunt aviators to Jefferson on a January Saturday. Captain Warren, who had served in the British Royal Flying Corps with Jock, the pilot for the stunt trio, narrates the story of Jock's frenetic inner turmoil. Another narrator describes the actions seen by the public, including the comic touches provided by a country woman. The plot is weak because the inextricable bond between the three aviators, the bond from which Capt. Warren urges Jock to remove himself for health reasons, is not explained or justified. [First published in *Scribner's Magazine*, XCI (January 1932), 34–42. First collected in *Doctor Martino and Other Stories* (1934); and included in *Collected Stories* (1950).]

Delta Autumn   First published in *Story*, XX (May–June 1942), 46–55. First collected in *Go Down, Moses* (1942) and included in *Big Woods* (1955). See the discussion of *Go Down, Moses*.

Divorce in Naples   "Divorce in Naples" is a finely wrought comic story focusing on the first breach in a marriage, which is, in this case, a very close friendship with slightly homosexual overtones. The central action is the futile attempt by George, a Greek-American merchant seaman, to prevent Carl, an eighteen-year-old messboy, from having his first sexual experience. George is trying to protect Carl with whom he has formed a strong camaraderie, because George says Carl is a virgin.

The comedy centers primarily on these two characters. George's frenetic search to find Carl who has sneaked off with a prostitute provides a broad, low comedy. Carl's reactions to his experience as George explains it to him present comedy of a subtle nature.

With an acute sense of periphrasis, Faulkner has cunningly handled the sailors' obscene language with discretion and wit. This story is recounted by a first person narrator in the role of observer, and the plot is tightly constructed. "Divorce in Naples" is one of Faulkner's most skillfully written humorous stories. [First published in *These 13* (1931). Included in *Collected Stories* (1950).]

Dr. Martino   The strange compact between Dr. Martino and Louise King is the dramatic focus of "Dr. Martino." The omniscient narrator uses the unusual relationship to provide the tension for the story. At the conclusion of the narrative the reason for the peculiar affinity is revealed in such a way that it dignifies Dr. Martino and Louise King.

This story is basically presented through Hubert Jarrod, the only character whose thoughts are related, and at the denouement the reader receives an insight into the deeper meaning of the action, just as Mr. Jarrod does. Lily Cranston, Proprietress of Cranston's Wells, Mississippi, serves for a time as expositor for the moral principle of the story. Mrs. Alvina King is a type-character representative of domineering, ambitious mothers. Mr. Jarrod seems as unaware as Mrs. King says he is. Dr. Martino, the pivotal character, uses his maturity and quiet bravery to infuse courage into Louise King. His struggle for life against a serious heart condition inspires Louise to swim and to ride a horse, and to conquer her fears.

Dr. Martino's philosophy, that having the fortitude to perform a deed one fears heightens one's sense of living, is perhaps too explicitly and too repeatedly emphasized. Though the plot is tightly organized, the characters' lack of vitality weakens the story. [First published in *Harper's Magazine*, CLXIII (November 1931), 733–43. First collected in *Doctor Martino and Other Stories* (1934) and included in *Collected Stories* (1950).]

Dry September   "Dry September" is a devastating anti-lynching polemic. The omniscient author uses characters to personify opposing points of view, but to the influences of logical argument and of irrational, hasty conclusions, he adds a third, more powerful factor: the dry hot weather of September. The fervid night overpowers the characters, engendering an animal violence in them, thus becoming the most potent force in the story.

The plot develops out of a rumor that Miss Minnie Cooper, thirty-eight or thirty-nine-year-old spinster has been assaulted or frightened or insulted by Will Mayes, Negro nightwatchman at the ice plant. None of the characters knows what has happened. Captain John McLendon, World War I hero, leads the mob, serving as its spokesman. He is not interested in facts. When a moderate asks if *it* really happened, he replies, "Happen? What the hell difference does it make? Are you going to let the black sons get away with it until one really does it?" (p. 171–2)[7] Henry Stribling (Hawkshaw) argues for calm reasoning. He is convinced that Will Mayes is a good Negro and would not have assaulted Miss Minnie. He suggests that Miss Minnie is suffering menopausal delusions and that the sheriff is the proper authority to conduct any action. In an attempt to prevent violence he accompanies the group to the ice plant, arguing constantly for Will's innocence. But in the confusion of capture, he becomes involved and even strikes Will himself. He does remove himself from the mob before murder occurs.

Miss Minnie is characterized as a disappointed unhappy woman. She becomes completely unhinged mentally while attending the picture show, her customary Saturday night activity. Her insanity strengthens the impression that Will Mayes *was* innocent.

---

[7] Quotation (marked by page number in parentheses) is from *Collected Stories of William Faulkner* (New York, 1950).

The virulence of the weather is emphasized in the final section. John McLendon returns to his home, where he snarls at his wife who has also been disturbed by the heat (or something), and then he stands undressed panting on the screened back porch, while the earth lies still and stricken.

A sense of overwhelming violence pervades this story so that most of the characters seem to act without volition, unapprehendingly. Consequently the characters lack depth of development. The tension of the story, however, achieves a frightening intensity. [First published *Scribner's Magazine,* LXXXIX (January 1931), 49–56. First collected in *These 13* (1931) and included in *Collected Stories* (1950).]

Elly   Two themes, the implacable hatred of Elly for her grandmother, and the sense of guilt Elly develops concerning her sexual exploits, are primary in "Elly," the story of an emotionally disturbed eighteen-year-old girl. Elly, whose real name is Ailanthia, is overcome with sexual desire, especially for Paul de Montigny, whom she believes has a tinge of Negro blood. The grandmother's silent disapproval of Elly's suspected sexual activities arouses Elly's sense of guilt, which in turn creates a violent loathing for the grandmother. Elly persistently believes that Paul will marry her after she has yielded to him in her first coition. When he refuses, as he had informed her from the beginning he would do, and after he has refused to murder the grandmother, Elly causes a wreck in which both Paul and the grandmother die. The story, told by the omniscient narrator, is weakened by the lack of motivation provided for Elly's intense hatred of her grandmother. [First published *Story,* IV (February 1934), 3–15. First collected in *Doctor Martino and Other Stories* (1934) and included in *Collected Stories* (1950).]

An Error in Chemistry   "An Error in Chemistry" is probably Faulkner's best detective story. The plot recounts the machinations of an escape artist who murders his wife and his father-in-law and almost leaves the scene with the blessings of the sheriff and Gavin Stevens, the County Attorney. With the exception of Joel Flint, the murderer who is an outsider, the characters are Yoknapatawpha citizens whom Faulkner depicts clearly and realistically. The tension in the story mounts as the criminal takes the initiative in actions which remain inexplicable to the reader as well as to the sheriff and Gavin until the moment of denouement. The climax occurs ironically as Joel Flint makes so simple and so obvious a mistake in a local custom he has vehemently denounced that even the young narrator (Gavin Stevens' nephew; probably Charles Mallison) recognizes the error. Flint fails through no flaw inherent in his ingenious plot but through his excessive pride in his own acting ability and his contempt for the local citizens. [First published *Ellery Queen's Mystery Magazine*, VII (June 1946), 5-19. First Collected in *Knight's Gambit* (1949).]

The Fire and the Hearth   First published in *Go Down, Moses* (1942). It includes revisions of "Gold is Not Always" and "A Point of Law." See the discussion of *Go Down, Moses*.

Fool About a Horse   First published *Scribner's Magazine*, C (August 1936), 80-6. Uncollected. See the discussion of *The Hamlet* (1940) into which this short story was incorporated.

Fox Hunt   Two antipathetic views of a fox hunt and the hunters involved are given in "Fox Hunt." A group of poor illiterate Carolina farmers gather to observe a rite incomprehensible to them. They discount the sport inherent in following the hounds; their ridicule of Harrison Blair's game is based on practical considerations. They also perceive the adulterous relationship between Mrs. Blair and Steve Gawtrey. Another deprecatory attitude toward the early morning activity is presented by Mr.

Blair's valet, Ernie, and the chauffeur. These two review the backgrounds of Mr. Blair, Mrs. Blair, and Steve; this informs the reader of the tensions between the major characters. Ernie has even collaborated in Gawtrey's pursuit of Mrs. Blair. The chauffeur and the valet, both city dwellers, cannot appreciate the hunt.

The story is concerned with the themes of marital unhappiness and with the difference between the rich and the poor. Perhaps because there is too much distance between the reader and the central figures, the story lacks force and realism. [First published *Harper's,* CLXIII (September 1931), 392–402. First collected in *Doctor Martino and Other Stories* (1934) and *Collected Stories* (1950).]

Go Down, Moses   First published *Collier's,* CVII (January 25, 1941), 19–20 ff. Revised for inclusion in *Go Down, Moses* (1942); see the discussion of *Go Down, Moses.*

Golden Land   Apparently working from his own experience in the area, Faulkner has written a rather puritanical protest against the easy life in California. "Golden Land" is that protest.

The characters are stereotyped figures who lack credibility. The situation is so patent as to be ineffective. Ira Ewing, Jr., has come from the harsh life of Nebraska, to the sunny reaches of California where he has married the daughter of a carpenter, has fathered two children, has become extremely wealthy from his Beverly Hills real estate dealings, and has suddenly discovered that his children are corrupt. The daughter whose film name is April Lalear, is involved in a sex orgy trial; the son is a transvestite. Ira Ewing, Realtor, has a forty-year-old mistress whose fourteen-year-old daughter he supports in boarding school. Complete with expansive mansion and Filipino chauffeur/valet, Mr. Ewing is the parvenu par excellence.

Since Faulkner works better with primitive characters, Mrs. Ira Ewing, Sr., widowed mother of Ira Ewing, Realtor, has more reality. But even she is made too pitiable in her desperate desire for a return to Nebraska. The fact that Ira Ewing uses his daughter's scandal for publicity purposes seems an extreme degradation contradicting the image Faulkner has created for Mr. Ewing. Unfortunately the sociological commentary of this narrative overpowers its literary art. [First published *American Mercury,* XXXV (May 1935), 1–14. First collected in *Collected Stories* (1950).]

Gold Is not Always   First published *Atlantic,* CLXVI (November 1940), 563–70. Extensively revised to become a part of "The Fire and the Hearth."

Hair   "Hair" is the story of a man who obeys his very strict sense of propriety, unconcerned with the opinion of society. Henry Stribling, (Hawkshaw) a quiet Jefferson barber who is in love with an orphan Susan Reed is the focal character. The narrator is a V. K. Ratliff-type traveling salesman, and it is he who discovers that Stribling's mysterious April vacations involve fidelity to a dead fiancee (Sophie Starnes) and her deceased parents.

Stribling's silent and ostensibly unrequited affection for Susan is a matter of gossipy anxiety for the townspeople who consider Miss Reed an immoral young woman. Because a cabal of Jefferson citizens tends to anticipate Stribling's disillusionment with Susan, the tension in the story hinges upon his ignorance of her moral condition. In the denouement that matter remains ambiguous. When Stribling has fulfilled his responsibilities to the Starnes family, he leaves Jefferson permanently taking Susan with him as his wife.

Two secondary themes, the innate badness of women and the contrast between a verbose person and a laconic person, support the primary emphasis, the patient goodness of Hawkshaw. The setting for the story principally involves Jefferson and Division;

the action begins in 1905 and culminates in 1930. The plot is well constructed, but the characters generally lack the realism typical in Faulkner's work. [First published *American Mercury*, XXIII (May 1931), 53–61. First collected in *These 13* (1931) and included in *Collected Stories* (1950).]

Hand Upon the Waters   Moving briskly from the discovery of the body to a tense scene in which Gavin Stevens almost gets killed, "Hand Upon the Waters" is a detective story filled with pertinent action. The murderer's punishment is poetically just though slightly illegal. Set in Yoknapatawpha County in July, the story, told by an omniscient narrator, concerns the murder of Lonnie Grinnup (a corruption of his real name Louis Grenier) who is the last descendant of one of the first settlers of Yoknapatawpha County. The nature of the crime is appropriate to the rural area about which Faulkner writes, and the characters are the rustic figures at which Faulkner excels. The economic plot builds to a dramatic climax and stresses the idea that justice is not always with the law. [First published *Saturday Evening Post*, CCXII (November 4, 1939), 14–15 ff. First collected in *Knight's Gambit* (1949).]

Honor   The most salient characteristic of "Honor" is the construction of its plot. The narrative includes two stories; one is enveloped by another. The story of the restlessness of Buck Monaghan, ex-World War I pilot, provides the frame for the story of Buck's relationship with Mildred and Howard Rogers. The inner story is cleverly inserted between two sentences in a conversation, when a reference to the label on an office door evokes an extended interior monologue. The frame story is simply an incident illustrating the dissatisfaction of Monaghan who discovered a life he enjoyed, only to have it ended by an armistice. The inner story depicts Buck's volatile affair with Mildred and the maturity of Howard. The title seems to refer to the sense of honor and decency displayed by Howard toward a man who has injured him unfairly, a sense of honor with which Howard defeats Buck. The story of the Rogers-Monaghan relationship implies that Buck Monaghan lives the erratic life illustrated by the framing incident, because he has lost his sense of personal honor and has been unable to acclimate himself to the commonplace world. [First published *American Mercury,* XX (July 1930), 268–74. First collected in *Doctor Martino and Other Stories* (1934) and included in *Collected Stories* (1950). Reprinted *American Mercury*, LXIII (October 1946), 485–93.]

The Hound First published in *Harper's,* CLXIII (August 1931), 266–74. First collected in *Doctor Martino and Other Stories* (1934). See the discussion of *The Hamlet* (1940) into which this short story was incorporated. Cf. *The Mansion* (1959).

Idyll in the Desert Random House published "Idyll in the Desert" in a limited edition in 1931; it has not been reprinted. It focuses on the ironic and coincidental situation in which Darrel Howes (or House) deserts the paramour who nurses him back to health from a case of tuberculosis; she contracts the disease and ultimately dies when she realizes he is never coming back for her. Ironically Darrel and his recent bride pass the paramour at the Blizzard depot, but he does not recognize her. The narrator is Lucas Crump, a mail carrier; who is a witty, clever character. The scene is apparently in Arizona.

A Justice Primitive justice as it is meted out by the Choctaw Indian chief is the focus of "A Justice." This comic tale has a double frame; Sam Fathers tells the story to Quentin Compson, age twelve; an older Quentin relates the story as he remembers its having been told.

The plot is concerned with the rise to power of Ikkemotubbe (alias David Callicoat; later Doom, the Man) and with the birth and naming of Sam Fathers, the Negro-Indian carpenter on Jason Compson II's farm. One action centers on the dragging of a wrecked steamboat from the river to the Indian plantation; the other is Crawfish-ford's attempt to obtain the married Negress whom he desires. The events are richly comic to the reader, though they were not meaningful to the young Quentin.

Most of the comedy is found in Crawfish-ford (Sam Fathers's father) and his naive insights. Crawford (as he was often called) and Herman Basket soon learn to agree with Doom, who demonstrates his cunning by feeding "New Orleans salt" (p. 347)[8] to an active puppy which immediately sickens and dies. Later the chief, Ikkemotubbe's maternal uncle, and his son also mysteriously sicken and die, leaving Ikkemotubbe as head of the tribe. In another instance, Crawford pretends to be ill so that he can remain at the plantation with the Negress while her husband helps move the steamboat. After several days, Doom slyly ends that ruse with a suggestion that the cuckolded husband build a fire by the mineral spring and accompany Crawfish-ford as he soaks his illness away. When a child of strangely un-Negroid coloring is born to the Negress, the Negro who has already shown himself quite clever, complains to Doom of the invasion of privacy. The scene in which Doom has to decide what to do with the issue of the illicit union is a comic inversion of the scene in I Kings 3, in which Solomon has to decide between the two women who both claimed a living child. Doom names the infant Had-Two-Fathers and passes a just sentence on Crawfish-ford.

Faulkner has written the dialogue of the Indians with a marvelous turn of phrase which underscores the wit and sense of justice. It is significant that Quentin Compson, a character later to be destroyed by his sister's sexual immorality, should be the narrator of a story whose good humor centers on sexual misconduct. It is even more significant that the tale does not, at the

---

[8] Quotations (marked by page numbers in parentheses) are from *Collected Stories of William Faulkner* (New York, 1950).

148   FAULKNER'S ART AND CHARACTERS

time, make sense to Quentin. This is a finely wrought narrative which employs clever comedy and reflects importantly on its narrator. [First published in *These 13* (1931). Included in *Collected Stories* (1950). Partially used for the second interlude of *Big Woods* (1955).]

Knight's Gambit "Knight's Gambit," providing the name for the collection of stories in which it was published, is a story of intrigue, of maturing youth, and of love. Though an omniscient narrator is presenting the story, the narrative focuses on the reactions of Charles Mallison, son of Gavin Stevens' sister Margaret. The conflict in the plot derives from the attempt of Max Harriss to bring about the departure or, failing that, the death of Captain Sebastian Gualdres, Argentine army captain who is a house guest at the Jefferson estate of Mrs. Harriss, Max's mother.

Once the major action is introduced via an interruption of the chess game between Gavin and Charles, the chess game from which the story takes its name, a thirty-page flashback presents the history of Mrs. Harriss. Legend reports that Mrs. Harriss, the daughter of a Yoknapatawpha aristocrat, was once engaged to some local swain, but she broke that engagement to marry Mr. Harriss who was considerably older than she and who became immensely wealthy, possibly from bootlegging during prohibition. After Mr. Harriss had rebuilt Mrs. Harriss's home into a fabulous mansion, he conveniently died, whereupon Mrs. Harriss and her son and daughter mourned suitably and then continued their traveling in South America (Europe being interdict by World War II), whence they returned accompanied by Captain Gualdres.

The plot pivots on the ill will Max feels for Captain Gualdres. This antipathy which leads Max to violent actions toward Captain Gualdres seems to arise not because Gualdres might marry Max's sister or his mother, nor because Gualdres is a better equestrian and fencer than Max, but because Max resents Gualdres's attentions to Miss Cayley to whom Max has given an engagement ring. But the murder attempt is thwarted and turned to advantage by Gavin Stevens, aided by his nephew.

Charles Mallison, almost eighteen when the story begins in 1941, is the admiring companion of his fifty-year-old uncle Gavin Stevens, Phi Beta Kappa—Harvard, Ph.D.—Heidelberg. The narrator relates most of the story as Charles has heard it, observed it, or performed it. He is a strong portrait of a young man striving for manhood; he wishes to outwit his clever uncle, and he is eager to earn glory in the war. The explicit discussions of the case at hand transpire between Gavin and Charles, and most of the important action occurs in Charles's presence. Through the coincidence of Charles's almost unconscious awareness that Rafe McCallum has sold a dangerous horse, the story is brought to a crisis. Once the Gualdres-Harriss case is successfully concluded, the scene shifts to follow Charles as he passes through Jefferson on his way from preflight to basic training.

"Knight's Gambit" is probably the most complimentary view of Gavin Stevens in Faulkner's canon. Gavin is the gentlemanly son of a successful lawyer; he is the scion of an aristocratic Jeffersonian family; he is a scholar who has made a twenty-year hobby of translating the Bible back into classical Greek. But more important than these things—Gavin is successful in this story as he is not in later works. He is witty, subtle, and ingenious. Since Gavin is a student of language, the reader accepts without qualms his conversing with Captain Gualdres in Spanish, though no prior hint has been given that Mr. Stevens had the slightest interest in Spanish. Gavin wins his wager with the Argentinean, he arranges the marriage of Captain Gualdres and Miss Harriss, and he persuades Max Harriss to enlist in the military. But Gavin is more than successful, he is warmly human because he himself turns out to be the local swain Mrs. Harriss was once engaged to, and he then claims the chief object of his gambit. Since the reader has been kept ignorant of Gavin's genuine interest in the Harriss affairs, the revelation of Gavin's affection serves as a satisfying denouement uniting all aspects of the story. [First published in *Knight's Gambit* (1949).]

The Leg   In one of his most subtle and most symbolic stories, "The Leg," Faulkner utilizes as a central figure, the first person narrator who is suffering from a manic-depressive psychosis. The structure of the story appropriately resembles the pattern of recurring periods of depression which a manic depressive experiences. The name Everbe Corinthia provides a clue to the symbology with which the author is working as he presents the hallucinations of the deranged man.

Section one, set in England in 1914, is the period of normalcy preceding the insanity. In this beginning section, George, an Englishman, and Davy, an American, are close friends and fellow students at Oxford. George is enamored of Everbe Corinthia Rust, daughter of a Thames lock keeper. Her name seems to be a pun on the Grecian city of Corinth.[9] At the end of this section George is killed in World War I. The second section presents the hallucinations apparently induced in Davy by the death of George and the amputation of Davy's leg. The bereavement for his friend and the nerve sensations (common with amputees), which cause Davy to think that he can still feel his leg, inspire hallucinations in which the apparition of George visits Davy and tries to find the amputated leg and kill it. Near the end of section two, Davy thinks that he has developed that "certitude of the young which so arbitrarily distinguishes between verities and illusions, establishing with such assurance that line between truth and delirium which sages knit their brows over" (p. 833).[10] He recognizes that his illness is past.

---

[9] In Greek mythology, Ephyre was an ancient city which later became known as Corinth.

[10] Quotations (marked by page numbers in parentheses) are from *Collected Stories of William Faulkner* (New York, 1950).

Section three, however, poses a problem for the reader and Davy as well. Jotham Rust, Everbe Corinthia's brother, deserts the army and tries to kill Davy because he believes that Davy is responsible for the mysterious death of his sister. A photograph of Davy, taken at a time when Davy was in one of his deepest states of depression, and inscribed to Corinthia with an obscenity, ostensibly in Davy's handwriting, provides incontrovertible evidence of Davy's part in Everbe Corinthia's death. As the story concludes, Davy seems to be sinking again into a manic-depressive state.

The symbology of the story is the key to its explication. Everbe Corinthia, with her Greek name, symbolizes, in Davy's mind anyway, the three aspects of the goddess Artemis: 1) Luna 2) Diana 3) Hecate. The moon figures prominently in Davy's hallucinations; Everbe Corinthia disappears mysteriously on a night when there is a bright moon. Earlier Davy has referred to George as a lunatic. At the beginning of the story, George, in courting Everbe, quotes the second speech of Comus, in which Comus says that the lady's voice is sweeter than that of the siren's who can rob sweet madness of itself. In this scene Everbe Corinthia is also a figure of the chaste maiden, as Artemis, in the role of Diana, is. Later, during the hallucinations, the apparition is associated with Everbe, now in the aspect of Hecate who could summon spirits and dreams. Davy's madness reaches its greatest intensity in a "dream" about sulphurous odors and a maid with him in a boat upon the moonlit river. These circumstances prevail on the night of Everbe's disappearance. George's apparition seems to be a signal that Davy is experiencing a period of depression, and the search for the leg becomes mingled with Davy's grief over the death of George, so that the search for the leg is also a search for the earlier happy relationship. Since Everbe Corinthia is associated in Davy's mind with George and the prewar experiences, he apparently visits her while he is attending the Observer's School. It is at this time that his final, most violent dream comes, and at this time Corinthia disappears only to reappear twelve hours later to die in a deranged condition.

Dramatic irony exists in Davy's inability to recognize that what he has related as a dream has, for the most part, been reality. Seemingly Davy, while in a psychotic state has visited Everbe Corinthia, so frightening her that she has died trying to scream after she has screamed herself hoarse. That the artificial leg should have saved Davy's life is ironic because the amputated leg has occasioned his insanity. "The Leg" is one of Faulkner's most complex and most rewarding short stories. [First published as "Leg" in *Doctor Martino and Other Stories* (1934); included in *Collected Stories* (1950) as "The Leg."]

Lion   First published *Harper's*, CLXXII (December 1935), 67–77. Incorporated into "The Bear" in *Go Down, Moses* (1942). See the discussion of *Go Down, Moses*.

Lizards in Jamshyd's Courtyard   First published in *Saturday Evening Post*, CCIV (February 27, 1932), 12–13 ff. See the discussion of *The Hamlet* (1940) into which this short story was incorporated.

Lo!   "Lo!" is a comic sketch deriving its humor from the situation of a United States President[11] besieged in the White House by peaceful Indians who have come to him for settlement of a legal question. The scene is Washington in the winter and spring of a year in the first half of the nineteenth century, and an omniscient narrator tells the story. Differences between the customs of the Chickasaw Indians from Mississippi and those of the white people of Washington and its environs provide a comic

---

[11] "Mountain Victory" repeats part of the story and states that Andrew Jackson was President. The President here, however, has a wife.

satire on the attitudes of each group toward the other. Though only one character, Francis Weddel (Vidal), is named and though the other figures are type characters, Faulkner is quite successful in his exploitation of a comic circumstance. [First published in *Story*, V (November 1934), 5–21. First collected in *Collected Stories* (1950).]

Miss Zilphia Gant Published in a special edition for the Book Club of Texas in 1932, "Miss Zilphia Gant" has never been reprinted. The story centers on the hatred Mrs. Jim Gant develops because her husband deserted her for another woman. Filled with hatred for men, Mrs. Gant becomes a Jefferson seamstress, who dominates and warps the life of her daughter Zilphia by constant scrutiny. Zilphia's pitiable situation becomes even more pathetic when Mrs. Gant prevents the consummation of Zilphia's marriage to a house painter. After the death of her mother Zilphia continues the seamstress business and adopts the orphaned daughter of the house painter and his second wife. The story ends as Miss Zilphia seems to be repeating her mother's pattern of child-rearing, but some hope is ambiguously provided by Zilphia's friendliness toward other people.

Mistral "Mistral" combines facetious, travelogue commentary by two walking American tourists in Italy, with the telling of a story appropriate to the background of the mistral, "That black chill wind full of dust like sparks of ice" (p. 876).[12] This short story is told by a nameless first person narrator, aged twenty-two, who accompanies a friend named Don, aged twenty-three.

The story which the tourists discover in the little village concerns a priest, his intractable ward (a young woman), the ward's dead fiancé, and the ward's lover, Giulio Farinzale. The plot of the priest's story centers on the postponement of the ward's mar-

---

[12] Quotation (marked by page number in parentheses) is from *Collected Stories of William Faulkner* (New York, 1950).

riage until her wealthy fiancé has died. His funeral occurs as the tourists enter the village. The story also hints somberly that the priest has lusted for the maid. But Giulio, immediately preceding the tourists, has returned from the army and been reunited with the ward, while the priest is left to his lamentations.

None of the characters has a full development. Because the priest, his ward, and Giulio flit darkly in the background, they make as little impression on the reader as they do on the narrator and Don. The action of "Mistral" seems interminable, and the gloomily melancholy atmosphere seems oppressively brittle and artificial. [First published in *These 13* (1931); included in *Collected Stories* (1950).]

Monk The narrator for "Monk" is the nephew of Gavin Stevens (probably Charles Mallison), and the story he tells focuses on the inherent innocence of a mental retardate, Stonewall Jackson (Monk) Odlethrop. Monk's life seems to have been a pitiable mistake from its very conception. Deserted by his parents, orphaned by the death of his grandmother, and abandoned again through the death of a moonshiner who had adopted him, Monk came ultimately to Jefferson. Through his idiocy he was convicted of murder and sent to the state penitentiary where supposedly leading an outbreak, he killed the warden, a man to whom he had transferred his whole devotion and for whom he was knitting a sweater.

Filtered as it is, partially through both Gavin and the nephew, the story does not so much evoke pity for Monk who cannot comprehend the distinction between life and death as it arouses indignation at the society which could apathetically condone such legalized injustice.

The important conflict of the story poses Gavin Stevens and the Governor as foils. Gavin is idealistically concerned with ascertaining the truth and acting honorably on the conclusions. The Governor, a shrewd politician, is uninterested in the specific details of truth since knowledge of them might interfere with his opportunism. Because Gavin tries to clear the name of a poor, deceased moron, the Governor describes him as a gentleman trying to uphold 1860 idealism in twentieth century politics. "Monk" is a dramatic polemic favoring even an ineffective idealism above an unprincipled expediency. [First published *Scribner's Magazine,* CI (May 1937), 16–24. First collected in *Knight's Gambit* (1949).]

Mountain Victory The tension existing between Confederate and Union partisans immediately after the Civil War is the theme of "Mountain Victory." Vatch, an illiterate mountaineer, represents the Union sentiment, and Saucier Weddel, cultivated, aristocratic Choctaw-Caucasian, represents the Southern element. Consequently the distinction between economic castes becomes entangled in the antipathy which Vatch expresses toward Saucier. A third complication arises when Vatch's sister, overcome by the aura of grandeur about Weddel, evinces love and admiration for him. Even Hule, the younger brother of Vatch, is so impressed with Weddel's courage that he attempts to aid him and is accidentally killed for his effort. The story also stresses the obligatory relationship existent between upper class Southerners and their Negroes. The conclusion comes very quickly and dramatically. [First published *Saturday Evening Post,* CCV (December 3, 1932), 6–7 ff. First collected in *Doctor Martino and Other Stories* (1934) and included in *Collected Stories* (1950).]

Mule in the Yard First published *Scribner's Magazine,* XCVI (August 1934), 65–70. First collected in *Collected Stories* (1950). See the discussion of *The Town,* (1957) into which this short story was incorporated.

My Grandmother Millard and General Bedford Forrest and The Battle of Harrykin Creek Presenting quite a romanticized view of Southern experiences during the Civil War, "My Grandmother Millard . . ." has an episodic structure centered on the determination of a strong-willed woman.

Bayard Sartoris, son of Col. John Sartoris, narrates the story which occurs in 1862, when he was an early adolescent. For him and Ringo [Marengo] the entire incident was a game. The excitement, the color, and the gallantry of his father and other Confederates entrance Bayard. He explains early that this event occurred before Yankees were an unpleasant threat to Jefferson. The Southern families, composed mostly of women and children, continued the genteel life with grace and decorum.

The story has a principal plot line involving the meeting and marriage of Cousin Melisandre and Cousin Philip. Other anecdotes, however, are woven around this thread. Digressions concern Lucius and his ideas about the freedom of slaves, Mrs. Compson's saving of her silver by sitting in the privy, and General Joseph Wheeler's collaboration with the Yankees (thirty years later) in the Spanish-American War. These accounts are always joined to the primary story by relevant transitions, and they enrich the story, even though they impede the progress.

Mrs. Rosa Millard is another of Faulkner's admirable, stern-willed older women. She rules the Sartoris household firmly, seeming to be aware of everything, having the proper solution to practically all problems, and being possessed of an acute wit. She martials the forces for the wedding as though she were a general deploying troops. Only Col. John Sartoris, her son-in-law, is not intimidated by her authoritative manner, and he is even amused by her trunk drill.

Because the story is told through the eyes of a young boy, the narrative tends to have a disjointed appearance. Small details are brought into close perspective. Bayard virtually apotheosized his Grandmother Millard, and his emphasis on her ingenuity helps to unify the wandering story. Except for some of the digressions, a clear chronological pattern prevails. The narrative appropriately

concludes with the practice with which it begins—the burying of
the silver. [First published *Story*, XXII (March–April 1943),
68–86. First collected in *Collected Stories* (1950).]

Name for the City   First published *Harper's* CCI (October
1950), 200. See the discussion of *Requiem for a Nun* (1951) into
which this short story was incorporated.

The New Orleans Sketches[13]   In 1925, on his way to Europe,
William Faulkner stopped for six months in New Orleans. While
there, basking in the sunshine of a literary group headed by
Sherwood Anderson, he published sketches in the Sunday edition
of the *Times-Picayune.*

Most of the sketches would not be worth remembering were
they not the earliest efforts of a great writer. But a few (e.g., "Out
of Nazareth," "Sunset," "The Rosary," "Country Mice," and
"The Liar") will almost stand alone as full-fledged short stories.
One group of very short, type-character sketches in the form of
interior monologues appeared in the January–February 1925
issue of the *Double Dealer* (a New Orleans literary magazine)
under the title, "New Orleans." All of these sketches, though
amateurish, do imply some of the directions the genius of William Faulkner would later take.

The sketches reflect some of the themes, techniques, and subjects of the later Faulkner stories and novels. The glory of the
past and its influence on an individual is a focal point for
"Home," the story of Jean Baptiste, a French immigrant whose
argument with his conscience is rather unsubtly portrayed. This
theme is exemplified also in "The Cobbler," the story of a Spanish

---

[13] Originally published in the Sunday edition of the *Times-Picayune* in 1925.
They have been variously collected. The best collection is *New Orleans Sketches*
(New Brunswick, N.J.: Rutgers University Press, 1958). The introduction by
Carvel Collins is especially good. One seeking a fuller discussion of the sketches
should consult it.

immigrant who had lost his love many years before. But "Episode" is the best of the stories which show the influence of the past upon an individual. The striking effect here is achieved by the modulation of the subjects by the artist's request for a change in position. As the old blind man and the old woman adopt different stances, their psychological outlooks change. The stories and novels which are set in Yoknapatawpha often capture the individual in a moment which demonstrates the influence of the past upon him. "A Rose for Emily" and the stories of the Compson or Sartoris families are only three immediate examples of his using this same theme in later successful works.

"Out of Nazareth" which glorifies the innocence of an untrammeled human spirit almost verbally anticipates Lena Grove of *Light in August*. Consider this passage about the young man compared to a youthful David:

> He reminded one of a pregnant woman in his calm belief that nature, the earth which had spawned him, would care for him, that he was serving his appointed ends, had served his appointed end and now need only wait.[14]

Many of these early sketches, if they do not exemplify a theme of importance later in the Faulkner canon, do reveal a kinship in subject matter. The idiot in "The Kingdom of God" is a predecessor to Benjy in *The Sound and the Fury*. The picture of a confused, fleeing Negro is sympathetically drawn in "Sunset," one of the most emotional of these sketches. One feels compassion for the country Negro who is frustrated by the white river boat captains and the complexity of the city. The strength of imagination expressed here leads in a more disciplined expression to "Pantaloon in Black" and to parts of *Light in August*.

"Country Mice" is an interesting story though it suffers from

---

[14] William Faulkner, *New Orleans Sketches* (New Brunswick, N.J., 1958), p. 103.

the presence of the narrator—a fault which the later writings of Faulkner have eliminated. The praise of the perspicacity of constables, which serves as the center of the story, reappears in *The Reivers* in connection with Boon Hogganbeck, Everbe Corinthia, and Butch.

The delayed burial of a human body forced upon unwilling participants is a central part of "Yo Ho and Two Bottles of Rum." The same topic is handled masterfully later in *As I Lay Dying*. "Yo Ho and Two Bottles of Rum" is highly imitative of Conrad, an author whom Faulkner is known to have admired.

These early sketches show, too, the striving artist working toward the mastery of his technique. The shifting point of view in "Home," "The Cobbler," "The Kid Learns," and "Sunset" is generally obvious and lacking in smoothness but *The Sound and the Fury* proved that Faulkner had graduated from the dramatic monologue to complete control of the interior monologue, that he could utilize point of view to achieve cohesion and pattern. Since these items were simple short sketches for newspapers, it is to be expected that many of them are without plot. An interest in dialect writing reveals itself here in a varity of types from the New Orleans brogue to the supposed jocky jabber to the drawl of the country folk. It is only natural that Faulkner turned later to the dialect of the country people, a dialect writing in which he excelled. The tendency to allegory, exemplified in "Chance" and the tendency to didacticism at the end of "Sunset" are elements which Faulkner was able to sublimate in his later work to a more subtle expression.

The sketch however which presages most of the future is "The Liar." It is the earliest story in a rural setting which was to grow into Yoknapatawpha. The scene is Gibson's store, which might easily be Varner's. The men congregated on the porch might have been Armistids or Winterbottoms or Bookwrights. The reference to a frightened horse running through Mis' Harmon's house anticipates "Spotted Horses." And the narrator of the

story within the story carries the reader along with him easily
as he shifts back and forth from the frame story to the inner
story. It is a short story with a complete action, an excellent story
in the yarn tradition that is a large part of the Frenchman's Bend
Tales.

The sketches written in New Orleans form the earliest body
of Faulkner fiction and reveal some of the creative experimentation in a period when Faulkner's artistry was beginning to
develop.

Notes on a Horsethief   Separately printed by the Levee Press,
Greenville, Mississippi, during the week of November 4, 1950.
Nine hundred and fifty signed copies were offered for sale. In-
corporated into *A Fable* (1954). See the discussion of *A Fable*.

An Odor of Verbena   See the discussion of *The Unvanquished*
(1938) in which this section was first published.

The Old People   First published *Harper's*, CLXXXI (September 1940), 418–425. Included in *Go Down, Moses* (1942) and *Big
Woods* (1955). See the discussion of *Go Down, Moses*.

Once Aboard a Lugger   First published *Contempo,* I (February
1, 1932), 1 and 4. Uncollected.

Pantaloon in Black   First published in *Harper's* CLXXXI
(October 1940), 503–513. Included in *Go Down, Moses* (1942);
see the discussion of *Go Down, Moses*.

Pennsylvania Station   Through dramatic irony and ambiguity
"Pennsylvania Station" presents a pitiable story in an unsentimental fashion. The narrative is concerned with the profligate,
probably criminal, son of a New York charwoman and the manner in which he robbed her, causing her death.

The omniscient narrator introduces Mrs. Margaret Noonan Gihon's brother who tells the story of his sister and her son Danny. The old man is puzzled by parts of the story, but he never understands the import of what he is telling. The dramatic irony is made evident through the young man, also a tramp, to whom the uncle tells the story as they sit in Pennsylvania Station. The young man perceives immediately what Danny's nature is, and the questions of the younger transient serve as guides to the reader. To get the money his mother has been paying on a casket, Danny has forged the mother's name on a note to Mr. Pinckski, the mortician. This knowledge destroys Mrs. Gihon. The uncle, however, fails to recognize what has happened and persistently believes in his nephew's innocence when Danny is charged with grand larceny and the murder of a policeman in St. Augustine. Mrs. Sophie Zilich, a neighbor also recognized the potential evil in Danny; she helps the brother care for Mrs. Gihon. Because Danny is in Chicago with friends (perhaps gangsters) who secured his release from jail, he cannot return to New York for his mother's funeral and compounds the irony by sending a $200 wreath. The uncle continually reminds his listener of the wreath as a symbol of devotion.

A certain ambiguity about the coffin money and Mr. Pinckski's part in the swindle intimates ironic relationships. The implication that Mr. Pinckski may have been involved in the stealing of Mrs. Gihon's money is supported by two items: a reference by Danny about a man in New York who held out some money from him, and the fact that Mr. Pinckski deducts ten per cent interest from the amount he refunds to Danny, though Mr. Pinckski had explicitly stated that he would not charge any interest. This ambiguity adds subtle ironic shadings to the entire coffin affair.

Because this pathetic story is related by the naive uncle-brother, the ironic subtleties attenuate the emotional impact and stimulate the curiosity. [First published *American Mercury*, XXXI (February 1934), 166–74. First collected in *Collected Stories* (1950).]

A Point of Law   First published *Collier's* CV (June 22, 1940), 20–1 ff. Incorporated into "The Fire and the Hearth" in *Go Down, Moses* (1942). See discussion of *Go Down, Moses*.

Race at Morning   The final story in *Big Woods,* a collection of Faulkner's hunting stories, is "Race at Morning." The narrative recounts the day-long chase of a twelve-point buck which has previously eluded the hunters. Uncle Ike McCaslin presides over the group of hunters, and the tension of the chase is realistically developed. The story is narrated by a twelve-year-old boy, deserted two years ago by his parents and adopted by Mr. Ernest, a Delta farmer-hunter. From an early reference to the boy's lack of schooling, the author develops the theme of the boy's education, which must include understanding mankind as well as gathering facts and skills. The prime import of the story rests in the explicit statements about the reason for the chase and the responsibility of man in the world. The hunter, the hound and the deer participate in the hunt "because that was the thing they done the best and was proudest at" (p. 188).[15] The boy realizes that he and Mr. Ernest must perform their farming tasks well and honestly to earn the right to hunt. Mr. Ernest says that the boy must belong to the "business of mankind" (p. 196), so that he can know both what is right and wrong and why each is each. The race at morning refers not only to the pursuit of the deer, but also to the boy's beginning life. [First published *Saturday Evening Post,* CCXXVII (March 5, 1955), 26–27 ff. First collected in *Big Woods* (1955).]

Raid   First published *Saturday Evening Post,* CCVII (November 3, 1934), 18–19 ff. See the discussion of *The Unvanquished* (1938) into which this short story was incorporated.

---

[15] Quotations (marked with page numbers in parentheses) are from *Big Woods* (New York, 1955).

Red Leaves   The Indians in "Red Leaves" and for whom the story is named serve a double function. First of all they provide Yoknapatawpha with a period of legendary history just at the extremities of living memory. This short story, told by the omniscient author, occurs during the lifetime of Sam Fathers who appears only incidentally as Had-Two-Fathers (p. 336).[16] Consequently the action would have occurred early in the nineteenth century, a time when the white man dominated the Indians and influenced them to accept many facets of the white civilization. Part of this mythical experience involves the very colorful chief Doom (*du homme*) and his activities as the Man. An appreciation of the Indians' communal possession of property (both land and Negroes) is stressed. The advice which Herman Basket and Louis Berry give Moketubbe demonstrates the relative freedom of expression which the Indian enjoyed. The sense of decorum which the Indians seemed to possess innately is clearly delineated in the impetus for the plot. That is, the burial procedures required that the chief's dog, horse, and Negro be buried with him to serve him in the next life. Issetibbeha's forty-year-old Guinea body servant, recognizing that his master was dying, had begun his flight, a procedure that had itself become a part of the funeral ritual. The focus of the story is the pursuit and capture of Issetibbeha's Negro. A part of the Indians' sense of propriety is their attitude toward time. On the sixth day of the casual search, the Indians say, "We will give him time. . . . Tomorrow is just another name for today" (p. 337). But on the seventh day Herman Basket says to the Negro, "Let us go now. . . . It is today" (p. 338). But decorum must be served; the Negro is offered food and drink before his execution. Thus the Indians display an orderly pattern of conduct in this early stage of Yoknapatawpha history.

A second purpose of the Indians is to parody the white,

---

[16] Quotations (marked by page numbers in parentheses) are from *Collected Stories of William Faulkner* (New York, 1950).

civilized Southern aristocrat. The Indians have acquired Negroes, whom they did not want and for whom they had no use, from the white man. The problems of keeping the Negroes occupied poses as much a problem for the Indian masters as for their paleface counterparts. The plantation owners' attempts to subdue the wilderness, to create imposing homes of foreign architecture, and to establish a veneer of social conventions are mimicked in the actions of the Indians. Ikkemotubbe (Doom), on his return from a sojourn of gambling in New Orleans, dragged an abandoned steamboat up to the central area and attached it to a lean-to thus creating a semblance of the white man's Georgian home. Since the tribal council could think of no other way to dispose of the Negroes, Ikkemotubbe began to purchase more Negroes, as well as breeding his own, to cultivate more land, a process which became a tiresome cycle. Issetibbeha, mirroring his white neighbors, went to Paris, whence he returned with household appointments such as the unused bed and the girandoles. He even bought a pair of red-heeled slippers which pose a challenge to Moketubbe, the son Issetibbeha impulsively begot of a field worker. Particularly do the comments of the Indians parody the complaints of their Caucasian duplicates. One old Indian says, "This world is going to the dogs. . . . It is being ruined by white men" (p. 323). Another Indian remarks, "When have they [the Negroes] ever been anything but a trial and a care to us?" (p. 333). Even the mutual pretensions of the plantation owner and his slaves are parodied in the Indians' feigned ignorance of the Negroes' drums and in the complacent pursuit of Issetibbeha's Negro, who for several days circles the steamboat house. All of this mockery gives a delightfully comic air to action about which the characters are deadly earnest. "Red Leaves," one of Faulkner's best, is a fine story well told. [First published *Saturday Evening Post*, CCIII (October 25, 1930), 6–7 ff. First collected in *These* 13 (1931); included in *Collected Stories* (1950), and *Big Woods* (1955).]

Retreat First published *Saturday Evening Post,* CCVII (October 13, 1934), 16–17 ff. See the discussion of *The Unvanquished* (1938) into which this short story was incorporated.

A Rose for Emily "A Rose for Emily" is one of Faulkner's most carefully constructed stories. Miss Emily Grierson, the last member of a decayed aristocratic family, was a Jeffersonian tradition, and the story begins with her death. It is told by a first person narrator who has actually observed part of the action[17] and has heard the earlier parts recounted. The narration moves backward in time from Emily's death to the encounter in which she routs the city tax officials, to another moment thirty years earlier when an unusual odor emanated from her house, and finally to an event two years before that, when her father had died. After the account of her father's death, the progress assumes a forward chronological movement. Emily seems to be characterized as a crotchety old lady who cannot cope with the changing world. After she loses her father and later her lover, her life becomes a withdrawal. With a stroke of master craftsmanship, Faulkner in the very last words reveals that the story has a deeper, pathetic significance; thus the title implies a tribute to Emily. The "strand of iron-gray hair" (p. 130)[18] is the most significant detail in the entire story.[19]

The touch of insanity in the Grierson family is subtly called to the attention of the reader several times. At first the narrator recalls that "old Lady Wyatt, her [Emily's] great-aunt, had gone completely crazy at the last" (p. 123), and the townspeople had

[17] He seems to be a part of the newer generation which "became the backbone and the spirit of the town," (p. 128) and he says, "Each December *we* [Italics added] sent her a tax notice" (p. 128).

[18] Quotations (marked by page numbers in parentheses) are from *Collected Stories of William Faulkner* (New York, 1950).

[19] John V. Hagopian and Martic Dolch, "Faulkner's 'A Rose for Emily,'" *The Explicator,* Vol. XXII, No. 8 (April, 1964), note 68.

attributed it in part to the extreme pride of the Griersons. Again at the death of Emily's father, the reader is reminded, "We did not say she was crazy then" (p. 124), though the implication is strong that such a label could be applied later.

But it is the iron-gray strand of hair on the pillow which creates the revelatory moment. The reader and the narrator simultaneously recognize the deeper implications of Emily's situation. Details which had seemed glibly presented as town gossip become viable intimations of Miss Emily's unhappy demented condition. Thus "A Rose for Emily" becomes for the reader a genuine epiphany.

In the reevaluation occasioned by the strand of hair, the depth of Emily's lamentable insanity becomes apparent. When Emily first appears after her father's death, she is described as having "a vague resemblance to those angels in colored church windows —sort of *tragic* and serene" (p. 124—Italics added). And the fact that her hair was cut, an act peculiar enough for a woman of her age near the turn of the century, may have had ceremonial significance (See footnote 19). The death of Homer Barron and the retention of his body is Emily's successful endeavor to hold onto the past, "to cling to that which had robbed her, as people will" (p. 124). It reflects Emily's earlier refusal to accept the death of her father.

Homer Barron is a character who has dash and apparently no intention of marrying. The townspeople suggest that Emily cannot marry Homer because he is a Yankee and a day laborer; then they tend to hope she will. No indication is given in the story, however, that he has ever proposed matrimony. In fact the description of Homer plus an earlier comment, "even with insanity in the family she [Emily] wouldn't have turned down all of her chances if they had really materialized" (p. 123) suggest that marriage was not his aim. But the box of poison bears the inscription "For rats" (p. 126) which reflects ironically on Homer.

Miss Emily, in her role as town Sphinx, as Jefferson's accepted responsibility, does not seem very real. Her aloofness is indeed indispensable if her position as living tradition is to be maintained. Miss Emily preserves an icy remoteness from the townspeople, and even the narrator views her from a respectful distance. But the contents of the up-stairs bedroom changes all of that. Emily Grierson in retrospect becomes pathetically and fallibly human, the sympathy of the reader is aroused, and the story ends poignantly, superbly. [First published *Forum*, LXXXIII (April 1930), 233–8. First collected in *These 13* (1931) and included in *Collected Stories* (1950).]

Shall Not Perish A well defined structure does not compensate for the basic inappropriateness of language and the melodrama of the action in "Shall Not Perish." The title, taken from the last sentence of Lincoln's "Gettysburg Address," implies that Faulkner's purpose, like Lincoln's, is to encourage Americans to be resolute in defending freedom and to console those mourning for dead sons. The dramatic situation in which the Griers, who lost Pete three months before, comfort Major de Spain in his recent loss of his son, a twenty-three-year-old aviator, complements such a purpose.

The language, however, is rather conventional in its treatment of the problem. Consider the young Grier's thoughts,

May be we had forgotten that it could and was going to [happen], again and again, to people who loved sons and brothers as we loved Pete, until the day finally came when there would be an end to it. (p. 102) [20]

In addition to its trite diction, the story contains long paragraphs of such exposition which are inappropriate to a nine-year-old nar-

[20] Quotations (marked by page numbers in parentheses) are from *Collected Stories of William Faulkner* (New York, 1950).

rator; he becomes too mature, too understanding, to remain in character. The language of Major de Spain is sheer fustian. He rejects his son's allegiance to the United States in these words of outrageous bombast: "In the interests of usury, by the folly and rapacity of politicians, for the glory and aggrandisement of organized labor!" (p. 108), and he adds, "How can poltroonery and rapacity and voluntary thralldom know shame and grief?" (p. 108) Mother's reply is excessively platitudinous. "All men are capable of shame, ... Just as all men are capable of courage and honor and sacrifice" (p. 108).

The actions of this pivotal episode are rather melodramatic. Major de Spain is prepared to commit suicide, but Mrs. Grier boldly takes the gun from him and tells him to find solace in weeping. Instantaneously his bitterness becomes tears of tender remorse and in gratitude he offers to send the Griers home in his automobile. This excess of sentiment destroys empathy.

Following the de Spain scene, a digression, involving a visit to an art museum and a reminiscence about Grandpap at the movies, stresses the continuity of the United States' progress and the unity of its people; the Civil War is viewed as just a step in America's expansion.

The story concludes with this crescendo of exposition, unsuitable for the young narrator:

and still coming, North and South and East and West, until the name of what they did and what they died for became just one single word, louder than any thunder. It was America, and it covered all the western earth. (p. 115)

The elegant wording of the closing paragraph betrays Faulkner's poorly disguised attempt to console grieving Americans. He has thus written a quite patriotic exhortation but a weak dramatic narrative. [First published *Story*, XXIII (July–August 1943), 40–47. First collected in *Collected Stories* (1950).]

Shingles for the Lord The tendency of country folk to enjoy matching wits with one another, especially in barter, to interpret striking a shrewd bargain as a psychological and moral victory, is the comic focal point of "Shingles for the Lord." The humor of the story derives from the general ineptitude of the central character, Res Grier. He is a bumbling character who diffuses his strength by expending more energy than is required for any given chore. Consequently in his exultation over his shrewd deal with Solon Quick and in his exuberance for his task, he destroys the whole project. He fails in overreaching himself.

The point of view is that of a first person observer, in this case, the son of Res. The Reverend Whitfield is quite sympathetically presented. The title refers to the work with which the story begins, work donated to the reroofing of the church. This story seems to lack the vitality of many of Faulkner's other comic tales. [First published *Saturday Evening Post,* CCXV (February 13, 1943), 14–15 ff. First collected in *Collected Stories* (1950).]

Skirmish at Sartoris First published *Scribner's Magazine,* XCVII (April 1935), 193–200. See the discussion of *The Unvanquished* (1938) into which this short story was incorporated.

Smoke In "Smoke" Gavin Stevens, as County Attorney, bluffs a murderer into condemning himself. Unfortunately the author overplays his own hand, having the omniscient narrator discuss tension which the story has not created, having Stevens so overstate his hoax that the reader perceives and rejects the specious reasoning, thus nullifying the impact of the story. The unimaginative trick which Gavin employs is perhaps the oldest bit of chicanery known to the criminal prosecutor; he conjectures evidence until the guilt-ridden party cracks under the tension and commits himself. Gavin conjures up a confession which would warrant the grand jury's indicting the murderer, but he rambles on until the criminal unjustifiably discloses himself before the most ephemeral evidence.

Set in Jefferson, the story abounds with Yoknapatawpha types common to Faulkner's work. Gavin Stevens presents an unusually loquacious appearance. The plot operates rather methodically as it revolves around the twins who lack realism because one is excessively impetuous while the other is overly restrained. [First published *Harper's*, CLXIV (April 1932), 562–78. First collected in *Doctor Martino and Other Stories* (1934) and included in *Knight's Gambit* (1949).]

Spotted Horses   First published *Scribner's Magazine*, LXXXIX (June 1931), 585–97. See the discussion of *The Hamlet* (1940) into which this short story was incorporated.

The Tall Men   As the title implies, the theme of "The Tall Men" is moral stature. The McCallums are not physically tall nor corporally large, but they take a fierce pride in independence. They are, and they symbolize, courageous, self-reliant farmers who prefer their own unfettered actions to the acceptance of government subsidies, who accept their mistakes with resolution, and who adhere to a code of honor, admirably demanding.

The plot is simple, being distinguished by Buddy's fortitude during the amputation of his mangled leg. Though the story is told by an omniscient author, Mr. Gombault also serves as spokesman with his homespun didacticism. He remarks, "We have slipped our backbone; we have about decided a man don't need a backbone any more; to have one is old fashioned" (p. 59).[21] Later he becomes even more explicit; he stresses the importance of "honor and pride and discipline that make a man worth preserving, make him of any value" (p. 60). By just such expostula-

---

[21] Quotations (marked by page number in parentheses) are from *Collected Stories of William Faulkner* (New York, 1950).

tions, Faulkner expounds his sermon to the detriment of his narrative. [First published *Saturday Evening Post*, CCXIII (May 31, 1941), 14-15 ff. First collected in *Collected Stories* (1950).]

That Evening Sun   Three levels of consciousness operate within the richness of "That Evening Sun." On one level are the adults at the time of the action, that is Mr. and Mrs. Jason Compson III, Dilsey, Nancy, and Jesus; a second level exists in the minds of the children Jason, Caddy, and Quentin Compson; the third level is the awareness of an older Quentin. Beginning with a reminiscence fifteen years later, Quentin narrates the story, but as he moves into a recollection of the major incident, his perspective becomes that of the nine-year-old uncomprehending child that he was when Nancy's fear was at its apex.

Each of the varying degrees of awareness permits the reader to share in the story in a different way. Quentin's *ex post facto* knowledge presented early in the narration gives the reader information concerning Nancy's relationship with a white man, information imperative to a comprehension of later events and of Jesus' motivation in particular. The discrepancy between the adults' understanding and the naivete of the children provides a grim humor which intensifies the ominous effect of Nancy's fear. Nancy's insistence upon the imminence of her murder becomes more frightening in contrast with two attitudes toward it. Mr. Compson claims helplessness in the situation. " 'What could the officers do?' father said. 'If Nancy hasn't seen him, how could the officers find him?' " (p. 299)[22] Because of Mrs. Compson's simpering agitation, he refuses Nancy the former sanctuary of his house. The children, aged nine, seven, and five, do not comprehend the references to Nancy's swelling stomach, nor father's suggestion that Nancy leave white men alone, nor Nancy's story about a

---

[22] Quotations (marked by page numbers in parentheses) are from *Collected Stories of William Faulkner* (New York, 1950).

queen approaching a ditch where a bad man was hiding. Caddy's unanswered questions are used to emphasize important details about Nancy's fear, to lead the reader to draw clear inferences of Nancy's situation. The innocence of the children accentuates Nancy's guilt.

The attitudes of Nancy, Jesus, and Dilsey toward the problem are noteworthy also. Nancy tries to escape the moral problems of her predicament by saying several times, "I just a nigger. It ain't no fault of mine" (p. 309). In fact this is her final statement. Jesus justifiably resents the association between Nancy and the white man. He remarks bitterly, "I cant hang around white man's kitchen. . . . But white man can hang around mine" (p. 292). Dilsey, however, stands as a clear refutation of Nancy's excuse, a striking reminder of Nancy's culpability, and a marked contrast to Jesus' rancor. Dilsey too is a Negro but she has not been involved in such reprehensible activities. In a truly charitable spirit, Dilsey suggests that Nancy seek the protection of the law, and then she offers her the sympathy and security of her own home. Nancy refuses Dilsey's ministrations. Nancy's moral cowardice paralyzes her with fear; all she can do is sit in her cabin with the lamp flaring and wait for her fate.

In this excellent short story, Faulkner has so maneuvered the points of view that the petrifying fear of a poor Negro washerwoman illuminates the moral decay of an entire society. [Cf. the discussion of *Requiem for a Nun*. First published *American Mercury*, XXII (March 1931), 257-67. First collected in *These* 13 (1931) and included in *Collected Stories* (1950).]

That Will Be Fine Desire for money and sexual lust serve as the two subtly interwoven themes of "That Will Be Fine." These themes are personified by the young uncomprehending narrator and the profligate uncle, both common character devices in Faulkner's work. Georgie, the seven-year-old narrator, does not understand the ironic comments made by his parents and other adults about Uncle Rodney, but he does recognize that he can gain nickels and quarters by helping his uncle with his "business."

Georgie's mercenary nature is emphasized by Rosie's comments and by Georgie's thoughts. Rosie, the Negro cook, once says, "You and money! If you ain't rich time you twenty-one, hit will be because the law done abolished money or done abolished you" (p. 265).[23] Georgie constantly remembers the quarters he has earned by watching for returning husbands while Uncle Rodney meets with the ladies. The possibility of gaining ten quarters, or even twenty, leads Georgie to lie to the sheriff and to abet the planned escape of his uncle.

The lecherous nature of Uncle Rodney, who is the youngest brother of Georgie's mother, is often depicted through the ironic comments of adults. George, Georgie's father, is the most prominent enunciator of these ironies. But Georgie's reminiscences of earning small change from supporting Uncle Rodney's actions in Jefferson and Mottstown complete the characterization of Rodney.

The comedy of this story develops from the dramatic irony of Georgie's lack of comprehension. The two primary themes are neatly joined at the conclusion by a unifying third theme introduced early by Rosie; it is the idea of a present for Grandpa. Rodney's body is ironically carried to Georgie's grandfather as a present "From all the husbands in Mottstown" (p. 286). But Georgie's lack of understanding prevails. He intends to make a profit from his present for Grandpa and to combine that money with the quarters he plans to collect from Uncle Rodney. Then he will have twenty-one quarters, and "that will be fine" (p. 288). [First published *American Mercury*, XXXV (July 1935), 264-76. First collected in *Collected Stories* (1950).]

There Was a Queen   The theme of "There Was a Queen" is "quality" versus "unquality." Elnora, the miscegenated half-

[23] Quotations (marked by page numbers in parentheses) are from *Collected Stories of William Faulkner* (New York, 1950).

sister to old Bayard Sartoris, considers Miss Jenny (Mrs. Virginia Sartoris Du Pre) as the last example of "quality"; she relegates Narcissa Benbow Sartoris, widow of young Bayard, to the odious position of "unquality." Set in Jefferson, Yoknapatawpha, in June of 1926,[24] the story told by an omniscient narrator, presents the last chapter in the Sartoris saga. The son of Narcissa and Bayard is the only remaining Sartoris male, and because he is named Benbow instead of John or Bayard, his role as a Sartoris seems diminished.

The narcissistic nature of Mrs. Bayard Sartoris is very strongly emphasized in this story, and the derogatory comments of Elnora seem justified by Narcissa's trip to Memphis. She has committed adultery with a Yankee Jew to retrieve some obscene letters written to her thirteen years earlier by a Jefferson bank cashier. In Miss Jenny's opinion Narcissa is not a lady because she enjoyed the letters and was willing to do anything to get them back. This knowledge seems directly related to Miss Jenny's death. At the conclusion of the story, the situation is as the title implies: there *was* a queen; there *is* a quean. [First published *Scribner's Magazine*, XCIII (January 1933), 10–16. First collected in *Doctor Martino and Other Stories* (1934) and included in *Collected Stories* (1950).]

Thrift   First published *Saturday Evening Post,* CCIII (September 6, 1930), 16–17 ff. Uncollected. Reprinted in *O. Henry Memorial Award Prize Stories of 1931.*

Tomorrow   "Tomorrow" is the explanation of a mistrial. Bookwright, a respected citizen, kills the rowdy young man who is eloping with the seventeen-year-old Bookwright daughter. Although it is discovered that the roughneck already had a legal

---

[24] Internal evidence: Mrs. Du Pre came to Jefferson in 1869, 57 years earlier. Information from *Sartoris* would indicate 1931 as the date of the story's content.

wife, one man on the jury refused to free the father. Gavin Stevens, who was defending Bookwright, determines to know the reason why S. J. Fentry would not acquit the father. The search leads Gavin and his nephew, (probably Charles Mallison) who narrates the story, into the hill country where Fentry lived and into Frenchman's Bend where Fentry once worked. The explanation, pieced together from neighbors and employers, neglects the crime to emphasize man's often underestimated capacity for love. The understanding which Gavin gains gives the reader an insight into the author's concept of man. The story suffers from the lack of action and the overt sentimentality. [First published *Saturday Evening Post*, CCXIII (November 23, 1940), 22-3 ff. First collected in *Knight's Gambit* (1949).]

Turnabout The theme of "Turnabout" is the incredible courage which men calmly display during the excessively dangerous duties of a war. The tension in the story is posited in the conflict between what the American flyers condescendingly assume to be the responsibility of a young British naval officer and what that responsibility actually entails. The straightforward plot is presented by an omniscient narrator, the scene is France during World War I, and the title refers to an exchange of visits during battle missions between Captain Bogard of the American Air Force and Midshipman L. C. W. Hope of the British Royal Navy.

The grim humor of the story arises from the satirized pomposity of the American flyers and from Captain Bogard's recognition of the irony inherent in the attitude of the Americans toward the British. The equanimity with which the young British officers perform their dangerous task evokes a profound admiration from Captain Bogard. His reaction to the experience is both humorous and inspired. Dramatic irony also exists in Claude Hope's praise of the Americans' accidental, unconscious bravery and his depreciation of his own deliberate, cognitive intrepidity. This is perhaps Faulkner's best war story. [First published *Saturday Eve-*

ning Post, CCIV (March 5, 1932), 6–7 ff. First collected in *Doctor Martino and Other Stories* (1934), and included in *Collected Stories* (1950).]

Two Soldiers   In a display of Faulkner's virtuosity, "Two Soldiers" evokes laughter and tears. The humor rises from the ingenuousness of the narrator, who is Pete Grier's young brother. The expression of deep, genuine—almost non-verbal—emotions in language which avoids the conventional, the trite, and the mawkish, arouses sincere responses.

The young narrator provokes amusement by his fiercely independent, simple-minded attitude. When Pete states his intention of fighting the Japanese, the brother plans to go along. He reasons, "You'll whup the big uns and I'll whup the little uns," (p. 83) [25] After having walked the twenty-two miles from Frenchman's Bend to Jefferson by himself at night, he is asked if he thinks he can find Pete in Memphis. He replies, " 'I reckon I can,' I said. 'I ain't got but one [brother] and I have knowed him all my life. I reckon I will know him again when I see him' " (p. 91). While the brother is with Pete in Memphis, the lieutenant asks if he can get home by himself. He remarks, "I don't live in but one place. I don't reckon it's moved" (p. 96). The facetious wit of the bus agent in Jefferson also serves as a foil to the unintentional humor of the narrator's comments. The young boy is sometimes used as comic relief in situations that might tend to become surcharged with emotion. The discrepancy between what adults recognize as the narrator's actual position in the world and his own opinion of his prominence is demonstrated while Pete and his parents are first discussing Pete's decision. " 'You hush your mouth!' maw said, crying. 'Nobody's talking

---

[25] Quotations (marked by page numbers in parentheses) are from *Collected Stories of William Faulkner* (New York, 1950). This story can be profitably studied in contrast to its sequel, "Shall Not Perish."

to you! Go and get me a armful of wood! That's what you can do!' " (p. 85)

The pathos is aroused by the sincere comments of several characters. In trying to explain to his brother that war is grim, Pete, nearly twenty, points out "Folks don't go to wars for fun. A man don't leave his maw crying just for fun" (p. 86). The mother accepts the son's decision with a maturity that belies her proclaimed lack of comprehension as she finally says, "You got to go, and so I want you to go. But I don't understand it, and I won't never, and so don't expect me to" (p. 85). Finally after he has tracked Pete to Memphis, the younger brother tries to persuade Pete to allow him to come also by exclaiming, "I got to go too. I got to. It hurts my heart, Pete" (p. 96).

Though the narrator, telling the story in retrospect, does not realize how agitated he was, Pete and the readers do. The fact that young Grier draws a knife on people in two separate instances indicated his emotional tension. Because Pete's brother is unaware of the depth and meaning of his inner turmoil (an impression supported by the narrator's lack of comprehension at his own tears), maudlin sentiment is forestalled in the reader.

In this narration, told with economy, the McKellogg episode seems to disrupt the unity of the story and weaken the plot slightly. Mrs. McKellogg's entrance lacks justification. By contrast, the choice of narrator and the careful wording could hardly have been more felicitous. Faulkner handled a difficult subject superbly. [First published *Saturday Evening Post* CCXIV (March 28, 1942), 9–11 ff. First collected in *Collected Stories* (1950).]

Uncle Willy An individual's struggle to get fun out of life is the theme of the story "Uncle Willy." The narrative is presented by a fourteen-year-old boy who is Uncle Willy's ally. Those who represent hampering forces are the do-gooders and the swindlers.

The story is the narrator's attempt to explain that he voluntarily aided Uncle Willy and that he was not trolled away.

The narrator abets Uncle Willy Christian's addiction to drugs, to liquor, and to flying. The boy early explains his devotion to Uncle Willy:

> I went because Uncle Willy was the finest man I ever knew, because even women couldn't beat him, because in spite of them he wound up his life getting fun out of being alive and he died doing the thing that was the most fun of all because I was there to help him. (p. 225)[26]

The lawyer father of the narrator and most other adults excuse the boy's actions on the grounds of his impressionable youth. The genuinely unselfish actions of the boy and Mr. Christian's two Negro employees contrast with the machinations of the do-gooders and the criminals.

The do-gooders, consisting principally of Mrs. Merridew and Rev. Schultz, determine to "save" Uncle Willy from a forty-year drug addiction. Though they loudly proclaim their Christian charity, Uncle Willy says to them, "Won't you please go to hell and just let me come on at my own gait?" (p. 231) One of the swindlers, the Memphis prostitute who marries Uncle Willy and willingly divorces him for a bribe, is a foil to Mrs. Merridew. Her honesty in taking Mr. Christian's money contrasts sharply with the idea that Mrs. Merridew, the Christian lady, will never forgive Uncle Willy for becoming bankrupt. The clerk whom the do-gooders hire to operate Uncle Willy's drugstore turns out to be an embezzler; he disappears quietly after having stolen as much as possible from the store.

The comedy of the story arises from the satire directed against the religious figures who appear more interested in Uncle Willy's

---

[26] Quotations (marked by page numbers in parentheses) are from *Collected Stories of William Faulkner* (New York, 1950).

material assets than in the needs of his soul. The cooperation
which the young boys of Jefferson give Uncle Willy in his clandestine efforts to preserve his right to independent action creates
humor also. The poignancy of the story resides in the inconsistency between the attitudes of the adults toward Uncle Willy and
the attitude of the narrator toward him, an attitude which causes
the boy to consider Uncle Willy's philosophy more valid than the
philosophy of his society. [First published *American Mercury,*
XXXVI (October 1935), 156–68. First collected in *Collected
Stories* (1950).]

The Unvanquished First published *Saturday Evening Post,*
CCIX (November 14, 1936), 12–13 ff. See the discussion of *The
Unvanquished* (1938) into which this short story was incorporated
as "Riposte in Tertio."

Vendee First published *Saturday Evening Post,* CCIX (December 5, 1936), 16–17 ff. See the discussion of *The Unvanquished*
(1938) into which this short story was incorporated.

Victory Beginning *in medias res,* "Victory" immediately
plunges the reader into a sequence of events in which time is
treated with a sophistication typical of Faulkner's work. The
story begins four years after the end of World War I, three years
after Captain Alec Gray, M.C., DSM, has taken a position with
the officers' association, and it focuses on his return to the "dead
scenes of his lost and found life" (p. 456).[27] No names are given
in this section. From that point the story moves backward to the
incident of Alec's insubordination. Then the plot moves all the
way back to the beginning of the story, presenting a family scene
in which Alec Gray decides to go to war as a soldier rather than
to follow the two-hundred-year family tradition of ship building.

---

[27] Quotations (marked by page numbers in parentheses) are from *Collected
Stories of William Faulkner* (New York, 1950).

Faulkner is vitally concerned throughout the canon of his work
with people in conflict with tradition, most often family tradition.
Such a conflict unifies the "Victory." From section three the story
moves forward chronologically, but by the time the reader has
read sections one and two, he is thoroughly enmeshed in the
actions of the excellently depicted characters and puzzled about
the future of Alec Gray.

But it is not the skillful manipulation of time which gives the
story its artistic merit; it is the irony. That "Victory" is located
in "The Wasteland" section of *Collected Stories* is appropriate
because it is the period of depression and dejection after World
War I on which the story centers. The title itself has a strikingly
ironic implication which becomes patently clear by the end of the
story. Many of the events of Alec Gray's military career involve
ironies. The letters between Alec and his family develop a subtle
discrepancy between what the family imagines Alec's situation
to be and what his situation actually is. In the battle for which
Alec receives his first citation, he murders the sergeant-major who
had earlier helped send him to the guard house for insubordination. After Alec becomes a captain, he sneers at a young Scottish
soldier; ironically performing an act similar to the one for which
he himself had killed an officer. The references to pride also have
ironic overtones. Matthew Gray, the simple shipwright, warns
his son against becoming an officer. He writes an admonition
against "the pride and vainglory of going for an officer" (p. 447).
After the war when Captain Alec informs his parents that he
intends to return to London to work with the Officers' Association, Matthew again reads "a paragraph of pride" (p. 455) from
the Book. Alec is proud of his rank and his association with
gentlemen; he joys in the Empire. The pride itself becomes an
instrument of irony as it forces Alec to prefer a life of begging
above a return to the simplicity of his family's life and to the
manual occupation of his forebears. From his valor in the victory
of war, Captain Alec Gray acquired a sense of self-esteem which

converted his plain of delight into a wasteland, his victory into a defeat.

This story is carefully constructed to emphasize the gradual depreciation of Alec's life, a change characteristic of many disillusioned souls after World War I. Walkley, who went to rural Canada and prospered, is provided as a foil to show that such a self-defeating pride was unnecessary. But what could have been a superior short story is marred by a somewhat sentimentalized juxtaposing of virtuous rural life with corrupting city life and by the needless exposition of the final paragraph. [First published *These* 13 (1931). Included in *Collected Stories* (1950).]

Was First published in *Go Down, Moses* (1942). See the discussion of *Go Down, Moses.*

Wash First published *Harper's,* CLXVIII (February 1934), 258–66. First collected in *Doctor Martino and Other Stories* (1934) and included in *Collected Stories* (1950). See the discussion of *Absalom, Absalom!* (1936) into which this short story is incorporated.

Dictionary of Characters

◆◆◆◆◆◆◆◆◆◆◆◆◆◆◆◆◆◆◆◆◆◆◆◆◆◆◆◆◆◆

HEADNOTE

This dictionary consists of an alphabetical listing of all the characters which appear in William Faulkner's books of fiction. Characters which appear in uncollected short stories are not included.

Following the name of the character, is a notation which reveals his race. After the notation of race, is found the title of the work or works in which the figure appears. A separate observation is made for each work in which the entity is found. Subsequent to each title is placed the earliest date of publication and an abbreviation which denotes the importance of the role the character plays in that particular work. *Major* means a major character; *Minor* denotes a minor role; *Bkg.* labels a background character. A character is considered major if he is important to the entire story or novel. He is accounted minor if he only supplements the action throughout the story or if he is quite important in only a segment of it. A background character may be a servant who stands quietly and serves all through the work, or a character who is simply mentioned in passing but who contributes to the atmosphere Faulkner is trying to create.

Abbreviations for race are *Neg.* for Negro, *Cau.* for Caucasian, and *Ind.* for Indian. Japanese is written out in the instances where it applies. Combinations of abbreviations are used to explain miscegenated characters, of whom there are not a few. The appropriate abbreviations appear with a diagonal mark between. Octoroon and quadroon are written out when Faulkner has so labeled the character.

The novels and short stories are arranged within each entry in chronological order of publication. The stories from *New Orleans Sketches* (1958) are dated from their first publication in the New Orleans *Times-Picayune*. All information within each notation has been derived from the particular work.

Although the first six chapters of *The Unvanquished* (1938) were published as short stories over a period of three years from 1934-36, all characters have been listed with the title of the novel and date of publication of the novel. See also the bibliographical information in the short story commentary.

A

Abe: Neg.—*Sartoris* (1929)—Bkg.—Caretaker of Doc Peabody's fishing pond.

Acey: Neg.—"Pantaloon in Black" (1940)—Bkg.—Attended the funeral of Rider's wife.

Adams, Mr. and Mrs.: Cau.—*The Town* (1957)—Bkg.—The mayor when Flem Snopes first came to town; she is called "Miss Eve Adam."

Adams, Theron: Cau.—*The Town* (1957)—Bkg.—The youngest son of Mayor Adams.

Ailanthia: Cau.—"Elly" (1934)—Major—The grandmother hatred for whom drives Elly, her own granddaughter, to attempt suicide.

Akers: Cau.—*Absalom, Absalom!* (1936)—Bkg.—Coonhunter who informs the town of Sutpen's activities.

Albert: Cau.—*As I Lay Dying* (1930)—Bkg.—The soda clerk of Mottson who told Moseley the Bundren story.

Albert: Cau.—"Turnabout" (1932)—Bkg.—Hope's British M.P. friend.

Albert: Cau.—*The Mansion* (1959)—Bkg.—A cohort of Mink Snopes in the Goodyhay episode.

Alec, Uncle: Neg.—"Pantaloon in Black" (1940)—Bkg.—Husband of the aunt who raised Rider.

Aleck Sander: See Sander, Aleck.

Alford, Dr.: Cau.—*Sartoris* (1929)—Minor—The young doctor, in indeterminate thirties, nephew of an old resident; he and Miss Jenny took Bayard (old) to Memphis specialist. Slightly interested in Narcissa Benbow. *As I Lay Dying* (1930) —Bkg.—Mentioned as doctor upstairs over drugstore.

Alice: Cau.—*Light in August* (1932)—Bkg.Twelve-year-old companion of Joe Christmas at Memphis orphanage.

Alice: Neg.—*The Reivers* (1962)—Bkg.—Miss Ballenbaugh's helper.

Allanovna, Myra: Cau.—*The Mansion* (1959)—Bkg.—A famous New York tie designer.

Allen: Cau. or American Indian—"Fox Hunt" (1931)—Bkg.—Childhood sweetheart of Mrs. Harrison Blair; marries a show girl.

Allen, Bobbie: Cau.—*Light in August*—(1932)—Minor—A prostitute who was eighteen-year-old Joe Christmas' first girl.

Allison, Miss: Cau.—*The Mansion* (1959)—Bkg.—de Spain cousin to whom Linda Snopes Kohl returns the mansion.

Allison, Howard: Cau.—"Beyond" (1933)—Bkg.—Judge Allison's ten-year-old son who died while riding his pony, eighteen years earlier. (b. April 3, 1903—d. August 22, 1913).

Allison, Judge: Cau.—"Beyond"—(1933)—Major—The sixty-five-year-old central character who dies and visits Heaven or Purgatory, but returns to his affirmation of death.

Allison, Sophia: Cau.—"Beyond" (1933)—Bkg.—The Judge's indulgent mother.

Ames, Dalton: Cau.—*The Sound and the Fury* (1929)—Bkg.— The father of Caddy's illegitimate child, Quentin.

Andrews: Cau. ?—"Fox Hunt" (1931) Bkg. A house servant of some sort.

Angelique: Cau.—*A Fable* (1954)—Bkg.—Old woman opposed to Corporal.

Anse: Cau.—*The Sound and the Fury* (1929)—Bkg.—The marshal who arrests Quentin for allegedly kidnapping the little Italian girl.

Antonio: Cau.—"Jealousy" (1925)—Major—The old, jealous husband who kills his suspected rival.

Armstead: See Armstid

Armstid: Mentioned in *The Hamlet* (1940) as family name of early Yoknapatawpha settlers. Spelled *Armstead* in *Intruder in the Dust* (1948).

Armstid, Mr. and Mrs. (Henry): Cau.—*As I Lay Dying* 1930)—Bkg.—Neighbors who aid the Bundrens when they cross the river; she is Lula here. *Light in August* (1932)—Bkg. —He gives Lena Grove a wagonride; she (Martha here) gives Lena money. *The Hamlet*—(1940)—Minor—Henry takes her money which has been saved for chaps' shoes and buys a spotted horse; He is also a victim in the Frenchman's place swindle. "Shingles for the Lord" (1943)—Bkg.—Farm couple living near Whitfield's church. *The Town* (1957)—Bkg.—A tricked partner of Ratliff on a gold deal which drove Henry insane; now in an asylum. *The Mansion* (1959)—Bkg.—Mentioned as tricked into buying Frenchman's place with Ratliff and Odum Bookwright.

Artist: Cau.—"New Orleans" (1925)—Major—His speech praises the creative fire. *Artist* is a label, not a name.

Ash, Old Man: Neg.—"A Bear Hunt" (1934)—Major—Major de Spain's hunting camp servant who is revenged on Butch Provine. His father is called Ash Wylie in *Big Woods* (1955) version of the story. "The Old People" (1940)—Bkg.—The camp cook. "The Bear" (1942)—Bkg.—The camp cook who is jealous of Ike McCaslin's first deer.

Atkins, Miss: Cau.—*Light in August* (1932)—Bkg.—The dietitian whose clandestine love affairs gets Joe Christmas into his first trouble.

Atkinson: Cau.—*Pylon* (1935)—Bkg.—Plane building partner of Matt Ord.

Aunt: Neg.—"Pantaloon in Black" (1940)—Bkg.—Rider's aunt. Alec's wife.

Avant, Jim: Cau.—*The Reivers* (1962)—Bkg.—Mentioned as expert on dogs.

Ayers, Mr. Freddie: Cau.—"Yo Ho and Two Bottles of Rum" (1925)—Major—The mate who accidentally kills Yo Ho.

Ayers, Major: Cau.—*Mosquitoes* (1927)—Major—The Britisher who is interested in selling a new laxative to Americans.

B

Backhouse, Mrs. Melisandre: Cau.—"My Grandmother Millard . . ." (1943)—Major—Falls in love with a young Confederate officer and they are married.

Backhouse, Philip St. Just: Cau.—"My Grandmother Millard . . ." (1943)—Major—A young Confederate officer who marries Bayard Sartoris's cousin Melisandre.

Backus, Melisandre: Cau.—*The Town* (1957)—Bkg.—Mentioned as girl Gavin Stevens ought to marry. *The Mansion* (1959)—A young friend of Gavin Stevens whom she later marries. See Mrs. Harriss.

Backus, Mr.: Cau.—*The Mansion* (1959)—Bkg.—Father of Melisandre.

Baddrington, Harold: Cau.—*The Mansion* (1959)—Bkg.— Mentioned as pilot of plane in which Charles Mallison was shot down.

Baird, Dr.: Cau.—*Soldiers' Pay* (1926)—Minor—A specialist from Atlanta who praises Mrs. Powers' evaluation and plan of action.

Baker, Joe (Jobaker): Ind.—"The Old People" (1940)—Bkg. —A friend of Sam Fathers; called Jobaker. "The Bear" (1942) —Bkg.—Mentioned as friend of Sam Fathers.

Ball: Cau.—*A Fable* (1954)—Bkg.—dead R.F.C. flyer.

Ballenbaugh (I): Cau.—*The Reivers* (1962)—Bkg.—First acquired Wyott's Crossing and is the ancestor of Miss Ballenbaugh who now runs the hostel at the Iron Bridge.

Ballenbaugh (II): Cau.—*The Reivers* (1962)—Bkg.—Son of Ballenbaugh (I); maker of whiskey; took over outpost in 1865 after which it became lawless until Hightower cleaned it up.

Ballenbaugh, Miss: Cau.—*The Reivers* (1962)—Minor—She runs the hostel at the Iron Bridge and her cooking attracts guests; descendant of Ballenbaugh (I, II). Lucius Priest and Boon Hogganbeck stop overnight there.

Ballenbaugh, Boyd: Cau.—"Hand Upon the Waters" (1939)— Major—Tyler Ballenbaugh's brother who murders Lonnie Grinnup.

Ballenbaugh, Tyler: Cau.—"Hand Upon the Waters" (1939)— Major—Owner of the life insurance on Lonnie Grinnup.

Ballott, Mr. and Mrs.: Cau.—*The Reivers* (1962)—Bkg.—He was the white foreman at the livery stable; his first wife had been the daughter of Dan Grinnup.

Baptiste, Jean: Cau.—"Home" (1925)—Major—The homesick French immigrant about to undertake some illegal job, but is reminded of his home by the saw-violinist. He ponders the reactions of the General, Pete and Tony.

Barbour, Mr.: Cau.—"Uncle Willy" (1935)—Bkg.—Teacher of the boys' Sunday School class that Uncle Willy always attended.

Barger, Sonny: Neg. ?—"Uncle Willy" (1935)—Bkg.—Storekeeper in Negro section.

Barker: Cau.—*A Fable* (1954)—Bkg.—R.F.C. hero.

Barron, Homer: Cau.—"A Rose for Emily" (1930)—Major—Emily Grierson's lover; a Northerner; day laborer.

Barron, Jake: Cau.—*The Mansion* (1959)—Bkg.—Convict at Parchman killed while trying to escape.

Bascomb, Maury: Cau.—*The Sound and the Fury* (1929)—Bkg. —The flamboyantly shiftless brother of Mrs. Caroline B. Compson.

Basket, Herman: Ind.—"A Justice" (1931)—Minor—A friend of Crawfishford, Sam Fathers' father. "A Courtship" (1948) —Bkg.—He and his sister live with his aunt who is important because of her relation to David Colbert, Chief of the Chickasaws.

Basket, John: Ind.—"A Bear Hunt" (1934)—Bkg.—One of the moonshining Indians who frighten Butch Provine.

Beale, Colonel: Cau.—*A Fable* (1954)—Minor—Thought he had seen the corporal (whom he calls Boggan) killed in action.

Bean, Capt.: Cau.—"Uncle Willy" (1935)—Bkg.—Would not let Uncle Willy learn to fly without a doctor's permit.

Beard: Cau.—*The Sound and the Fury* (1929)—Bkg.—Mentioned as owner of vacant lot used by carnival.

Beard, Virgil: Cau.—*Sartoris* (1929)—Minor—Unwittingly penned Byron Snopes's letters to Miss Narcissa Benbow. Son of Mr. and Mrs. Will C. Beard.

Beard, Will C.: Cau.—*Sartoris* (1929)—Bkg.—Operated grist mill; his wife runs boarding house; father of Virgil.

Beard, Mrs. Will C.: Cau.—*Sartoris* (1929)—Bkg.—Operated boarding house where Byron Snopes lived; Virgil's mother. *Light in August* (1932)—Bkg.—Operated boarding house where Byron Bunch stayed.

Beauchamp, Amodeus McCaslin: Son of Tomey's Turl and Tennie Beauchamp. Born and died 1859.

Beauchamp, Bobo: Neg./Cau.—*The Reivers* (1962)—Minor— Gets the horse-car trade started through his gambling; Mr. Van Tosch's groom; cousin to Ned McCaslin.

Beauchamp, Callina: Daughter of Tomey's Turl and Tennie Beauchamp; born and died 1862.

Beauchamp, Henry: Neg./Cau.—"The Fire and the Hearth" (1942)—Bkg.—Son of Molly and Lucas Beauchamp; childhood comrade of Roth Edmonds.

Beauchamp, Hubert Fitz-Hubert: Cau.—"The Bear" (1942)— Bkg.—Pretended to bequeath Isaac a silver cup filled with gold, but he had spent it before his death; brother of Sophonsiba B. McCaslin. "Delta Autumn" (1942)—Bkg.—Mentioned as man Buddy McCaslin won Tennie Beauchamp from. "Was" (1942)—Major—A bachelor who owns a farm about one-half day's ride from the McCaslins; brother of Sophonsiba Beauchamp.

Beauchamp, James Thucydus (Thucydides)—(Tennie's Jim): Neg./Cau.—"The Old People" (1940)—Bkg.—A servant at hunting camp. "The Bear" (1942)—Bkg.—A servant at hunting camp until he runs away on his twenty-first birthday, forfeiting the inheritance from his father; born December 29, 1864. "Delta Autumn" (1942)—Bkg.—The grandfather of the Negro girl who bears Roth Edmonds' child. *The Reivers* (1962)—Bkg.—Mentioned as former worker at de Spain hunting camp; grandfather of Bobo Beauchamp.

Beauchamp, Lucas Quintus Carothers McCaslin: Neg./Cau. —"Pantaloon in Black" (1940)—Bkg.—Oldest tenant on Roth Edmonds' place; his hearth fire inspired Rider and Mannie. "Go Down, Moses" (1941)—Bkg.—Mentioned as Molly's husband. "The Bear" (1942)—Bkg. Mentioned as born 17 March, 1874; son of Tomey's Turl and Tennie Beauchamp. "Delta Autumn" (1942)—Mentioned as uncle to woman with whom Roth Edmonds has an affair. "The Fire and the Hearth" (1942) —Major—The son of Tomey's Turl and Teenie Beauchamp; the grandson of old Carothers McCaslin; as a sixty-seven-year-old man, he tries to protect his moonshine activities and to find a pile of money. This is the story of his life, his strength of character. *Intruder in the Dust* (1948)—Major—Lucas, a proud almost insolent Negro, is saved from hanging unjustly by Charles Mallison. *The Reivers* (1962)—Bkg.—Mentioned as being very much like his ancestor, L.Q.C. McCaslin.

Beauchamp, Molly Worsham: Neg.—"Go Down, Moses" (1941)—Major—The grandmother of Sam W. Beauchamp who is electrocuted by law; wife of Lucas; name spelled *Mollie*. "Delta Autumn" (1942)—Bkg.—Mentioned as Aunt Mollie, aunt of woman Roth Edmonds has an affair with. "The Fire and the Hearth" (1942)—Minor—Lucas's wife; she rears Roth Edmonds; Lucas thinks Zackary used her as a mistress. *Intruder in the Dust* (1948)—Bkg.—Deceased wife of Lucas; Miss Habersham's former friend.

Beauchamp, Nathalie: See Wilkins, Mrs. Nathalie B.

Beauchamp, Philip Manigault: Neg.—*A Fable* (1954)—Bkg. —A Mississippi soldier involved in the killing of General Gragnon; a future undertaker.

Beauchamp, Samuel Worsham (Butch): Neg./Cau.—"Go Down, Moses" (1941)—Major—Mollie Worsham Beauchamp's electrocuted grandson whose body is shipped home from Illinois to Jefferson.

Beauchamp, Sophonsiba: See McCaslin, Mrs. Sophonsiba B.

Beauchamp, Sophonsiba (Fonsiba): Neg./Cau.—"The Bear" (1942)—Minor—Marries a Negro who is considered a pseudo-intellectual, and moves to Arkansas; receives three dollars per month from inheritance; born 1869. "The Fire and the Hearth" (1942)—Bkg.—A daughter of Tennie Beauchamp and Tomey's Turl; Marries and moves to Arkansas; to receive three dollars a week from inheritance, according to this version.

Beauchamp, Tennie: Neg.—"The Bear" (1942)—Bkg.—Twenty-one years old in 1859; slave won from Hubert F. Beauchamp by Amodeus; married to Tomey's Turl in 1859. "Delta Autumn" (1942)—Bkg.—Mentioned as won in a card game. "Was" (1942)—Major—The Negress of Mr. Hubert Beauchamp's that Tomey's Turl runs away to see. "The Fire and the Hearth" (1942)—Minor—The wife of Tomey's Turl; mother of Lucas.

Beauchamp, Tomey's Turl: Neg.—*The Town* (1957)—Minor—The night fireman at the electric plant; likely a descendant of Tomey's Turl, father of Lucas Beauchamp.

Bedenberry, Brother: Neg.—*Light in August* (1932)—Bkg.—Attacked by Joe Christmas while Joe is a fugitive.

Beggar: Cau.—"Mirrors of Chartres Street" (1925)—Major—One-legged beggar who derides the policeman until the paddy wagon arrives.

Benbow, Mrs. Belle (Mitchell): Cau.—*Sartoris* (1929)—Minor—A self-centered society leader who left Harry Mitchell for Horace Benbow; mother of "little" Belle Mitchell. *Sanctuary* (1931)—Bkg.—Horace Benbow's wife of ten years; mother of "little" Belle Mitchell.

(Benbow), "little" Belle Mitchell: See Mitchell, "little" Belle.

Benbow, Cassius Q. (Uncle Cash): Neg.—*The Unvanquished* (1938)—Bkg.—Former Benbow coachman whom carpetbag Burden's are running for U. S. Marshal in Jefferson.

Benbow, Francis: Cau.—*Sartoris* (1929)—Bkg.—Mentioned as ancestor of Horace and Narcissa.

Benbow, Horace: Cau.—*Sartoris* (1929)—Major—The playful, thirty-three-year-old brother of Narcissa Benbow; just back from World War I, he takes Belle Mitchell away from her husband. *Sanctuary* (1931)—Major—A brother of Mrs. Narcissa Benbow Sartoris; Lee Goodwin's lawyer; a generally inept, ineffective, rather idealistic man who is conquered by realities of conventional life.

Benbow, Judge: Cau.—*Absalom, Absalom!* (1936)—Bkg.— Managed Goodhue Coldfield estate. *The Unvanquished* (1938) —Bkg.—Arranged the end of Sartoris-Redmond partnership. *The Hamlet* (1940)—Bkg.—Mentioned. [These may be different Benbows] See Benbow, Will.

Benbow, Narcissa: See Sartoris, Mrs. Narcissa B.

Benbow, Percy: Cau.—*Absalom, Absalom!* (1936)—Bkg.—Son of Judge Benbow.

Benbow, Will and Julia: Cau.—*Sartoris* (1929)—Bkg.—The parents of Horace and Narcissa. *Sanctuary* (1931)—Bkg.— Clarence Snopes refers to Horace's father as Judge Benbow.

Berry, Ben: Cau.—"An Error in Chemistry" (1946)—Bkg.—A deputy sheriff.

Berry, Louis: Ind.—"Red Leaves" (1930)—Major—One of those hunting for Issetibbeha's Negro.

Best, Henry: Cau.—*The Town* (1957)—A Jefferson alderman.

Bidet: Cau.—*A Fable* (1954)—Bkg.—A glory seeking French military leader.

Bidwell: Cau.—"Hair" (1931)—Bkg.—Storekeeper at Division. He showed narrator through the Starnes home.

Biglin, Mr. and Mrs. Luther: Cau.—*The Mansion* (1959)— Bkg.—He was Flem's bodyguard, unknown to Flem; she is mentioned.

Binford, Mr. and Mrs. Dewitt: Cau.—*The Town* (1957)—

Bkg.—They took Byron Snopes's children on contract; she was a Snopes.

Binford, Lucius: Cau.—*Sanctuary* (1931)—Bkg.—Miss Reba Rivers' man; landlord of her brothel for eleven years; died two years earlier. *The Mansion* (1959)—Bkg.—Miss Reba Rivers' now deceased man. *The Reivers* (1962)—Bkg.—The man who keeps order at Miss Reba Rivers' bordel but whose gambling is betrayed by Otis.

Bird, Tom Tom: Neg.—"Centaur in Brass" (1932)—Major— The sixty-year-old, two hundred pound day fireman with the high-yellow wife; responsible for Flem Snopes's monument. Last name not given here. *The Town* (1957)—Minor—The day fireman at the power plant; helps Flem Snopes steal brass.

Bird, Uncle: Neg.—*Sartoris* (1929)—Bkg.—A church member who helped get church money from Simon Strother.

Birdsong: Cau.—"Pantaloon in Black" (1940)—Minor—The sawmill nightwatchman; owner of a crooked dice game; killed by Rider; has many relatives.

Birdsong, Preacher: Cau.—*The Town* (1957)—Bkg.—Having learned to box in France, he fought once with Matt Levitt.

Bishop: Cau.—*A Fable* (1954)—Bkg.—R.F.C. hero.

Bishop, Ephraim: Cau.—*The Mansion* (1959)—Bkg.—Young Hub Hampton's alternating partner in the sheriff's office; once had similar arrangement with old Hub.

Black: Cau.—"Death Drag" (1932)—Bkg.—Stunt flyers rode to Jefferson with him.

Blair, Harrison: Cau.—"Fox Hunt" (1931)—Major—a cuckold; owner of the horses; his extermination of the fox bodes ill for Mrs. Blair; a former Carolinian, now a New Yorker.

Blair, Mrs. Harrison: Cau.—"Fox Hunt" (1931)—Major—An Oklahoman unhappily married to a sneering man whom she cannot please.

Blair, John: Cau.—"Artist at Home" (1933)—Major—The

young Shelley who has a love affair with Mrs. Howes and writes his one poem.

Blake, Jim: Cau.—"Hand Upon the Waters" (1939)—Bkg.— Paid a share of Lonnie Grinnup's funeral expenses.

Bland: Cau.—"Ad Astra" (1931)—Major—A very handsome Rhodes Scholar and a member of the R. A. F.; a Southerner, possibly Gerald Bland.

Bland, Gerald: Cau.—*The Sound and the Fury* (1929)—Minor —A fellow Harvard student and friend of Quentin Compson; from Kentucky.

Bland, Mrs.: Cau.—*The Sound and the Fury* (1929)—Bkg.— Gerald's bragging mother.

Bledsoe:?—*The Wild Palms* (1939) in "Old Man"—Bkg.—Person at Parchman Penitentiary.

Bledsoe, Sergeant: Cau.—*A Fable* (1954)—Bkg.—Soldier opposed to military Runner's plan for peace.

Bleyth, Captain: Cau.—*Soldiers' Pay* (1926)—Bkg.—R.A.F. pilot Julian Lowe remembered.

Blum, Major: Cau.—*A Fable* (1954)—Bkg.—French soldier.

Bob: Cau.—"Sunset" (1925)—Bkg.—White man known to "Black Desperado," the protagonist.

Bogard, Captain H. S.;—Cau.—"Turnabout" (1932)—Major— A daring American Air Force war pilot who discovers that the British seamen have extraordinary nerves.

Boggan: Cau.—*A Fable* (1954)—Col. Beale's name for the Corporal. See Stefan.

Bolivar, Uncle Dick: Cau.—*The Hamlet* (1940)—Bkg.—Mentioned as aid in seeking old Frenchman's place money.

Bon, Charles: Neg./Cau.—*Absalom, Absalom!* (1936)—Major —Son of Thomas Sutpen and Eulalia Bon; he had a son by his octoroon mistress. While he attended the University of Mississippi, he courted Judith Sutpen, thus forcing the destruction of Sutpen's dream; born 1829—died 1865.

Bon, Charles Etienne de Saint Velery: Neg./Cau.—*Absalom, Absalom!* (1936)—Bkg.—Son of Charles Bon and an octoroon. b. 1859—d. 1884.

Bon, Eulalia: Neg./Cau.—*Absalom, Absalom!* (1936)—Bkg.— Daughter of a Haitian sugar planter; married Thomas Sutpen (1827); bore Charles Bon; divorced 1831.

Bond, Jim: Neg./Cau.—*Absalom, Absalom!* (1936)—Bkg.— The idiot great-grandson of Thomas Sutpen; Sutpen's only living descendant; son of Charles E. de St. V. Bon and a full-blooded Negress; b. 1882.

Bonds, Jack: Cau.—"A Bear Hunt" (1934)—Bkg.—A rowdy companion of Luke Provine in their younger days.

Bookwright: Mentioned in *Intruder in the Dust* (1948) as family name of early Yoknapatawpha settlers.

Bookwright: Cau.—"Tomorrow" (1940)—Bkg.—Killed Buck Thorpe who was eloping with seventeen-year-old Bookwright daughter.

Bookwright, Cal (Calvin): Cau.—*The Town* (1957)—Bkg. —His youngest daughter, Letty, married Zack Houston. *The Mansion* (1959)—Bkg.—Aged bootlegger makes excellent whisky; sells to Ratliff. *The Reivers* (1962)—Bkg.—Uncle Calvin is a moonshiner of consummate skill.

Bookwright, Herman: Cau.—*The Mansion* (1959)—Bkg.— One of the trio that courted the unwed Eula Varner.

Bookwright, Homer: Cau.—"Shingles for the Lord" (1943)— Bkg.—Poor farmer working on church. "Shall Not Perish" (1943)—Bkg.—Grier rides to Jefferson on Homer's cattletruck. *The Mansion* (1959)—Bkg.—Townsperson.

Bookwright, Letty (Mrs. Zack Houston): Cau.—*The Town* (1957)—Bkg.—Youngest daughter of Cal Bookwright; school teacher; married Zack Houston; killed by stallion. Cf. Houston, Zack; and Pate, Lucy.

Bookwright, Odum: Cau.—*The Hamlet* (1940)—Minor—One

of Ratliff's partner's in the treasure hunt. *The Mansion* (1959)
—Bkg.—He, Henry Armstid, and V. K. Ratliff bought Frenchman's place looking for treasure.

Bootlegger: Cau.—"Country Mice" (1925)—Major—Narrator's
friend who learned better than to belittle hick cops.

Bouc, Pierre: Pseudonym for Zsettlani, Piotr.

Bowden, Matt: Cau.—*The Unvanquished* (1938)—Bkg.—A
partner with Major Grumby in the horse business.

Bowen, Captain: Cau.—*The Unvanquished* (1938)—Bkg.—
Yankee Captain.

Boy: Cau.—"Race at Morning" (1955)—Major—Twelve-year-
old narrator; ward of Mr. Ernest.

Boyd, Mr. and Mrs.: Cau.—"The Brooch" (1936)—Major—
She is Howard's domineering mother who has already driven
Mr. Boyd away; her father was a wealthy merchant.

Boyd, Mrs. Amy: Cau.—"The Brooch" (1936)—Major—She
loses her husband, Howard, to his mother; the daughter of a
railroad conductor.

Boyd, Howard: Cau.—"The Brooch" (1936)—Major—The only
son of a wealthy invalid mother who ruins his life; commits
suicide.

Bradley, Mr. and Mrs.: Cau.—*The Wild Palms* (1939) in
"Wild Palms"—Bkg.—Neighbors who gave their leftover food
to Charlotte and Harry.

Brandt, Dr.: Cau.—*Sartoris* (1929)—Bkg.—The unnecessary
blood and glandular disease specialist in Memphis.

Breckbridge, Gavin: Cau.—*The Unvanquished* (1938)—Bkg.
—Drusilla Hawk's fiance who died at Shiloh.

Bridesman, Captain: Cau.—*A Fable* (1954)—Bkg.—A British
flight chief.

Bridger: Cau.—*The Unvanquished* (1938)—Bkg.—A partner to
Grumby whom he turns over to Marengo (Ringo) and Bayard
Sartoris.

Briggins, Lycurgus: Neg.—*The Reivers* (1962)—Minor—Helps

Ned and Lucius in the horse episodes; the grandson of Uncle Parsham Hood, with whom he and his mother live.

Briggins, Mary: Neg.—*The Reivers* (1962)—Bkg.—Lycurgus' mother.

Broussard, Mr.: Cau.—*Mosquitoes* (1927)—Bkg.—Owner of Broussard's Restaurant in New Orleans.

Brown, Joe: See Burch, Lucas.

Brownlee, Percival: Neg.—"The Bear" (1942)—Bkg.—Mc-Caslin slave bought from N. B. Forrest; worthless except for preaching; renamed Spintrius.

Brummage, Judge: Cau.—*The Mansion* (1959)—Bkg.—Judge at Mink Snopes's trial.

Brzewski: See Stefan.

Buchwald: Cau.—*A Fable* (1954)—Bkg.—American soldier from Brooklyn; he understands the plot to kill Gragnon.

Buck: Cau.—*Sartoris* (1929)—Bkg.—Marshal in Jefferson who "arrests" young Bayard Sartoris and gives him his own bed. Cf. Conner, Buck and Connors, Buck.

Buckner, Mr. and Mrs. (Buck and Billie): Cau.—*The Wild Palms* (1939) in "Wild Palms"—Minor—He is the manager of the Utah mine; she is Harry Wilbourne's first and only successful abortion patient.

Buckworth, Deputy Warden: Cau.—*The Wild Palms* (1939) in "Old Man"—Minor—In charge of the convicts working on the levee; reported Tall Convict drowned; transferred to highway patrol.

Bud, Uncle: Cau.—*Sanctuary* (1931)—Bkg.—Little boy who is spending a week with Miss Myrtle, a friend of Miss Reba Rivers; gets drunk on beer.

Buffaloe, Mr.: Cau.—*The Town* (1957)—Bkg.—Electrician who had made the first car in Jefferson (1904). *The Mansion* (1959)—Bkg.—His car frightened Bayard (old) Sartoris's team. *The Reivers* (1962)—Minor—Jeffersonian who built his own car and taught Boon Hogganbeck how to drive.

Buford: Cau.—*Light in August* (1932)—Bkg.—Deputy sheriff.

Bullitt, Mr. and Mrs. R. Q. (Bob): Cau.—*Pylon* (1935)—Bkg. —Flyer and his wife at the New Valois meet.

Bunch, Byron: Cau.—*Light in August* (1932)—Major—His affair with Lena Grove provides continuity; revitalizes Gail Hightower; a selfless, kind man.

Bundren, Mrs.: Cau.—*As I Lay Dying* (1930)—Bkg.—Anse Bundren's new wife; a duck-shaped woman.

Bundren, Addie: Cau.—*As I Lay Dying* (1930)—Major—First wife of Anse Bundren; execution of her dying wish—to be buried in Jefferson—involves the family in a series of unreasonable catastrophes which all resolve rather too smoothly; once a school teacher.

Bundren, Anse: Cau.—*As I Lay Dying* (1930)—Major—Slothful, selfish husband of Addie Bundren; her funeral trip happens to him.

Bundren, Cash: Cau.—*As I Lay Dying* (1930)—Major—Oldest child of Anse and Addie; made the coffin; suffered a broken leg in the process of the trip; carpenter.

Bundren, Darl: Cau.—*As I Lay Dying* (1930)—Major—Second Bundren child; seems to be most loving toward Addie, but he insanely burns Gillespie's barn; sent to state mental institution in Jackson. "Uncle Willy" (1935)—Bkg.—Mentioned as example of an insane person.

Bundren, Dewey Dell: Cau.—*As I Lay Dying* (1930)—Major —Addie's fourth child, who at seventeen is pregnant with Lafe's illegitimate child; quiet, sloven girl.

Bundren, Jewel: Cau.—*As I Lay Dying* (1930)—Major—The illegitimate son of Addie Bundren and Rev. Whitfield; owned a spotted horse which he sacrifices to buy mules to get his mother to Jefferson.

Bundren, Vardaman: Cau.—*As I Lay Dying* (1930)—Major —Addie's youngest child; unable to accept her death.

Burch, Lucas (alias Joe Brown): Cau.—*Light in August*

(1932)—Major—Joe Christmas' partner; father of Lena Grove's child; tries to collect reward by informing on Joe Christmas.

Burchett, Mr. and Mrs.: Cau.—"Hair" (1931)—Minor—Adopted parents of Susan Reed.

Burden: Family tree—Cau.—from *Light in August* (1932)—Bkg. Nathaniel Burrington (I) begot Calvin Burden who married Evangeline and begot Vangie (f.), Beck (f.), Sarah (f.), and Nathaniel (m.) who married Juana and begot Calvin (II). Nathaniel married a second time and begot Joanna.

Burden, Calvin and Calvin: Cau.—*Light in August* (1932)—and *The Unvanquished* (1938)—Bkg.—Grandfather and grandson from Missouri who are killed by Col. John Sartoris while trying to get a Negro elected U.S. Marshal.

Burden, Joanna: Cau.—*Light in August* (1932)—Major—Joe Christmas' mistress who is murdered when she tries to reform Joe; descendant of carpetbaggers; Negrophile. *The Mansion* (1959)—Bkg.—Her mailbox is used by young boys as a direction to France.

Burgess, Mr. and Mrs.: Cau.—*The Sound and the Fury* (1929)—Bkg.—Parents of girl assaulted by Benjy Compson.

Burk: Cau.—*A Fable* (1954)—Bkg.—R. A. F. hero.

Burke: Cau.—"Fox Hunt" (1931)—Bkg.—Mrs. Harrison Blair's Irish maid; likely Irish-American.

Burney, Mr. and Mrs.: Cau.—*Soldiers' Pay* (1926)—Minor—Parents of Dewey Burney who died in the war.

Burney, Dewey: Cau.—*Soldiers' Pay* (1926)—Bkg.—A rather worthless boy whose death in World War I gave his mother a place in society; killed Lt. Powers.

Burnham, Lt. Frank: Cau.—*Pylon* (1935)—Bkg.—First pilot who fatally crashes in the New Valois meet; burns to death.

Burrington, Nathaniel (II): Cau.—*Light in August* (1932)—Bkg.—Joanna Burden's nephew of St. Exeter, New Hampshire, who offered a thousand dollar reward for capture of murderer. Cf. Burden family tree above.

Burt: Cau.—"Turnabout" (1932)—Bkg.—Crewmember of Hope and Smith's torpedo boat.

Bush, Lem: Cau.—*Light in August* (1932)—Bkg.—Milly Hines went to circus in his wagon.

Butch: Cau.—"Dry September" (1931)—Minor—Encouraged mob action against Will Mayes. Possibly Butch (Luke) Provine.

C

Cain: Cau.—*The Hamlet* (1940)—Bkg.—A store owner in Ratliff's youth; Mrs. Vynie Snopes bought milk separator from him.

Cajan: Cau.—*The Wild Palms* (1939)—in "Old Man"—Bkg.—Alligator hunting partner of the Tall Convict.

Caldwell, Sam: Cau.—*The Reivers* (1962)—Minor—Railroad flagman who as a favor to Miss Corrie (whom he patronizes) helped get Lightning (Coppermine) to Parsham.

Callaghan: Cau.—"Fox Hunt" (1931)—Bkg.—Mrs. Harrison Blair's riding instructor.

Callaghan, Miss: Cau.—"Uncle Willy" (1935)—Bkg.—Narrator's school teacher.

Callaghan: Cau.—*The Wild Palms* (1939) in "Wild Palms"—Bkg.—Sells stock in defunct Utah mine; hires Harry to go to Utah as mine physician.

Callicoat, David: Cau.—"Justice" (1931)—Bkg.—Name of man who once guided the steamboat which ultimately became part of Ikkemotubbe's house. Cf. Ikkemotubbe.

Callie, Aunt: Neg.—*The Reivers* (1962)—Bkg.—Mrs. Maury Priest's cook; a long time family retainer.

Captain: Cau.—"Crevasse" (1931)—Major—Leader of a detachment of British soldiers in World War I; they almost suffocate in cavern.

Carl: Cau.—"Divorce in Naples" (1931)—Major—Virgin male whom George is trying to protect; learns about sex in this story.

Carruthers, Miss: Cau.—*Light in August* (1932)—Bkg.—Once the organist in Gail Hightower's church.

Carter, Mr.: Cau.—"Black Music" (1934)—Bkg.—Wilfred Midgleston's boss in New York firm; chief architect.

Caspey: See Strother, Caspey

Casse-tete: Cau.—*A Fable* (1954)—Bkg.—An idiot-murderer executed with the Corporal.

Cavalcanti: Cau.—"Mistral" (1931)—Bkg.—Tavern keepers in the small Italian town where the story is set; aunt and uncle of returned soldier.

Cayley, Hence: Cau.—"Knight's Gambit" (1949)—Bkg.—Father of girl to whom Max Harriss gives an engagement ring.

Cayley, Miss: Cau.—"Knight's Gambit" (1949)—Minor—Daughter of Hence Cayley; possessor of Max Harriss' ring; her mother was a Mossop.

Chance, Vic: Cau.—*Pylon* (1935)—Bkg.—Builder of racing planes.

Charley: Cau.—*Light in August* (1932)—Bkg.—Intern who was having an affair with Miss Atkins.

Charley: Cau.—"Tomorrow" (1940)—Bkg.—Another lawyer; possibly Charles Mallison, Sr.; Gavin Stevens' brother-in-law.

Charley: Cau.—*The Reivers* (1962)—Bkg.—Railroad man, possibly switchman, who aids in the horse maneuvers.

Charley, Uncle: Neg.—"Dr. Martino" (1931)—Bkg.—Servant at Cranston's Wells, Mississippi.

Charlie: Cau.—*The Sound and the Fury* (1929)—Bkg.—One of Caddy Compson's early lovers.

Chlory: Neg.—"Beyond" (1933)—Bkg.—House servant to Judge Allison; sang mournfully at his death.

Christian, Walter: Neg.—*The Town* (1957)—Bkg.—Uncle Willy Christian's drugstore janitor.

Christian, Uncle Willy: Cau.—"Uncle Willy" (1935)—Major—Jefferson druggist who survives cures for drug and liquor addiction but finally dies piloting his plane; his sister, married to Texas oil millionaire, is mentioned. His father also is mentioned as founder of the drugstore in 1850. *The Town* (1957) —Bkg.—His drugstore robbery led to the conviction of M. W. Snopes on liquor charges. *The Mansion* (1959)—Bkg.—His drugstore was the site of Linda Snopes's rendezvous with Gavin Stevens. *The Reivers* (1962)—Bkg.—Mentioned as owner of drugstore below Doc Peabody's office.

Christian, Mrs. Willy: Cau.—"Uncle Willy" (1935)—Minor— Prostitute who married Uncle Willy and then divorces him for a thousand dollars.

Christmas, Joe: Probably Neg./Cau.—*Light in August* (1932) —Major—An orphan and a psychological misfit whose pathetic search for identity is told here; grandson of Mr. and Mrs. Eupheus Hines; son of Milly Hines and a carnival worker; once adopted by Mr. and Mrs. Simon McEachern; lover and murderer of Joanna Burden.

Church, Mrs.: Cau.—"That Will Be Fine" (1935)—Bkg.— Once called on Mrs. Pruitt.

Cinthy: Neg.—*Light in August* (1932)—Bkg.—Servant of Gail Hightower's father.

Clapp, Walter: Cau.—*The Reivers* (1962)—Bkg.—Mr. Van Tosch's horse trainer.

Clay, Sis Beulah: Neg.—*The Sound and the Fury* (1929)— Bkg.—Mentioned as dead Negress who has been "moaned."

Clefus: Neg.—*The Town* (1957)—Bkg.—Gavin Stevens' office janitor.

Clytemnestra (Clytie): Neg./Cau.—*Absalom, Absalom!* (1936)—Major—Daughter of Thomas Sutpen and a slave; serves all the Sutpens, then burns the mansion with herself and Henry Sutpen inside. b. 1834—d. 1910.

Cobbler: Cau.—"The Cobbler" (1925)—Major—Tuscan immigrant, who had lost his sweetheart in his youth, speaks this dramatic monologue.

Cofer: Cau.—*The Wild Palms* (1939) in "Wild Palms"—Bkg.

—Real estate agent who leased Mississippi coast cabin to Harry Wilbourne and Charlotte Rittenmeyer.

Colbert, David: Ind.—"A Courtship" (1948)—Bkg.—Great chief of the Chickasaws in northern Mississippi; Herman Basket's aunt was the second cousin by marriage to the grand-niece of David Colbert's wife.

Coldfield, Ellen: See Sutpen, Mrs. Ellen C.

Coldfield, Goodhue: Cau.—*Absalom, Absalom!* (1936)—Minor —Merchant father of Ellen and Rosa Coldfield; partner of Thomas Sutpen in some nefarious business deal; moved to Jefferson in 1828; died 1864.

Coldfield, Rosa: Cau.—*Absalom, Absalom!* (1936)—Major— Ellen Coldfield Sutpen's sister; narrates part of the story to Quentin Compson; part of it they experience; hates Thomas Sutpen; b. 1845—d. 1910.

Coleman, Mrs.: Cau.—*Soldiers' Pay* (1926)—Bkg.—Resident of Charlestown, Georgia.

Collier: Cau.—"Turnabout" (1932)—Bkg.—American flyer with a mandolin.

Collyer: Cau.—*A Fable* (1954)—Bkg.—R.A.F. hero.

Compson, Benjamin (first named Maury): Cau.—*The Sound and the Fury* (1929)—Major—Thirty-three-year-old idiot son of Jason III and Caroline Bascomb Compson; Part I is told through his consciousness. He loved Caddy, the pasture, and firelight. [Appendix to the Modern Library Edition (1946) states that following his widowed mother's death, Jason IV sends him to the state asylum and sells Compson home.] *The Mansion* (1959) Bkg.—Returned from asylum, Benjy burned himself and the Compson home about ten years before events of this novel.

Compson, Candace (Caddy): Cau.—*The Sound and the Fury* (1929) Major—Daughter of Jason Richmond and Caroline Bascomb; begets an illegitimate daughter (Miss Quentin) by Dalton Ames; divorced by Herbert Head when he discovers her pregnancy; very kind to Benjy. [Appendix to Modern Library Edition (1946) places her in Europe just prior to World War II] "That Evening Sun" (1931)—Major—As a seven-year-old child, Caddy provides contrast with Nancy. "A Justice" (1931)—Bkg.—Mentioned as younger sister of narrator. *The Mansion* (1959)—Bkg.—Mentioned as Miss Quentin's absent mother.

Compson, Caroline Bascomb (Mrs. Jason Richmond): Cau. —*The Sound and the Fury* (1929)—Major—Ego-centric, psychically invalided mother of principal characters. [Appendix to Modern Library Edition (1946) posits her death and the sale of the family home for a boarding house.] *The Mansion* (1959) —Bkg.—Lives with Jason IV in new brick house, Benjy having returned from asylum and burned himself and old one.

Compson, Charles Stuart: Cau.—Appendix to the Modern Library Edition (1946) of *The Sound and the Fury* (1929)— peg-legged son of Quentin Maclachan; father of Jason Lycurgus.

Compson, General: See Compson, Jason Lycurgus (II).

Compson, Jason Lycurgus: Cau.—Appendix to the Modern Library Edition (1946) of *The Sound and the Fury* (1929)— Bkg.—Son of Quentin Maclachan; first owner of Compson's Domain (one mile square piece of property), which he bought from Ikkemotubbe with a racing mare in 1861. *Requiem for a Nun* (1951)—Bkg.—Mentioned as first acquiring large Compson estate. Cf. Quentin Maclachan Compson (II).

Compson, Jason Lycurgus II (Brigadier, General): Cau. —Appendix to Modern Library Edition (1946) of *The Sound and the Fury* (1929)—Bkg.—Ostensibly son of Governor Quentin Maclachan Compson; General in the Confederate Army; put first mortgage on Compson property; grandfather of Candace, Quentin, Benjy, and Jason IV; d. 1900 in de Spain hunting camp. "A Justice" (1931)—Bkg.—Mentioned as grandfather of narrator; owner of farm where Sam Fathers worked. "A Bear Hunt" (1934)—Bkg.—Mentioned as old hunter. *Absalom, Absalom!* (1936) Many details of this story are told to General Compson by Thomas Sutpen; grandfather of Quentin, (III). *The Unvanquished* (1938)—Bkg.—Mentioned as General Compson. "The Old People" (1940)—Minor —Known as General Compson; an elder statesman sort of hunter. "The Bear" (1942)—Minor—Old hunter who recognizes Ike McCaslin's maturity. "Delta Autumn" (1942)—Bkg. —Mentioned as deceased hunting friend of Isaac McCaslin's. "My Grandmother Millard" (1943)—Bkg.—Mentioned as General Compson. *Intruder in the Dust* (1948)—Bkg. Mentioned as a hunter at de Spain's camp. *Requiem for A Nun* (1951) —Bkg.—Erstwhile partner with Col. John Sartoris and Redmond in the railroad venture; son of first Jason. [Cf. notation from Appendix to Modern Library Edition of *The Sound and the Fury* above.] Here referred to as General. *The Town* (1957)—Bkg.—Mentioned as Confederate brigadier and governor of Mississippi for two days. Cf. Quentin Maclachan Compson (II). *The Reivers* (1962)—Bkg.—Made a woodsman out of Boon Hogganbeck; called General Compson.

Compson, Mrs. Jason Lycurgus (II) (General): Cau.—"My Grandmother Millard" (1943)—Bkg.—General Compson's wife who saved the family silver by sitting on it in the privy. *The Town* (1957)—Bkg.—Mentioned as General Compson's wife who had given Het a toque fifty years prior.

Compson, Jason Richmond (III): Cau.—*The Sound and the Fury* (1929)—Major—Father of Quentin, Candace, Jason (IV) and Benjy; husband to Caroline Bascomb Compson; becomes an alcoholic; pessimist; gradually sells off remaining portions of Compson estate to finance Candace's wedding and Quentin's year at Harvard; lawyer by profession; discussed in Appendix to Modern Library Edition (1946) of *The Sound and the Fury*. "That Evening Sun" (1931)—Major—The father of Candace, Quentin, and Jason; tries to help relieve

Nancy's fear. *Absalom, Absalom!* (1936)—Minor—Quentin's father who tells many of the details of the Sutpen myth and surmises portions of the story that he does not know for certain.

Compson, Jason (IV): Cau.—*The Sound and the Fury* (1929)—Major—Selfish, embittered, sardonic second son of Jason Richmond and Caroline Bascomb Compson; narrator of section III; becomes employee in hardware store, cotton speculator, and embezzler of Miss Quentin's money which she successfully steals back. [Appendix to Modern Library Edition (1946) of *The Sound and the Fury* calls him the first sane Compson in America; says he sent Benjy to state asylum after death of his mother, and sold home for boarding house.] "That Evening Sun" (1931)—Minor—Five-years-old at time of story; whining, tattling son of Jason Richmond Compson. "A Justice" (1931)—Bkg.—Mentioned as younger brother of the narrator. *The Town* (1957)—Bkg.—Collects rent on his mother's building which houses M. W. Snopes's atelier. *The Mansion* (1959)—Bkg.—Owner of McCaslin Hardware Company which he manipulated from Earl Triplett who manipulated it from Ike McCaslin. Living with his mother in a new brick house because Benjy, returned from state asylum, burned himself and the old Compson place ten years before events of this novel.

Compson, Quentin Maclachan (I): Cau.—Appendix to Modern Library Edition (1946) of *The Sound and the Fury* (1929) —Bkg.—First Compson in U.S.; at eighty fled into Kentucky with infant grandson in 1779.

Compson, Quentin Maclachan (II) (Governor): Cau.— Appendix to the Modern Library Edition (1946) of *The Sound and the Fury* (1929)—Bkg.—Governor (of what is not specified) who caused Compson estate to long be called the Old Governor's place; ostensibly son of Jason Lycurgus (I), and father of Jason Lycurgus (II). *The Mansion* (1959)—Bkg.—

Mentioned as person to whom Mohataha (Chickasaw matriarch) had granted the land of the Compson estate in 1821. Cf. Jason Lycurgus Compson (II).

Compson, Quentin (III): Cau.—*The Sound and the Fury* (1929)—Major—Oldest son of Jason Richmond and Caroline Bascomb Compson; committed suicide after one year at Harvard because he was so shaken by his sister's sexual promiscuity; narrator of very involved section. His emotional problems are further dissected in the Appendix to the Modern Library Edition (1946) of *The Sound and the Fury*. "That Evening Sun" (1931)—Major—Narrator of story that occurred fifteen years earlier when he was nine; Nancy's fear is the focus of the story. "A Justice" (1931)—Major—As a twelve-year-old child, he listens to Sam Fathers tell this story; though unnamed, circumstances indicate his identity. *Absalom, Absalom!* (1936)—Major—Narrates most of the story to Shrevlin McCannon, his Harvard roommate; b. 1891—d. 1910. His reaction to Sutpen myth indicates ambivalent attitude toward South.

[Compson], Miss Quentin: Cau.—*The Sound and the Fury* (1929)—Major—Illegitimate daughter of Candace Compson and Dalton Ames; steals back the money which Jason (IV) has been embezzling from her and her mother; elopes with a carnival worker. Further details given in Appendix to the Modern Library Edition (1946) of *The Sound and the Fury*. *The Mansion* (1959)—Bkg.—Mentioned as eloping with carnival worker.

Compson, Mrs.: Cau.—*The Unvanquished* (1938)—Bkg.— Loaned Mrs. Rosa Millard a hat and helped force the marriage between Col. John Sartoris and Drusilla Hawk. Her husband, who shoots potatoes from the heads of young Negroes seems to be distinct from General Compson; possibly Quentin Maclachan (II).

Comyn: Cau.—*Sartoris* (1929)—Bkg.—Irish man Bayard Sartoris had known in England. "Ad Astra" (1931)—Major—An

Irish soldier in World War I; in group with Bayard Sartoris.

Confrey, Max and Mame: Cau.—*Light in August* (1932)—Bkg.—Owners of the Jefferson cafe where Bobbie Allen works.

Conner, Buck: Cau.—*Light in August* (1932)—Bkg.—Marshal . who keeps Joe Brown. Cf. Connors, Buck; and Buck.

Connors, Buck: Cau.—"Centaur in Brass" (1932)—Bkg.—Town marshal of Jefferson. *The Town* (1957)—Minor—Town marshal in the M. W. Snopes case. Cf. Conner, Buck.

Connors, Buck, Jr.: Cau.—*The Town* (1957)—Bkg.—Young companion of Chick Mallison's.

Conventicle: Cau.—*A Fable* (1954)—Bkg.—British flyer.

Convict, (Tall): Cau.—*The Wild Palms* (1939) in "Old Man" —Major—Convict who worked so hard getting back to Parchman with woman and boat.

Convict, (Plump one, second convict): Cau.—*The Wild Palms* (1939) "Old Man"—Minor—Foil for Tall Convict; lost from skiff.

Cook, Celia: Cau.—*The Unvanquished* (1938)—Bkg.—Scratched her name on window pane in Oxford when N. B. Forrest rode down street. Cf. Farmer, Cecilia.

Cooper: Cau.—*Pylon* (1935)—Bkg.—Reporter on same paper that *the* Reporter worked for.

Cooper, Miss Minnie: Cau.—"Dry September" (1931)—Major —Fortyish, mentally unbalanced old maid who imagines rape; her mother and an aunt are mentioned.

Cop: Cau.—"New Orleans" (1925)—Major—Gives his thoughts on becoming a cop—the duties, sorrows, and advantages.

Corporal: See Stefan.

Corrie, Miss: See Hogganbeck, Everbe Corinthia.

Cotton, Ernest: Cau.—"The Hound" (1931)—Major—Murderer of Houston. Cf. Snopes, Mink.

Cowan, Mrs.: Cau.—"Hair" (1931)—Bkg.—Operator of boarding house where Henry Stribling and Mitch Ewing lived.

Cowrie, Capt.: Cau.—*A Fable* (1954)—Bkg.—Sharer of Bridesman's hut; R. A. F. flyer.

Crack: Cau.—*The Mansion* (1959)—Bkg.—Member of Sartoris Rifles. See McLendon, John.

Crain, Mr. and Mrs. Amos: Cau.—"Artist at Home" (1933) —Bkg.—Average young farming couple in the Valley of Virginia; shocked by Howes's visitors.

Cranston, Lily: Cau.—"Dr. Martino" (1931)—Minor—Spinster proprietress of Cranston's Wells, Mississippi, site of a major portion of the action.

Crawfishford: Ind.—"A Justice" (1931)—Major—Father of Sam Fathers; outwitted by Doom and the husband of Sam Fathers' mother.

Crawford, Dr.: Cau.—"The Bear" (1942)—Bkg.—Doctor summoned to aid Lion, Boon Hogganbeck, and Sam Fathers.

Crenshaw, Jack: Cau.—*The Town* (1957)—Bkg.—Federal revenuer.

Crowe: Cau.—*The Wild Palms* (1939) in "Wild Palms"—Bkg. —Artist at whose party Charlotte and Harry meet.

Crump, Lucas: Cau.—*Idyll in the Desert* (1931)—Major—Mail rider who narrates the story; witty; humorous.

Cunninghame, Sergeant: Cau.—"Victory" (1931)—Bkg.— Young Alec Gray's sergeant at inspection during shaving incident.

D

Dad: Cau.—*The Mansion* (1959)—Bkg.—Compatriot of Mink Snopes in the Goodyhay episode.

Daingerfield, Miss: Cau.—*The Sound and the Fury* (1929) —Bkg.—Girl at Mrs. Bland's picnic.

Daisy: Neg.—"The Bear" (1942)—Bkg.—de Spain's cook.

Damuddy: Cau.—*The Sound and the Fury* (1929)—Bkg.— Grandparent who dies in an early scene; probably the maternal grandmother, judging from the reaction of Mrs. Caroline Compson.

Dan: Neg.—"The Fire and the Hearth" (1942)—Bkg.—Edmonds' Negro.

Dandridge, Miss Maggie: Cau.—*Intruder in the Dust* (1948)— Bkg.—Maiden name of Chick Mallison's grandmother, likely maternal.

David: See Tramp.

Davies, Rhys: Cau.—*A Fable* (1954)—Bkg.—R. F. C. hero.

Davy: Cau.—"The Leg" (1934)—Major—Lost a leg in a World War I battle; thereafter suffered delusions of a supernatural nature; loss of leg related to Everbe Corinthia Rust's death.

Deacon: Cau.—*Sartoris* (1929)—Bkg.—Proprietor of store-cafe where Bayard (young) and Rafe MacCallum drink.

Deacon: Neg.—*The Sound and the Fury* (1929)—Bkg.— Porter at Harvard.

De Marchi: Cau.—*A Fable* (1954)—Bkg.—R. A. F. hero.

Demont, M. and Marthe: Cau.—*A Fable* (1954)—He (Bkg.) is a French farmer, married to Marthe (Magda); she (Major), a half-sister to Corporal, raises him from infancy and pleads with General for Corporal's life.

De Montigny: Cau.—*The Wild Palms* (1939) in "Wild Palms" —Bkg.—Mentioned as medical student whose suit Harry wears.

De Montigny: Cau.—*A Fable* (1954)—Bkg.—French army officer.

de Montigny, Paul: Cau. or Mixed?—"Elly" (1934)—Major— Elly's lover who may have Negro blood; dies in auto crash.

De Pre, Mrs. Virginia: See Du Pre, Mrs. Virginia S.

de Spain, Major (Cassius) de Spain (I): Cau.—[Name *Cassius* does not occur in any of Faulkner's prose, but appears on Yoknapatawpha map drawn for 1951 Modern Library Edition of *Absalom, Absalom!*]—"A Bear Hunt" (1934)— Bkg.—Mentioned as father of present Major de Spain; major in Confederate Army. "Wash" (1934)—Bkg.—Mentioned as sheriff who comes to capture Wash Jones. *Absalom, Absalom!* (1936)—Bkg.—Same capacity as in "Wash." "Barn Burning" (1939)—Minor—Wealthy aristocrat who leases farm to Ab

Snopes. *The Hamlet* (1940)—Bkg.—His experience with Ab Snopes is repeated. "The Old People" (1940)—Bkg.—Hunts occurred at his Tallahatchie bottom hunting camp. "The Bear" (1942)—Minor—Owner of hunting camp; former Confederate soldier; leases land to lumber company. "Delta Autumn" (1942)—Bkg.—Mentioned as deceased hunting friend of Ike McCaslin; cavalry commander of Theophilus McCaslin. *Intruder in the Dust* (1948)—Bkg.—hunter. *The Town* (1957)—Bkg.—Confederate major; father of Manfred. *The Mansion* (1959)—Bkg.—Father of Manfred. *The Reivers* (1962)—Bkg.—Father of Manfred; owner of hunting camp.

de Spain, Mrs. Lula: Cau.—"Barn Burning" (1939)—Bkg.—Major de Spain's wife whose rug is ruined by Ab Snopes. *The Hamlet* (1940)—Bkg.—She and her rug are mentioned.

de Spain, Major (II): Cau.—"A Bear Hunt" (1934)—Son of Major de Spain; banker; called *Major* though he did not have military career; his hunting camp was the site of the story's events. "Shall Not Perish" (1943)—Major—Banker; lost his twenty-three-year-old son as aviator in a Pacific battle. Cf. Holland, Mr.

de Spain, Mrs. (Major II): Cau.—"A Bear Hunt" (1934)—She and some married daughters are mentioned.

de Spain, Manfred: Cau.—*The Town* (1957)—Minor—Successful rival of Gavin Stevens for Eula V. Snopes; President of Sartoris Bank; Mayor of Jefferson; Veteran of Spanish-American War; son of Major de Spain (I). *The Mansion* (1959)—Major—Mayor of Jefferson; President of Bank; Eula V. Snopes is his mistress; son of Major de Spain (I); leaves town when Will Varner objects to his affair with Eula. *The Reivers* (1962)—Bkg.—Mentioned as proprietor of first car in Jefferson; son of Major de Spain (I); seller of hunting camp.

Despleins, Jules: Cau.—*Pylon* (1935)—Bkg.—Flyer at New Valois meet.

de Vitry, Soeur-Blonde: Cau.—"Red Leaves" (1930)—Bkg.—

Friend of Doom's and later of Issetibbeha's in Paris. "The Old People" (1940)—Bkg.—Mentioned as Ikkemotubbe's comrade. "A Courtship" (1948)—Bkg.—Mentioned as accompanying Doom to plantation.

Devries, Col.: Cau.—*The Mansion* (1959)—Bkg.—Opposed Clarence Snopes for state senator; dog thicket won for him.

Dicey: Neg.—"Wash" (1934)—Bkg.—Midwife for Milly Jones.

Dick, Col. Nathaniel G.: Cau.—*The Unvanquished* (1938)— Minor—An Ohio Yankee colonel who has respect for Rosa Millard.

Dilazuck: Cau.—*The Mansion* (1959)—Bkg.—Owner of livery stable.

Dilsey: See Gibson, Dilsey.

Doc: Cau.—*Sanctuary* (1931)—Bkg.—Jefferson boy who knew about Temple Drake's morals.

Doctor and Mrs. (Martha): Cau.—*The Wild Palms* (1939)— in "Wild Palms"—Minor—He sent Charlotte to hospital and Harry to jail; she is pragmatist.

Dodge, Granby: Cau.—"Smoke" (1932)—Major—Cousin to the Holland twins; plotted three murders; accomplished two.

Dollar: Cau.—*Light in August* (1932)—Bkg.—Storeowner in Mottstown.

Don: Cau.—"Mistral" (1931)—Major—Twenty-three-year-old walking friend of the narrator; both Americans.

Doom: See Ikkemotubbe.

Doshey: *The Hamlet* (1940)—Bkg.—Family name of people who moved into Frenchman's Bend after Frenchman; Eustace Graham's wife was a Doshey.

Dough, James: Cau.—*Soldiers' Pay* (1926)—Bkg.—Returned crippled soldier.

Downs, Mrs: Cau.—*Intruder in the Dust* (1948)—Bkg.—Mentioned as fortune teller.

Drake, Hubert (Buddy): Cau.—*Sanctuary* (1931)—Bkg.— One of Temple's four brothers.

Drake, Judge: Cau.—*Sanctuary* (1931)—Bkg.—Temple's father who takes her to Europe after Goodwin trial; a Jackson judge.

Drake, Temple: Cau.—*Sanctuary* (1931)—Major—Judge Drake's eighteen-year-old daughter who goes on a joy ride, is raped, becomes a prostitute, and is partially rehabilitated. See Stevens, Mrs. Temple D.

Dukinfield, Emma: Cau.—"Smoke" (1932)—Bkg.—Daughter who brought Judge Dukinfield the brass box from Europe.

Dukinfield, Judge: Cau.—"Smoke" (1932)—Minor—Murdered during probation of Anselm Holland, Sr.'s will. *The Town* (1957)—Bkg.—Judge in case of stolen brass. *The Mansion* (1959)—Bkg.—Appointed Judge Stevens to hear impeachment proceedings against Mayor Manfred de Spain.

Du Pre, Mrs. Virginia Sartoris (Miss Jenny; Aunt Jenny): Cau.—*Sartoris* (1929)—Major—Youngest sister of Col. John Sartoris; Now eighty-year-old witty, efficient manager of Sartoris household; aunt of Bayard (old); great-great-aunt of twins John and Bayard; friend of Narcissa Benbow who marries Bayard (young). "All the Dead Pilots" (1931)—Bkg.— Mentioned as great-aunt of pilot (John Sartoris) who is killed; mistakenly called Mrs. Virginia Sartoris. *Sanctuary* (1931)— Minor—Sharp-tongued, ninety-year-old aunt-in-law of Mrs. Narcissa B. Sartoris; called Genevieve. "There Was a Queen" (1933)—Major—Sister to first John Sartoris; ninety-year-old invalid confined to wheelchair; dies. *The Unvanquished* (1938)—Minor—Encourages Bayard (elder) not to kill Redmond; sister of Col. John Sartoris; same age as Mrs. Drusilla Hawk Sartoris. *Requiem for a Nun* (1951)—Bkg.—Mentioned as Col Sartoris' sister; spelled De Pre. *The Town* (1957)— Bkg.—Labeled Bayard (old) Sartoris's sister; ruler of his household. *The Mansion* (1959)—Bkg.—Mentioned as arranging Narcissa Benbow-Bayard (young) marriage.

E

Earl: See Triplett, Earl.

Ed: Cau.—*Soldiers' Pay* (1926)—Bkg.—Policeman who tries to arrest Gilligan for drunkenness.

Ed: Cau.—*Mosquitoes* (1927)—Bkg.—Captain of *Nausikaa*.

Ed: Cau.—*The Reivers* (1962)—Bkg.—Night telegrapher who judges the races.

Edmonds, Alice: Cau.—"The Bear" (1942)—Bkg.—Wife of McCaslin Edmonds.

Edmonds, Carothers McCaslin (Cass): Cau.—"A Bear Hunt" (1934)—Bkg.—Hunter at de Spain's camp. "The Old People" (1940)—Minor—Ike McCaslin's cousin (sixteen years older than Ike); hunter; guardian of McCaslin estate. "Was" (1942) —Major—Nine-year-old orphaned grandson of Theophilus and Amodeus McCaslin's sister; b. 1850. "The Bear" (1942)— Major—Cousin with whom Isaac argues about patrimony; important hunter; inherits rejected McCaslin estate. "Delta Autumn" (1942)—Bkg.—Mentioned as grandfather of Roth and as deceased hunter. "The Fire and the Hearth" (1942) —Bkg.—Father of Zachary Edmonds; McCaslin on mother's side; dispossessed Ike McCaslin. *The Town* (1957)—Bkg.— Mentioned as Roth Edmonds' father. *The Reivers* (1962)— Bkg.—Mentioned as man to whom Ike McCaslin abdicated; father of Zackary.

Edmonds, Carothers (Roth): Cau.—"Pantaloon in Black" (1940)—Bkg.—Land owner from whom Rider rents. "Go Down, Moses" (1941)—Bkg.—Land owner. "The Fire and the Hearth" (1942)—Major—Bachelor son of Zachary Edmonds; owner of land farmed by Lucas Beauchamp; reared by Molly Beauchamp; forty-three years old. "Delta Autumn" (1942)— Major—Father of the part-Negro girl's child; cousin of Isaac McCaslin. *Intruder in the Dust* (1948)—Bkg.—Lucas Beauchamp lives on his plantation. "Race at Morning" (1955)— Minor—Scotch-drinking, poker-playing hunter. *The Town*

(1957)—Bkg.—One signer of Lucius Hogganbeck's auto loan note; called son of McCaslin Edmonds.

Edmonds, Louisa: Cau.—*The Reivers* (1962)—Bkg.—Wife of Zack Edmonds.

Edmonds, Zachary (Zack): Cau.—"The Fire and the Hearth" (1942)—Minor—Father of Roth Edmonds; grandson of L.Q.C. McCaslin; after the death of his wife, he keeps Molly Beauchamp for six months; he and Lucas Beauchamp were childhood companions. *The Reivers* (1962)—Bkg.—He and his wife Louisa are cousins of Lucius Priest; it is at their home (McCaslin Place) that Lucius is supposed to be staying.

Ek: Cau.—"The Liar" (1925)—Major—The liar whose tale, quite credible, rewards him with a gunshot.

Elly: Cau.—"Elly" (1934)—Major—Emotionally imbalanced, vicious, eighteen-year-old; lived in Jefferson; caused wreck in which her grandmother and Paul de Montigny are killed; real name is Ailanthia.

Elma, Miss: Cau.—*The Town* (1957)—Bkg.—Wife of Sheriff Hampton's predecessor; office clerk. Cf. Bishop, Ephraim.

Elnora: Neg./Cau.—*Sartoris* (1929)—Minor—Cook for Sartoris family; daughter of Simon; sister to Caspey; mother of Isom. "All the Dead Pilots" (1931)—Bkg.—Mentioned as Sartoris Negro. "There Was a Queen" (1933)—Major—Servant of Virginia Du Pre; half-sister to Bayard (old) Sartoris; wife of Caspey; mother of Joby, Isom, and Saddie.

Emmaline: Neg.—"That Will Be Fine" (1935)—Bkg.—Louisa's baby's nurse.

Emmy: Cau.—*Soldiers' Pay* (1926)—Minor—Rector's housekeeper who had an affair with Donald Mahon before he went to war.

Ephraim: Neg.—*Intruder in the Dust* (1948)—Bkg.—Father of Paralee.

Ephum: Neg.—*The Reivers* (1962)—Bkg.—Negro worker at Ballenbaugh's.

Ernest, Mr.: Cau.—"Race at Morning" (1955)—Major—Hunter-protector-friend of the boy.

Ernie: Cau.—"Fox Hunt" (1931)—Bkg.—Narrator of a major section of the story; valet of sorts.

Eunice: Neg.—*Sartoris* (1929)—Bkg.—Benbow cook who makes such good chocolate pies.

Eunice: Neg.—"The Bear" (1942)—Bkg.—Mother of Tomasina (Tomey) by L.Q.C. McCaslin; grandmother of Tomey's Turl; bought in New Orleans (1807) by L.Q.C. McCaslin, her lover. Married to Thucydides (1809); Drowned herself (Christmas Day, 1832) six months before Tomasina bore Tomey's Turl to L.Q.C. McCaslin.

Eustace: See Graham, Eustace or Grimm, Eustace.

Everbe Corinthia: See Hogganbeck, E. C.

Ewell, Bryan: Cau.—"An Error in Chemistry" (1946)—Bkg.—Deputy sheriff.

Ewell, Walter: Cau.—"A Bear Hunt" (1934)—Bkg.—Hunter at de Spain's camp. "The Old People" (1940)—Minor—Highly respected hunter; his rifle never misses. "The Bear" (1942)—Minor—Excellent hunter; respected marksman. "Delta Autumn" (1942)—Bkg.—Deceased hunter. "Race at Morning" (1955)—Bkg.—Poker-playing hunter. *The Mansion* (1959)—Bkg.—Hunter. *The Reivers* (1962)—Bkg.—Hunter at Major de Spain's camp.

Ewing, Mr. and Mrs. Ira (Elder): Cau.—"Golden Land" (1935)—Parents of Ira Ewing, Realtor. Mr. Ewing, Sr., a minister-farmer died in Nebraska. Mrs. Ewing, Sr., named Samantha, lives in Glendale home provided by her son; major character.

Ewing, Mr. and Mrs. Ira (Realtor): Cau.—"Golden Land" (1935)—He, a major character, is a successful realtor, corrupted by wealth. She, a minor character, daughter of a carpenter, is his wife in name only. He has a Filipino valet-chauffeur, and a forty-year-old mistress whose fourteen-year-old daughter he supports in boarding school.

Ewing, Mitch: Cau.—"Hair" (1931)—Bkg.—Depot freight agent; lived at Mrs. Cowan's where Henry Stribling boarded. Cf. Mitch.

Ewing, Samantha (April Lalear): Cau.—"Golden Land" (1935)—Minor—Reveals a sex orgy that presents the crux of story; daughter of Ira Ewing, Realtor.

Ewing, Voyd: Cau.—"Golden Land" (1935)—Minor—Delinquent, transvestite son of Ira Ewing, Realtor.

F

Fairchild, Mr. Dawson: Cau.—*Mosquitoes* (1927)—Major—New Orleans novelist and friend of Mrs. Maurier. Portrait of Sherwood Anderson; his conversation provides much of the subject matter of the novel.

Falls, Will (Old Man Will): Cau.—*Sartoris* (1929)—Bkg.—Ninety-three-year-old man; good friend of Col. John Sartoris, about whom he reminisces; cures wen on Bayard Sartoris's face.

Farinzale, Giulio: Cau.—"Mistral" (1931)—Bkg.—Lover of priest's ward.

Farmer: Cau.—*Requiem for a Nun* (1951)—Bkg.—Turnkey during Civil War.

Farmer, Cecilia: Cau.—*Requiem for a Nun* (1951)—Bkg.—Daughter of turnkey above; scratched her name on pane of jail window; cf. Cook, Celia.

Farr, George: Cau.—*Soldiers' Pay* (1926)—Major—Loved Cecily Saunders passionately and ultimately married her.

Fathers, Sam (Had-Two-Fathers, Uncle Blue Gum): Neg./Ind.—"A Justice" (1931)—Major—Sam explains how Doom became Chief and how he (Sam) was born to Crawfishford and a Negress, the wife of another Negro slave; thus his name Had-Two-Fathers. "The Old People" (1940)—Major—Son of Chickasaw Indian chief Doom and a quadroon slave girl. Trains Isaac McCaslin in woodsmanship. "The Bear" (1942)—

Major—Son of Chickasaw Indian chief and Negro slave; dies after Old Ben (the bear) is killed. "Delta Autumn" (1942)— Bkg.—Deceased woodscraft mentor of Ike McCaslin. *Intruder in the Dust* (1948)—Bkg.—Mentioned as hunter at de Spain's camp. *The Reivers* (1962)—Bkg.—Mentioned as hunter.

Faulkner: Cau.—*Mosquitoes* (1927)—Bkg.—Presumably William who had conversed with Jenny Steinbauer; professional liar.

Feinman, Col. H. I.: Cau.—*Pylon* (1935)—Minor—Jewish lawyer; head of New Valois Sewage Board; airport is named for him; supervises air meet.

Fentry, G. A.: Cau.—"Tomorrow" (1940)—Bkg.—S. J. Fentry's father—a rough, unfriendly cuss.

Fentry, Jackson and Longstreet: See Thorpe, Buck.

Fentry, Stonewall Jackson: Cau.—"Tomorrow" (1940)— Major—Man who hung the jury in the Bookwright murder trial because victim was his former son.

Ffolansbye: Cau.—"All the Dead Pilots" (1931)—Minor—Soldier who tells part of the story to the first person narrator.

Fibby: See Phoebe

Fittie, Aunt: Cau.—*The Reivers* (1962)—Bkg.—Madame of Arkansas brothel where Miss Corrie (Everbe Corinthia) worked.

Flint: Cau.—*The Wild Palms* (1939) in "Wild Palms"—Bkg.— Medical student roommate of H. Wilbourne whom he takes to French Town for a party.

Flint, Joel and Ellie Pritchel: Cau.—"An Error in Chemistry" (1946)—Major—He (once Signor Canova, disappearing artist) kills her and her father and almost gets away.

Fonzo: See Winbush, Fonzo

Foote: Cau.—"Two Soldiers" (1942)—Bkg.—Law officer in Jefferson.

Fortinbride, Brother: Cau.—*The Unvanquished* (1938)— Minor—Illiterate soldier-pastor of Miss Rosa Millard's church.

Fox, Matt: Cau.—"Hair" (1931)—Minor—Quiet but nosey barber who works with Hawkshaw at Maxey's Barbershop.

Frank: Cau.—*Sanctuary* (1931)—Bkg.—One of Ruby Lamar's earliest suitors.

Frankie: Cau.—*Sartoris* (1929)—Bkg.—Young girl tennis player at Belle Mitchell's.

Franz: Cau.—"Ad Astra (1931)—Bkg.—Younger brother to German pilot captured by Monaghan.

Fraser: Mentioned in *Intruder in the Dust* (1948) as family name of early Yoknapatawpha settlers.

Fraser: Cau.—"A Bear Hunt" (1934)—Bkg.—Hunter at de Spain's camp.

Fraser: Cau.—"Monk" (1937)—Bkg.—Moonshiner who taught Monk to make whisky.

Fraser, Squire Adam: Cau.—*Intruder in the Dust* (1948)—Bkg.—Store owner.

Fraser, Doyle: Cau.—*Intruder in the Dust* (1948)—Bkg.—Son of Squire Adam Fraser.

Frazier, Judge: Cau.—"Tomorrow" (1940)—Bkg.—Judge in Bookwright murder trial.

Fred: See Louisa.

Freeman, Mr. and Mrs.: Cau.—*The Hamlet* (1940)—Bkg.—Farming couple; he buys a spotted horse.

Frony: Neg.—*The Sound and the Fury* (1929)—Bkg.—Dilsey's daughter. [Appendix to Modern Library Edition (1946) says that she married Pullman porter and made a home for Dilsey in Memphis.] "That Evening Sun" (1931)—Bkg.—Dilsey's daughter.

Frost, Mark: Cau.—*Mosquitoes* (1927)—Minor—New Orleans' leading poet, he says; a pale, apathetic egoist.

G

Gabe: Neg.—*The Reivers* (1962)—Bkg.—Smith at the livery stable.

Gambrell, C. L.: Cau.—"Monk" (1937)—Bkg.—Warden of Parchman; killed by Monk whom he has befriended.

Gant, Jim: Cau.—*Miss Zilphia Gant* (1932)—Major—Father who deserted Zilphia and her mother; killed by his wife.

Gant, Mrs. Jim: Cau.—*Miss Zilphia Gant* (1932)—Major— Seamstress mother who ruined Zilphia's marriage.

Gant, Miss Eunice: Cau.—*The Town* (1957)—Bkg.—Clerk in Wildermark's store.

Gant, Miss Zilphia: Cau.—*Miss Zilphia Gant* (1932)—Major —Daughter of Mr. and Mrs. Jim Gant; marries, loses her husband and rears the child of her husband and his second wife.

Gargne, M. and Madame: Cau.—*A Fable* (1954)—Bkg.— Runner lives in garret of their house.

Garraway: Cau.—*The Town* (1957)—Bkg.—First person to transfer his money from the Sartoris bank to the Bank of Jefferson because of Flem Snopes.

Gary, Dr.: Cau.—*Soldiers' Pay* (1926)—Minor—Obnoxious young physician trying to court Cecily Saunders.

Gatewood, Jabbo: Neg.—*The Town* (1957)—Bkg.—Repairs Manfred de Spain's flat; son of Uncle Noon Gatewood.

Gatewood, Uncle Noon: Neg.—*The Town* (1957)—Bkg.— Gavin Stevens' hoe was sharpened in his blacksmith shop.

Gawtrey, Steve: Cau.—"Fox Hunt" (1931)—Major—A would-be consort of Mrs. Harrison Blair's.

Gene: Cau.—*Sanctuary* (1931)—Bkg.—Bootlegger friend of Red's who provided the liquor at Red's funeral.

George: Cau.—"Divorce in Naples" (1931)—Major—Old salt getting divorced from Carl; cook of Greek extraction.

George: Cau.—"The Leg" (1934)—Major—Oxford buddy of Davy; his apparition appears to Davy for a time.

George: Cau.—"That Will Be Fine" (1935)—Major—Owner of livery stable in Jefferson; father of narrator.

George: Cau.—*The Hamlet* (1940)—Bkg.—Deputy who helps take Mink Snopes to jail.

Georgie: Cau.—"That Will Be Fine" (1935)—Major—Narrator (age seven); helps Uncle Rodney for a quarter; very mercenary.

Gibson, Dilsey: Neg.—*The Sound and the Fury* (1929)—Major —Faithful Negress who understands and ministers to the Compsons; wife of Roskus; mother of Frony, T. P. and Versh. "That Evening Sun" (1931.)—Bkg.—Compson cook for whom Nancy substituted.

Gibson, Frony: See Frony

Gibson, Roskus: Neg.—*The Sound and the Fury* (1929)—Bkg. —Husband of Dilsey; a faithful Compson servant. "A Justice" (1931)—Bkg.—Carriage driver for Jason (II) and Jason (III).

Gibson, T. P.: Neg.—*The Sound and the Fury* (1929)—Bkg. —Son of Dilsey and Roskus; sometimes an attendant to Benjy. "That Evening Sun" (1931)—Bkg.—Mentioned.

Gibson, Versh: Neg.—*The Sound and the Fury* (1929)—Bkg. —Oldest son of Dilsey and Roskus; attendant to Benjy. "That Evening Sun" (1931)—Bkg.—Mentioned as possible protector for Nancy.

Gibson, Will: Cau.—"The Liar" (1925)—Major—Owner of store on porch of which the liar told the truth.

Gihon: Cau.—*The Mansion* (1959)—Bkg.—F. B. I. Agent checking on Linda S. Kohl's Communist activities.

Gihon, Danny: Cau.—"Pennsylvania Station" (1934)—Major —Profligate son of Mrs. Margaret Noonan Gihon.

Gihon, Mrs. Margaret Noonan: Cau.—"Pennsylvania Station" (1934)—Major—Widowed charwoman; mother of criminal son; her brother tells her story.

Gillespie: Cau.—*As I Lay Dying* (1930)—Bkg.—Neighborly farmer whose barn is burnt by Darl.

Gillespie: Cau.—*The Wild Palms* (1939) in "Wild Palms"— Bkg.—Part owner of McCord's cabin.

Gillespie, Mack: Cau.—*As I Lay Dying* (1930)—Bkg.—Helped get animals from his father's burning barn.

Gilligan, Joe: Cau.—*Soldiers' Pay* (1926)—Major—Took care of Donald Mahon; loved Mrs. Margaret Powers; nicknamed *Yaphank*.

Gillman: Cau.—*Light in August* (1932)—Bkg.—Foreman who succeeded Eupheus Hines at Arkansas sawmill.

Gilman: Cau.—"Country Mice" (1925)—Major—They are the country mice; father, a justice of the peace, arrests the bootlegger's brother Gus. Sons—one a deputy and one a pilot—help the bootlegger fly his "booze" to New Haven.

Ginotta, Joe: Cau.—*Mosquitoes* (1927)—Bkg.—Pete's elder brother who successfully runs the modernized family restaurant.

Ginotta, Mr. and Mrs.: Cau.—*Mosquitoes* (1927)—Bkg.— Pete's parents; Italian immigrants; He is dead; she is deaf.

Ginotta, Pete: Cau.—*Mosquitoes* (1927)—Major—Jenny's boyfriend who came along for the ride; flees Miss Jameson.

Ginsfarb: Cau.—"Death Drag" (1932)—Major—As Daredevil Duncan, he really takes a spill.

Gombault, Pete: Cau.—"The Tall Men" (1941)—Major— Deputy U.S. Marshal who teaches Mr. Pearson a lesson in government; just called Mr. Gombault. *Requiem for a Nun* (1951)—Bkg.—U.S. Marshal; called Uncle Pete Gombault. *The Town* (1957)—Bkg.—U.S. marshal.

Goodwin, Lee: Cau.—*Sanctuary* (1931)—Major—Bootlegger accused of raping Temple Drake and killing Tommy; lynched. Cf. Lamar, Ruby.

Goodwin, Pap: Cau.—*Sanctuary* (1931)—Lee Goodwin's blind father.

Goodyhay, Bro. Joe C.: Cau.—*The Mansion* (1959)—Bkg.— Ex-Marine sergeant-preacher who helps Mink Snopes.

Gordon: Cau.—*Mosquitoes* (1927)—Major—Sculptor tricked into coming on the cruise; active, red-haired person.

Gowan, Judge: Cau.—"The Fire and the Hearth" (1942)—Bkg.—Judge before whom Lucas Beauchamp and George Wilkins are arraigned for making illegal whiskey.

Gower, District Attorney: Cau.—*The Wild Palms* (1939) in "Wild Palms"—Bkg.—Prosecuted Harry for manslaughter.

Gowrie: Mentioned in *Intruder in the Dust* (1948) as family name of early Yoknapatawpha settlers.

Gowrie: Cau.—*The Town* (1957)—Bkg.—Delivers Gavin Stevens's liquor.

Gowrie, Amanda Workitt: Cau.—*Intruder in the Dust* (1948)—Bkg.—Deceased wife of N.B.F. Gowrie.

Gowrie, Bilbo: Cau.—*Intruder in the Dust* (1948)—Bkg.—Son of Nub Gowrie; twin of Vardaman.

Gowrie, Bryan: Cau.—*Intruder in the Dust* (1948)—Bkg.—Nub Gowrie's third son.

Gowrie, Crawford: Cau.—*Intruder in the Dust* (1948)—Major—Killed his brother Vinson from whom he was stealing lumber.

Gowrie, N. B. Forrest: Cau.—*Intruder in the Dust* (1948)—Bkg.—Oldest son of Nub Gowrie.

Gowrie, Nub (Old Man Nub): Cau.—*Intruder in the Dust* (1948)—Minor—Father of the murderer and the murdered. *The Mansion* (1959)—Bkg.—Farmer in Beat 9.

Gowrie, Vardaman: Cau.—*Intruder in the Dust* (1948)—Bkg.—Twin of Bilbo Gowrie; son of Nub Gowrie.

Gowrie, Vinson: Cau.—*Intruder in the Dust* (1948)—Bkg.—The murdered youngest son of Nub Gowrie.

Grady: Cau.—*Pylon* (1935)—Bkg.—New Valois reporter.

Gragnon, General Charles: Cau.—*A Fable* (1954)—Minor—Commander of the division in which the regiment revolted; killed by American soldiers.

Graham, Eustace: Cau.—*Sartoris* (1929)—Bkg.—Crippled lawyer who introduced Mr. Gratton to Bayard (young); only called Eustace. *Sanctuary* (1931)—Minor—District attorney prosecuting Goodwin case; clubfooted man who worked his way through the state university partially by winning at poker.

Grant, Joe: Cau.—*Pylon* (1935)—Bkg.—Flyer at New Valois meet.

Gratton: Cau.—*Sartoris* (1929)—Bkg.—Friend of Eustace (Graham); a returned soldier.

Gray, Alec (Captain): Cau.—"Victory" (1931)—Major— Typical war hero overcome with easy living; becomes degenerate.

Gray, Alec (old): Cau.—"Victory" (1931)—Bkg.—Grandfather of young Alec; a shipwright.

Gray, Jessie; John Wesley; Matthew, Jr.; and Elizabeth: Cau.—"Victory" (1931)—Bkg.—Sisters and brothers of Capt. Alec; Jessie is older than Alec; others are younger and are listed in order of age, oldest first.

Gray, Johnny: Cau.—"The Kid Learns" (1925)—Major—Kid who learns how hard it is to become the boss.

Gray, Matthew and Annie: Cau.—"Victory" (1931)—Bkg.— Parents of Capt. Alec; he is shipwright.

Gray, Simon: Cau.—"Victory" (1931)—Bkg.—Brother to Alec (old).

Green, Captain: Cau.—*Soldiers' Pay* (1926)—Bkg.—Raised a company of men in Donald's hometown; died in Europe.

Greenleaf: Mentioned in *Intruder in the Dust* (1948) as family name of early Yoknapatawpha settlers.

Grenier, Louis: Cau.—Hinted at in "Hand Upon the Waters" (1939) and *The Hamlet* (1940). *Intruder in the Dust* (1948)— Bkg.—Mentioned as one of founders of Yoknapatawpha. *Requiem for a Nun* (1951)—Bkg.—Huguenot who brought the first slaves into the area; first big cotton planter. *The Town* (1957)—Bkg.—Mentioned as one of Jefferson's founders. *The Reivers* (1962)—Bkg.—Mentioned as Huguenot plantation owner; one of Jefferson's founders.

Grier, Mrs.: Cau.—"Shingles for the Lord" (1943)—Minor—wife of Res Grier whom she doctors after church fire.

Grier, Mrs.: Cau.—"Two Soldiers" (1942)—Minor—Mother of Pete. "Shall Not Perish" (1943)—Major—Mother of deceased Pete; comforts Major de Spain (II) on loss of his son.

Grier, Pete: Cau.—"Two Soldiers" (1942)—Major—Nigh twenty-year-old son of a farm family; enlists to fight the Japanese. "Shall Not Perish" (1943)—Bkg.—Notification of his death comes to the family.

Grier: Cau.—"Two Soldiers" (1942)—Major—Almost nine-year-old younger brother of Pete; narrator of story; tries to enlist in Army. "Shall Not Perish" (1943)—Major—Narrator; explains Pete's death in glowing patriotic terms.

Grier: Cau.—"Shingles for the Lord" (1943)—Major—Son of Res Grier; possibly Pete (see above).

Grier: Cau.—"Two Soldiers" (1942)—and "Shall Not Perish" (1943)—Minor—Pete's father; not too aggressive farmer.

Grier, Res: Cau.—"Shingles for the Lord" (1943)—Major—Caused the church to burn; inept. *The Mansion* (1959)—Bkg.—Involved in dog-unit work with Solon Quick.

Grierson, Emily: Cau.—"A Rose for Emily" (1930)—Major—Lonely, frustrated old maid who retains the body of her dead lover; two female cousins visit for a time after the death of her father.

Grimm, Eustace: Cau.—*As I Lay Dying* (1930)—Bkg.—Groom who delivers a span of mules from Snopes to Anse Bundren. *The Hamlet* (1940)—Bkg.—Farmer; his mother was Ab Snopes's youngest sister.

Grimm, Percy: Cau.—*Light in August* (1932)—Minor—Disappointed would-be soldier who castrated and shot Joe Christmas.

Grinnup, Dan (Dan Grenier): Cau.—*The Reivers* (1962)—Bkg.—Scottish driver at the Priest livery stable.

Grinnup, Lonnie (Louis Grenier): Cau.—"Hand Upon

the Waters" (1939)—Minor—Murder victim; simpleton. Descendant of one of the three original Yoknapatawpha settlers.
Intruder in the Dust (1948)—Bkg.—Mentioned as descendant
of original Louis Grenier.

Grove, Lena: Cau.—*Light in August* (1932)—Major—Simple,
humble country girl whose story provides continuity; pregnant
and unworried, she pursues father of her child; captivates
Byron Bunch and takes him along.

Grove, McKinley: Cau.—*Light in August* (1932)—Bkg.—Lena
Grove's brother from Doane's Mill, Alabama.

Grumby, Major: Cau.—*The Unvanquished* (1938)—Minor—
Killed Rosa Millard; killed and skinned by Bayard (old)
and Marengo. *The Hamlet* (1940)—Bkg.—Mentioned as
murderer of Rosa Millard.

Grummet: Cau.—*As I Lay Dying* (1930)—Bkg.—Owner of
hardware store in Mottson where cement was bought for
Cash's leg.

Gualdres, Captain Sebastian: Cau.—"Knight's Gambit" (1949)
—Major—Argentine house guest of Mrs. Melisandre B. Harriss; Gavin Stevens defeated him by saving his life, forcing
him to marry Miss Harriss.

Gus: Cau.—"Country Mice" (1925)—minor—Brother of bootlegger.

Guster: Neg.—*The Town* (1957)—Bkg.—Wife of Big Top;
cook for Mallison-Stevens family; mother of Aleck Sander and
Little Top.

H

Habersham: Cau.—*The Unvanquished* (1938)—Bkg.—Bank
clerk; signed Col. John Sartoris's peace bond; wife is Martha.

Habersham, Mrs.: Cau.—"Two Soldiers" (1942)—Bkg.—Social
worker in Jefferson; helped Pete Grier's brother get to
Memphis.

Habersham, Emily: Cau.—*The Town* (1957)—Bkg.—Helps arrange return of Byron Snopes's children to Mexico. [Vintage edition (1961) attributes this act to Eunice. Possibly same role as Mrs. Habersham in "Two Soldiers."]

Habersham, Miss Eunice: Cau.—*Intruder in the Dust* (1948)— Major—Seventy-year-old friend of Molly Beauchamp because Molly's parents had been the slaves of Miss Habersham's grandparents. Cf. Miss Belle Worsham. *The Town* (1957)—Bkg.— Mentioned as truck farmer and bank stockholder.

Habersham, Mrs. Martha: Cau.—*The Unvanquished* (1938)— Bkg.—Helped force the marriage of Drusilla Hawk and Col. John Sartoris; her husband is bank clerk.

Habersham, Dr. Samuel: Cau.—*Intruder in the Dust* (1948)— Bkg.—Grandfather of Miss Eunice Habersham. *Requiem for a Nun* (1951) and The *Town* (1957)—Bkg.—Mentioned as one of Jefferson's founders.

Had-Two-Fathers: See Fathers, Sam.

Hagood: Cau.—*Pylon* (1935)—Minor—City editor of the paper for which Reporter works; humors Reporter.

Hait, Lonzo: Cau.—*The Town* (1957)—Bkg.—partner of I. O. Snopes in mule killing enterprise; train killed him three years prior to events of *The Town;* cf. Hait, Mannie. *The Mansion* (1959)—Bkg.—Horse trader.

Hait, Mannie: Cau.—"Mule in the Yard" (1934)—Major— Forty-year-old widow of Lonzo Hait, who was killed by train ten years earlier; outwits I. O. Snopes in mule trade. *The Town* (1957)—Minor—Received $8,500 for death of her husband on railroad; outwits I. O. Snopes and Flem Snopes.

Haley, Lem: Cau.—"The Liar" (1925)—Bkg.—His hounds caught Ek, causing him to have to wear shoes.

Halladay, Jim: Cau.—*Intruder in the Dust* (1948)—Bkg.— Apparently a district attorney.

Halliday: Cau.—*Light in August* (1932)—Bkg.—Caught Joe Christmas in Mottstown.

Hamblett, Jim: Cau.—*Absalom, Absalom!* (1936)—Bkg.—
Justice of the peace.

Hamp: Cau.—*The Wild Palms* (1939) in "Old Man"—Bkg.—
Person associated with animals at Parchman Penitentiary.

Hampton: Cau.—*The Reivers* (1962)—Bkg.—Mentioned as
sheriff who was an ancestor to the later Hampton sheriffs;
law officer in Boon Hogganbeck-Ludus fracas.

Hampton, Hope: Cau.—*Intruder in the Dust* (1948)—Major—
Sheriff who solves the case of the Gowrie murder; wife is
mentioned. Cf. Hampton, Hub.

Hampton, Hubert (Hub): Cau.—*The Hamlet* (1940)—Bkg.—
Sheriff who jails Mink Snopes. *The Town* (1957)—Bkg.—
Sheriff of Yoknapatawpha County. *The Mansion* (1959)—
Bkg.—Sheriff in M. W. Snopes case.

Hampton, Hub, Jr.: Cau.—*The Mansion* (1959)—Bkg.—
Inherits his father's position of alternating sheriff's terms
with Ephraim Bishop. *The Reivers* (1962)—Bkg.—Grandson
of Hampton who was sheriff in 1905; presently sheriff or
will be next term.

Hampton, Sally: See Priest, Mrs. Maurice.

Handy, Professor: Neg.—*The Town* (1957)—Bkg.—Leader
of the band for the Christmas dance.

Hank: Cau.—*Pylon* (1935)—Bkg.—Announcer for New Valois
air meet.

Hanley: Cau.—*A Fable* (1954)—Bkg.—R.A.F. hero.

Hare: Cau.—*Requiem for a Nun* (1951)—Bkg.—Bandit in past.

Harker: Cau.—"Centaur in Brass" (1932)—Minor—Narrates
portions; night engineer at city power plant. *The Town* (1957)
—Bkg.—Brass story repeated here.

Harker, Otis: Cau.—*The Town* (1957)—Bkg.—Relative of
engineer Harker for whom he substitutes a power plant; later
becomes town night marshal.

Harmon, Mrs.: Cau.—"The Liar" (1925)—Bkg.—A frightened
horse ran through her house.

Harpe, Wiley: Cau.—*Requiem for a Nun* (1951)—Bkg.— Mentioned as bandit-murderer.

Harper: Cau.—"Turnabout" (1932)—Bkg.—Gunner on Capt. Bogard's plane.

Harris: Cau.—*Sanctuary* (1931)—Bkg.—Proprietor of livery stable in which Eustace Graham played poker; Eustace bluffed him in an anecdotal game.

Harris: Cau.—"The Rosary" (1925)—Major—Poor man who hated above all else the song "The Rosary"; his wife and daughters are mentioned.

Harris: Cau.—"Death Drag" (1932)—Bkg.—Owner of only rental car in Jefferson.

Harris: Cau.—"Honor" (1934)—Bkg.—Owner of flying circus in which Buck Monaghan and Rogers meet.

Harris: Cau.—"Barn Burning" (1939)—Minor—Loses his lawsuit against Ab Snopes for barn burning. His affair with Snopes is reported in *The Hamlet* (1940) and *The Town.* (1957).

Harris, Elmer: Cau.—"Black Music" (1934)—Bkg.—Chief of police in Virginia town where W. Midgleston disappeared.

Harris, Meloney: Neg.—*Sartoris* (1929)—Bkg.—Belle Mitchell's maid; an attractive young Negress who presumably receives financing for her beauty shop from Simon Strother for his amour; Simon is killed in her home.

Harrison, Sergeant: Cau.—*The Unvanquished* (1938)—Bkg.— Lost the best horse in the regiment to Bayard and Ringo.

Harriss: Cau.—"Knight's Gambit" (1949)—Bkg.—Rumored to have been a bootlegger of immense wealth; married Jefferson girl [Melisandre Backus] and rebuilt her father's home into a fabulous show place; died suddenly; possibly murdered before events of this story occur. *The Mansion* (1959)—Bkg.—Gangster-type who married Melisandre Backus.

Harriss, Miss: Cau.—"Knight's Gambit" (1949)—Major—Mrs. M. B. Harriss's daughter; fights for and wins Capt. Gualdres.

Harriss, Mrs. Melisandre Backus: Cau.—"Knight's Gambit" (1949)—Minor—Only known as Mrs. Harriss here; Gavin was betrothed to her when she was sixteen and he was thirty; at the end of this story they marry. Cf. Backus, Melisandre and Stevens, Mrs. Melisandre B. H.

Harriss, Max: Cau.—"Knight's Gambit" (1949)—Major—Tried to kill Capt. Gualdres, but Gavin prevented him; son of Mrs. M. B. Harriss.

Harry, Mr.: Cau.—*A Fable* (1954)—Major—English groom who races the three-legged horse in America; killed with rebellious units. Negro calls him "Mistairy." Same role in *Notes on a Horsethief* (1950) which is included in *A Fable*.

Hatcher, Louis and Martha: Neg.—*The Sound and the Fury* (1929)—Bkg.—He gives Caddy driving lessons and goes coon hunting with Quentin (III); she is his wife.

Hawk, Dennison and Louisa: Cau.—*The Unvanquished* (1938)—Minor—He is deceased; she insisted on marriage for Drusilla Hawk and Col. John Sartoris; uncle and aunt of Bayard (old); she is the sister of Rosa Millard.

Hawk, Dennison, Jr. (Denny): Cau.—*The Unvanquished* (1938)—Bkg.—Son of Dennison and Louisa; lawyer after Civil War.

Hawk, Drusilla: See Sartoris, Mrs. Drusilla H.

Hawkshaw: See Stribling, Henry.

Head, Mr. Sydney Herbert: Cau.—*The Sound and the Fury* (1929)—Candace Compson's husband who divorces her when he discovers that she is pregnant with someone else's child; Indianian; scoundrel himself.

Henderson, Mrs.: Cau.—*Soldiers' Pay* (1926)—Bkg.—Inquisitive passenger on train with Donald Mahon.

Henri: Cau.—*A Fable* (1954)—Bkg.—French army commander.

Henry: Neg.—*Soldiers' Pay* (1926)—Bkg.—Porter on one of the trains the major characters take.

Henry, Uncle: Neg.—*Sartoris* (1929)—Bkg.—Coon hunt begins behind his house.

Henry: Cau.—*The Sound and the Fury* (1929)—Bkg.—Smart classmate of Mr. Quentin Compson in Jefferson.

Henry: Cau.—"The Fire and the Hearth" (1942)—Bkg.—Deputy marshal.

Henry: Cau.—*Requiem for a Nun* (1951)—Minor—Governor to whom Gavin Stevens takes Temple Drake Stevens for confession.

Henry: Neg.—*The Mansion* (1959)—Bkg.—Jack Houston's helper.

Het (Old): Neg.—"Mule in the Yard" (1934)—Major—Poorhouse Negro whom everyone contributes to; helps Mrs. Hait in the mule escapade with I. O. Snopes. Same role in *The Town* (1957) which includes "Mule in the Yard."

Hightower, Gail (I): Cau.—*Light in August* (1932)—Bkg.—Grandfather of Gail (D.D.); killed while robbing hen house during Civil War.

Hightower, Gail, D.D.: Cau.—*Light in August* (1932)—Major—Jefferson minister rejected by his congregation because he lived in a phantasy and because his wife committed suicide; forced back to life by Byron Bunch; much of the action of the novel occurs in his home; entranced with the "glory" of his Confederate grandfather; his father and mother are mentioned but unnamed.

Hightower, Mrs. Gail (D.D.): Cau.—*Light in August* (1932)—Bkg.—Deceased insane wife who did not like the religious life and could not cope with the coldness of Gail.

Hightower, Hiram: Cau.—*The Reivers* (1962)—Bkg.—Baptist minister who forcibly overcame the heathen at Ballenbaugh's Ferry in the summer of 1886.

Hilliard: Cau.—*The Unvanquished* (1938)—Bkg.—Owner of livery stable in Oxford.

Hines, Eupheus and Mrs.: Cau.—*Light in August* (1932)—
Minor—Joe Christmas's grandparents; he tries to get Joe
lynched; she tries to save Joe. He is fanatically religious; she is
the patient wife. He killed Joe's father and put Joe in an orphanage, believing that Joe had Negro blood.

Hines, Milly: Cau.—*Light in August* (1932)—Bkg.—Joe Christmas's mother who conceived him by a circus worker and died
at Joe's birth because her father refused to allow medical help.

Hipps, Buck: Cau.—*The Hamlet* (1940)—Bkg.—Texan who
brought the spotted horses to Frenchman's Bend.

Hoake: Cau.—*The Hamlet* (1940)—Bkg.—Father of Allison
Hoake; sat up with shotgun when she eloped.

Hogben: Cau.—*The Wild Palms* (1939) in "Wild Palms"—
Bkg.—engineer of ore train.

Hogganbeck, Boon: Ind./Cau.—"The Old People" (1940)—
Bkg.—Hunter with adolescent mentality; grandmother was
Chickasaw woman. "The Bear" (1942)—Major—Forty-year-old
hunter; greatly attached to Lion; an inept, semi-moron; one-
fourth Indian; general handyman for General Compson, Major
de Spain, and Cass Edmonds; kills Old Ben. "Delta Autumn"
(1942)—Bkg.—Mentioned as former hunting companion of Ike
McCaslin. *Intruder in the Dust* (1948)—Bkg.—Mentioned as
hunter. *The Town* (1957)—Bkg.—Mentioned as father of Lucius; former hunting handyman of Major de Spain. *The Reivers*
(1962)—Major—Middle-aged moron; crazy about cars; provides the impetus for much of the story; an institution supported by Compsons, Edmonds, de Spains; marries Everbe
Corinthia and fathers Lucius Priest Hogganbeck. [*Big Woods*
(1955) version of "A Bear Hunt" (1934) employs him in roles
mentioned above, especially father of Lucius; Neither he nor
Lucius appear in the earlier version as found in *Collected
Stories* (1950).]

Hogganbeck, David: Cau.—"A Courtship" (1948)—Major—

Riverboat pilot in love with Herman Basket's sister; vies with Ikkemotubbe.

Hogganbeck, Everbe Corinthia: Cau.—*The Reivers* (1962)—Minor—Prostitute who reforms from her career and marries Boon Hogganbeck; mother of Lucius Priest Hogganbeck.

Hogganbeck, Lucius Priest: Ind./Cau.—*The Town* (1957)—Bkg.—Owner of Jefferson's first Ford Model-T. *The Mansion* (1959)—Bkg.—Operator of taxi in Jefferson. *The Reivers* (1962)—Bkg.—Infant son of Boon and Everbe C. Hogganbeck; named for Lucius Priest. [In *Big Woods* (1955) version of "A Bear Hunt" (1934), a composite of Jack Bonds (q.v.) and Luke Provine (q.v.) from earlier version; role of Mrs. Luke Provine becomes Mrs. Lucius Hogganbeck.]

Hogganbeck, Melissa: Cau.—"Knight's Gambit" (1949)—Bkg.—Chick Mallison's history teacher; *The Town* (1957)—Bkg.—History teacher at the Academy in Jefferson.

Holcomb, Ashley: Cau.—*The Town* (1957)—Bkg.—Playmate of young Chick Mallison.

Holcomb, Sister Beth: Cau.—*The Mansion* (1959)—Bkg.—Led Mink Snopes to Brother Goodyhay.

Holland, Mr.: Cau.—"Tomorrow" (1940)—Bkg.—Foreman of the jury in Buck Thorpe manslaughter case.

Holland, Mr.: Cau.—*The Mansion* (1959)—Bkg.—President of the Bank of Jefferson; gives Essie Meadowfill a job for life; gives a $500 scholarship in honor of his son who died as a Navy pilot in one of the first Pacific battles of World War II. Cf. Major de Spain (II).

Holland, Anselm: Cau.—"Smoke" (1932)—Minor—Died leaving a peculiar will. *The Hamlet* (1940)—Bkg.—Ratliff's pap and Ab Snopes rented land from him at the same time; called Anse. [Possibly different roles.]

Holland, Anselm, Jr.: Car.—"Smoke" (1932)—Major—Younger twin son of Anse Holland with whom he quarreled bitterly.

Holland, Mrs. Cornelia Mardis: Cau.—"Smoke" (1932)—Bkg.
—Wife of Anselm, Sr.; mother of twins, Anselm and Virginius.

Holland, Virginius: Cau.—"Smoke" (1932)—Major—Soft-spoken elder twin son of Anselm Holland; inherited the farm.

Holmes, Miss: Cau.—*The Sound and the Fury* (1929)—Bkg.—One of the young ladies at Mrs. Bland's picnic.

Holmes, Jack: Cau.—*Pylon* (1935)—Major—Parachute jumper; one of Laverne Shumann's lovers; father of child she is carrying; dislikes Reporter.

Holston, Dr.: Cau.—"My Grandmother Millard" (1943)—Bkg. Mentioned as Jefferson citizen.

Holston, Mrs.: Cau.—*The Unvanquished* (1938)—Bkg.—Owner of the hotel.

Holston, Alexander: Cau.—Mentioned as one of founders of Jefferson; established Holston House (a tavern) later succeeded by Holston Hotel—in *Intruder in the Dust* (1948), *Requiem for a Nun* (1951), *The Town* (1957), and *The Mansion* (1959). Mentioned only as *Holston* in same role in *Absalom, Absalom!* (1936), "Hand Upon the Waters" and the Appendix to the Modern Library Edition (1946) of *The Sound and the Fury*.

Hood, Uncle Parsham: Neg.—*The Reivers* (1962)—Minor—Fine old Negro who is respected by everyone in the novel.

Hooper: Cau.—*Mosquitoes* (1927)—Bkg.—Type of the Northern industrialist; frenetic; Rotarian; smug.

Hope, Midshipman L. Claude W.: Cau.—"Turnabout" (1932)—Major—Daring young British naval officer who serves on torpedo boat; his courage wins Capt. Bogard's admiration.

Hopkins: Cau.—*The Sound and the Fury* (1929)—Bkg.—Cotton speculator.

Horn: Cau.—*A Fable* (1954)—Bkg.—Runner appropriates his uniform; British soldier.

Houston: Neg.—*Sartoris* (1929)—Bkg.—Negro waiter in the store-cafe where Bayard got drunk.

Houston: Cau.—*As I Lay Dying* (1930)—Bkg.—Neighbor who attended Addie Bundren's funeral.

Houston, Jack (Zack): Cau.—"The Hound" (1931)—Major—Killed by Ernest Cotton. *The Hamlet* (1940)—Bkg.—Tried to get his horse shod by Eck Snopes; married Lucy Pate; murdered by Mink Snopes. *The Town* (1957)—Bkg.—Called Zack; married to Letty Bookwright; killed by Mink Snopes. *The Mansion* (1959)—Minor—Overbearing bully killed by Mink Snopes.

Houston, Mrs. Jack (Zack): See Bookwright, Letty; and Pate, Lucy.

Hovis: Cau.—*The Town* (1957)—Bkg.—Cashier in Manfred de Spain's bank.

Hovis, Mrs.: Cau.—"Uncle Willy" (1935)—Bkg.—Mrs. Merridew's helper.

Howes, Mrs. Anne: Cau.—"Artist at Home" (1933)—Major—Her love affair with a young poet evokes a great poem.

Howes, (or House), Darrell (Dorry): Cau.—*Idyll in the Desert* (1931)—Major—Came to tuberculosis camp first, recovered, and deserted his paramour.

Howes, Roger: Cau.—"Artist at Home" (1933)—Major—Former advertisement writer turned novelist who is besieged by unexpected literary guests to his home in the Valley of Virginia; creates an excellent story from his wife's affair with John Blair.

Hoxey, Major: Cau.—"Centaur in Brass" (1932)—Bkg.—Mayor of Jefferson and lover of Flem Snopes's wife.

Hub: Cau.—*Sartoris* (1929)—Bkg.—Youth; drinking friend of young Bayard and Suratt.

Hub: Cau.—"An Error in Chemistry" (1946)—Major—Sheriff who helped solve the murder and escape; cf. Hampton, Hub.

Hughes, Manny: Cau.—*Idyll in the Desert* (1931)—Bkg.—Helped Lucas Crump send letters and telegrams to the woman's husband.

Hule: Cau.—"Mountain Victory" (1932)—Minor—Vatch's young brother; tries to help Weddel and gets killed.

Hulett, Mr.: Cau.—"The Fire and the Hearth" (1942)—Bkg.— Clerk of court from which Lucas and Molly Beauchamp do not get a divorce.

Hume: Cau.—"Ad Astra" (1931)—Bkg.—R.A.F. hero.

Hurtz, Mr. and Mrs.: Cau.—*Pylon* (1935)—Bkg.—She is Reporter's mother.

I

Idiot: Cau.—"The Kingdom of God" (1925)—Major—Bellows when his flower droops and causes his brother and an accomplice to be caught bootlegging whiskey; forerunner of Benjy Compson.

Ike: Cau.—"Hand Upon the Waters" (1939)—Bkg.—Took the body of Lonnie Grinnup for burial.

Ikkemotubbe (Doom): Ind.—"Red Leaves" (1930)—Bkg.— Called Doom; father of Issetibbeha; *Doom* is corruption of *du homme* as he was called by Chevalier Soeur Blonde de Vitry. "A Justice" (1931)—Major—Called Ikkemotubbe, alias David Callicoat; A Mingo, son of The Man's sister; becomes The Man (Chief of the Choctaws) through murder and threats. *Absalom, Absalom!* (1936)—Bkg.—Indian from whom Thomas Sutpen acquires land for Sutpen's Hundred. "The Old People" (1940)—Bkg.—Chickasaw chief; father of Sam Fathers; here Moketubbe abdicates and Ikkemotubbe becomes Chief. "The Bear" (1942)—Bkg.—Sells Sam Fathers, his mother (Negro) and her husband to L. Q. C. McCaslin; originally sold hunting land to Thomas Sutpen. Mentioned in same roles in Appendix to Modern Library Edition (1946) of *The Sound and the Fury*. "A Courtship" (1948)—Major—Nephew of Issetibbeha; cousin of Moketubbe whom he poisons; contends with David Hogganbeck for attentions of Herman Basket's sister. *Requiem for a Nun* (1951) Bkg.—Son of Mohataha; succeeded Issetibbeha, his uncle, as Chief of the Chickasaws. *The Town* (1957) and *The Reivers* (1962)—Bkg.—Mentioned as usurper of Chickasaw throne.

Ingraham: Mentioned in *Intruder in the Dust* (1948) as family name of early Yoknapatawpha County settlers; now Ingrum.

Ingrum, Willy: Cau.—*Intruder in the Dust* (1948)—Bkg.—Town marshal of Jefferson.

Irey: Cau.—*Notes on a Horsethief* (1950)—Minor—Turnkey who arrests Negro groom. Same role in *A Fable*.

Isham: Neg.—"Delta Autumn" (1942)—Minor—Eldest servant on the hunting trip.

Isom: Neg./Cau.—*Sartoris* (1929)—Bkg.—Sixteen-year-old son of Elnora; works Miss Jenny's flower beds. *Sanctuary* (1931)—Bkg.—Servant of Miss Jenny and Mrs. Narcissa B. Sartoris. "All the Dead Pilots" (1931)—Bkg.—Mentioned in Johnny's letter. "There Was a Queen" (1933)—Bkg.—Son of Elnora.

Issetibbeha: Ind.—"Red Leaves" (1930)—Minor—Chief who has just died and whose Negro is being hunted; nineteen when his father, Doom, died. "The Old People" (1940)—Bkg.—Maternal uncle of Ikkemotubbe who forces Moketubbe, son of Issetibbeha, to abdicate. "The Bear" (1942)—Bkg.—Mentioned as Ikkemotubbe's father. "A Courtship" (1948)—Bkg.—Old Chief who dies; maternal uncle of Ikkemotubbe (Doom); also father of Moketubbe who is poisoned. *Requiem for a Nun* (1951)—Bkg.—Predecessor of Ikkemotubbe. *The Town* (1957) —Bkg.—Mentioned as Ikkemotubbe's uncle. *The Reivers* (1962)—Bkg.—Chickasaw Chief.

J

Jabbo, Captain: Cau.—*The Mansion* (1959)—Bkg.—Parchman guard who shoots Jake Barron when he tries to escape.

Jack: Cau.—"Honor" (1930)—Bkg.—Buddy of Buck Monaghan's; refers Buck to Harris.

Jackie: Cau.—*The Reivers* (1962)—Bkg.—Miss Reba left her (one of the prostitutes) in charge of the House.

Jackson, Al: Cau.—*Mosquitoes* (1927)—Bkg.—In a yarn told by Dawson Fairchild, a descendant of Andrew Jackson.

Jackson, Art: Cau.—*Pylon* (1935)—Bkg.—Stunt flyer who hires Jiggs.

Jackson, Claude: Cau.—*Mosquitoes* (1927)—Bkg.—Al Jackson's brother who changed to a fish.

Jackson, "Old Man": Cau.—*Mosquitoes* (1927)—Bkg.—Father of Al and Claude; owner of sheep-fish ranch.

Jake: Cau.—"The Kingdom of God" (1925)—Major—Brother of Idiot; caught selling bootleg whisky because the Idiot bellows; shows loyalty to his brother.

Jake: Cau.—"Death Drag" (1932)—Minor—Partner of Ginsfarb and Jock.

Jake: Neg.—"Beyond" (1933)—Bkg.—Negro house servant to Judge Allison.

James, Lt. Colonel: Cau.—*A Fable* (1954)—Bkg.—Runner's group commander.

Jameson, Dorothy: Cau.—*Mosquitoes* (1927)—Minor—Woman who keeps trying to seduce Pete Ginotta or Mark Frost; sadly unattractive woman.

Jarrod, Hubert: Cau.—"Dr. Martino" (1931)—Major—Wealthy Oklahoman who marries Louise King.

Jean: Cau.—*A Fable* (1954)—Bkg.—Follower (m.) of the Corporal.

Jean-Baptiste: Cau.—"Home" (1925)—Major—Homesick French immigrant about to undertake some illegal job, but who is reminded of his home by the saw violinist.

Jenny: See Steinbauer, Genevieve.

Jerry: Cau.—"Turnabout" (1932)—Bkg.—American flyer who disparages Claude Hope.

Jesus: Neg.—"That Evening Sun" (1931)—Minor—Supposedly

Aunt Rachel's son; husband to Nancy who fears his retribution for her infidelity.

Jew, Wealthy: Cau.—"New Orleans" (1925)—Major—Interior monologuist who stresses the perseverance of the Jews.

Jiggs: Cau.—*Pylon* (1935)—Major—Roger Shumann's mechanic; helps present the story of the Shumanns; has a wife and two kids in Kansas.

Jim: Cau.—*The Hamlet* (1940)—Bkg.—Deputy Sheriff.

Jim: Neg.—*The Hamlet* (1940)—Bkg.—Artist in horse work and trading; works for Pat Stamper.

Jingus: Neg.—*The Unvanquished* (1938)—Bkg.—One of the faithful Negroes at Hawkhurst, home of Dennison and Louisa Hawk, Gihon County, Alabama.

Job, Uncle: Neg.—*The Sound and the Fury* (1929)—Bkg.— Works for Earl's hardware store; witty, indolent old man.

Job, Uncle: Neg.—"Smoke" (1932)—Bkg.—Judge Dukinfield's janitor who watched the door of the court house. Same role in *The Town* (1957).

Jobaker: See Baker, Joe.

Joby (I): Neg.—*Sartoris* (1929)—Bkg.—Old servant of Sartorises; remembered from Christmas 1869. *The Unvanquished* (1938)—Minor—Body servant of Col. John Sartoris; husband of Louvinia; trainer of Simon, Ringo's father; older than John Sartoris whom he had accompanied from North Carolina. "My Grandmother Millard" (1943)—Bkg.—Mentioned in same roles as above.

Joby (II): Neg./Cau.—"There Was a Queen" (1933)—Bkg.— Son of Elnora; lives in Memphis.

Jock: Cau.—"Death Drag" (1932)—Major—Very nervous pilot of the daredevil plane.

Jody: Cau.—*As I Lay Dying* (1930)—Bkg.—Young buck of Jefferson; employed in drugstore.

Joe: Cau.—*Sartoris* (1929)—Bkg.—Tennis player at Belle Mitchell's.

Joe: Cau.—*Sanctuary* (1931)—Bkg.—Boisterous friend of Red's.

Joe: Cau.—"The Hound" (1931)—Bkg.—Deputy sheriff.

Joe: Cau.—*Pylon* (1935)—Bkg.—Owner of a bar.

Joe: Neg.—*Intruder in the Dust* (1948)—Bkg.—Carothers Edmonds's helper.

Joe: Cau.—"Hand Upon the Waters" (1939)—Major—Deafmute who saved Gavin Stevens's life by avenging Lonnie Grinnup.

Joe: Cau.—"Episode" (1925)—Minor—Blind man who with his wife is sketched by Spratling.

Joe: Cau.—"Country Mice" (1925)—Major—Partner of the tricked bootlegger.

John Henry: Neg.—*Sartoris* (1929)—Bkg.—Saves Bayard Sartoris (young) from drowning after auto wreck.

John Paul: Neg.—"That Will Be Fine" (1935)—Bkg.—Driver of the hack.

Jonas: Neg.—"Was" (1942)—Minor—McCaslin Negro.

Jones (Doctor): Neg.—*Sartoris* (1929)—Bkg.—Janitor at Col. Sartoris's bank.

Jones: Cau.—"Death Drag" (1932)—Bkg.—Fair Secretary; responsible for airport.

Jones, Herschell: Cau.—*Sanctuary* (1931)—Bkg.—Mentioned as suitor of Narcissa Benbow Sartoris.

Jones, Januarius: Cau.—*Soldiers' Pay* (1926)—Minor—Tries unsuccessfully to seduce every female with whom he comes in contact; aged thirty-one.

Jones, Melicent: Cau.—*Absalom, Absalom!* (1936)—Bkg.—Daughter of Wash Jones; mother of illegitimate Milly.

[Jones], Milly: Cau.—"Wash" (1934)—Major—Mistress of Col. Sutpen; granddaughter of Wash Jones. This story is repeated as a part of *Absalom, Absalom!* (1936) where she occupies the same role, though her story is less important in context of the novel.

Jones, Wash: Cau.—"Wash" (1934)—Major—Poor white trash;

kills Col. Sutpen for rejecting Milly and her daughter; this version is told from Wash's point of view; story of his relations with Col. Sutpen is included in *Absalom, Absalom!* (1936) though told from Sutpen's point of view.

Jordan, Mrs.: Cau.—"That Will Be Fine" (1935)—Bkg.—Georgie and Rosie go to sleep at her house.

Jubal: Neg.—"Mountain Victory" (1932)—Major—Body servant of Saucier Weddel; killed with Weddel.

Jug: Cau.—*Pylon* (1935)—Bkg.—Photographer with same paper the Reporter works for.

Julio: Cau.—*The Sound and the Fury* (1929)—Bkg.—Italian who accuses Quentin Compson of kidnapping his sister.

Junkin, Professor: Cau.—*The Sound and the Fury* (1929)—Bkg.—School teacher; possibly principal of the school desultorily attended by Miss Quentin.

Jupe: Neg.—*Light in August* (1932)—Bkg.—Almost fights with Joe Christmas in the streets of Jefferson.

K

Kauffman, Julius: Cau.—*Mosquitoes* (1927)—Major—Referred to as "The Semitic man"; close friend to Dawson Fairchild for whom he is conversational foil; his grandfather of the same name helped Mr. Maurier to improve his fortune; brother of Eva Wiseman.

Kaye, Major C.: Cau.—"All the Dead Pilots" (1931)—Bkg.—Writer of letter informing Mrs. V. Sartoris of the death of Johnny Sartoris.

Kazimura: Japanese—"Golden Land" (1935)—Bkg.—Mrs. Samantha Ewing's gardener.

Kemp, Beasley: Cau.—*The Hamlet* (1940)—Bkg.—Ab Snopes got the trick horse from Beasley the first time.

Kennedy, Watt: Cau.—*Light in August* (1932)—Bkg.—Sheriff in Jefferson.

Kenny: Cau.—*The Sound and the Fury* (1929)—Bkg.—One of three young boys Quentin Compson meets near Cambridge.

Ketcham: Cau.—"Pantaloon in Black" (1940)—Bkg.—Jailer.

Killebrew, Miss: Cau.—*The Town* (1957)—Bkg.—Teller in Manfred de Spain's bank.

Killegrew, Mr. and Mrs.: Cau.—"Two Soldiers" (1942)—Bkg. —Because they are both deaf, they play the radio loud enough for Pete Grier and his brother to hear when they stand outside the window. "Shingles for the Lord" (1943)—Bkg.—Old, deaf farm couple; he is seventy years old. "Shall Not Perish" (1943) —Bkg.—He is mentioned as old deaf man.

Killegrew, Hampton: Cau.—"Knight's Gambit" (1949)—Bkg. —Town marshal of Jefferson.

Killegrew, Hunter: Cau.—*The Mansion* (1959)—Bkg.—Deputy who took M. W. Snopes to Parchman.

King, Mrs. Alvina: Cau.—"Dr. Martino" (1931)—Major— Conniving mother of Louise King.

King, Louise: Cau.—"Dr. Martino" (1931)—Major—Tricked by her mother into ending a valuable association with Dr. Martino and into marrying Hubert Jarrod.

Kitchener (Kit): Cau.—"All the Dead Pilots" (1931)—Bkg.— Nickname for Johnny Sartoris's girl.

Kneeland: Cau.—*The Town* (1957)—Bkg.—Suits for Christmas ball were rented from tailor Kneeland.

Kohl, Barton: Cau.—*The Mansion* (1959)—Bkg.—Linda Snopes Kohl's husband; killed in Spanish Civil War.

Kohl, Mrs. Linda Snopes: Cau.—*The Mansion* (1959)—Major —Daughter of Hoake McCarron and Eula Varner; social reformer; deaf war casualty; close friend of Gavin Stevens; responsible for getting Mink Snopes out of prison.

Kyerling, R.: Cau.—"All the Dead Pilots" (1931)—Bkg.— R. A. F. pilot who saw Johnny Sartoris shot down.

L

Labove: Cau.—*The Hamlet* (1940)—Bkg.—Young school teacher tortured by thoughts of seducing Eula Varner; his father, grandmother and other immediate relatives are mentioned.

Lafe: Cau.—"The Liar" (1925)—Minor—One of the listeners; keeps interrupting Ek's story.

Lafe: Cau.—*As I Lay Dying* (1930)—Bkg.—Father of child Dewey Dell Bundren is carrying.

Lalear, April: See Ewing, Samantha

Lallemont, General: Cau.—*A Fable* (1954)—Bkg.—Corps commander above Gragnon.

Lamar, Ruby: Cau.—*Sanctuary* (1931)—Major—Common law wife of Lee Goodwin; mother of his son; former prostitute.

Landry, Sergeant: Cau.—*A Fable* (1954)—Bkg.—In charge of group to secure body of Unknown Soldier.

Lapin: Cau.—*A Fable* (1954)—Bkg.—Executed with the Corporal.

Laura, Miss: Cau.—*The Sound and the Fury* (1929)—Bkg.—Quentin Compson's school teacher.

Lawington, Miss: Cau.—*As I Lay Dying* (1930)—Bkg.—Town lady associated with Cora Tull.

Leblanc: Cau.—*Pylon* (1935)—Bkg.—Policeman; friend of Reporter.

Ledbetter, Mrs.: Cau.—*The Town* (1957)—and *The Mansion* (1959)—Bkg.—Purchaser of sewing machine from Ratliff.

Legate, Bob: Cau.—*The Reivers* (1962)—Bkg.—Hunter.

Legate, Will: Cau.—"Delta Autumn" (1942)—Minor—Hunts with Roth Edmonds. *Intruder in the Dust* (1948)—Minor—Hampton's deputy who guards Lucas Beauchamp. "Race at Morning" (1955)—Bkg.—Hunter.

Legendre, Dr.: Cau.—*Pylon* (1935)—Bkg.—Mr. Hagood tells Reporter to get sleeping pills from him.

Lena, Missy: Neg.—*The Unvanquished* (1938)—Bkg.—Hawk servant.

Leonora: Neg.—*Pylon*—(1935)—Bkg.—Charwoman for Reporter.

Lessep, Grandfather and Grandmother: Cau.—*The Reivers* (1962)—Bkg.—His death occasioned the opportunity for the Memphis trip; Lucius Priest's maternal grandparents.

Lessep, Alexander: Cau.—*The Reivers* (1962)—Bkg.—Deceased great-uncle of Lucius Priest.

Levine, David: Cau.—*A Fable* (1954)—Minor—British flyer who chases the German commander's plane on its way to generals' conference.

Levitt, Matt: Cau.—*The Town* (1957)—Minor—Flashy beau of Linda Snopes; former Golden Glove boxer; owns racing car.

Lewis, Matt: Cau.—*Idyll in the Desert* (1931)—Bkg.—Operator of livery stable in Blizzard.

Lilley: Cau.—*Intruder in the Dust* (1948)—Bkg.—Operator of store; encourages lynching effort.

Linscomb, Colonel: Cau.—*The Reivers* (1962)—Bkg.—Owner of Acheron, horse which raced against Coppermine; lawyer.

Littlejohn: Cau.—*As I Lay Dying* (1930)—Bkg.—Neighbor farmer who attended Addie Bundren's funeral.

Littlejohn, Mrs.: Cau.—*The Hamlet* (1940)—Bkg.—Operator of hotel; takes care of Ike Snopes; widow. *The Town* (1957) —Bkg. Operates Littlejohn Hotel.

Lizzie: Cau.—"Barn Burning" (1939)—Bkg.—Mrs. Lennie Snopes's sister.

Log-in-the-Creek: Ind.—"A Courtship" (1948)—Major—Lazy, harmonica-playing Indian who marries Herman Basket's sister.

Long, Judge: Cau.—*The Town* (1957)—Bkg.—Federal Judge in the M. W. Snopes case. *The Mansion* (1959)—Bkg.—Same role as above.

Loosh: See Nelson, Loosh or Lucius.

Lorraine: Cau.—*The Sound and the Fury* (1929)—Bkg.—Jason (IV) Compson's girl friend from Memphis.

Lorraine, Miss: Cau.—*Sanctuary* (1931)—Bkg.—Thin prostitute friend of Miss Reba Rivers.

Louisa and Fred: Cau.—"That Will Be Fine" (1935)—Bkg.— Narrator's maternal aunt and her husband; their two children, Louisa and Fred, cousins of narrator are mentioned.

Louisa: Neg.—*The Wild Palms* (1939) in "Wild Palms"—Bkg. —Maid in a San Antonio brothel.

Louvinia: Neg.—*Sartoris* (1929)—Bkg.—Cook for the Sartoris family during the Civil War. *The Unvanquished* (1938)— Minor—Wife of Joby, mother of Simon and Lucius, and grandmother of Ringo; faithful Negro servant. "My Grandmother Millard" (1943)—Bkg.—Cook; Mother of Lucius.

Lovelady: Cau.—"That Evening Sun" (1931)—Bkg.—Collector of Negro burial insurance in Jefferson; his wife committed suicide.

Lovemaiden, Butch: Cau.—*The Reivers* (1962)—Bkg.—Deputy sheriff who plagues Boon and Miss Corrie.

Lowe, Julian: Cau.—*Soldiers' Pay* (1926)—Minor—Nineteen-year-old disappointed cadet who wrote love letters to Mrs. Powers.

Lucius: Neg.—*The Unvanquished* (1938)—Minor—Son of Joby and Louvinia; husband of Philadelphy; follows the Union soldiers away from Sartoris after showing them the silver; called Loosh; later returns. "My Grandmother Millard" (1943)— Minor—Eager to use his new freedom; Philadelphia's husband; son of Louvinia.

Ludus: Neg.—*The Mansion* (1959)—Bkg.—Husband of Minnie; lazy, lecherous Negro.

Ludus: Neg.—*The Reivers* (1962)—Bkg.—Driver whose tom-catting got him in dutch with Boon Hogganbeck.

Lufbery: Cau—*Soldiers' Pay* (1926)—Bkg.—Mentioned.

Luis: Cau.—"Carcassonne" (1931)—Bkg.—Operator of the cantina.

Luke: Cau.—*Sanctuary* (1931)—Bkg.—One of the Jefferson youths who knew about Temple Drake's immorality.

Luluque: Cau.—*A Fable* (1954)—Bkg.—Follower (m.) of the Corporal.

Luster: Neg.—*The Sound and the Fury* (1929)—Minor—Son of Frony; keeper to Benjy at the time of three sections of the work; mentioned in Appendix to Modern Library Edition (1946) of *The Sound and the Fury*. *Absalom, Absalom!* (1936) —Bkg.—A Compson servant.

Luster: Neg.—*The Reivers* (1962)—Bkg.—Helped Gabe shoe a horse and aided in Ludus-Boon Hogganbeck fracas.

Lytle, Horace: Cau.—*The Reivers* (1962)—Bkg.—Wealthy man in Parsham who owns fine bird dogs.

M

Mac: Cau.—*The Sound and the Fury* (1929)—Bkg.—Drugstore clerk who discusses baseball with Jason (IV) Compson.

Mac: Cau.—*Pylon* (1935)—Bkg.—Desk policeman who releases Jiggs to the Reporter.

MacCallum: Family name spelled *MacCallum* in *Sartoris* (1929); Spelled *McCallum* in later works. All members of this family are listed together under *McCallum*.

MacGowan, Skeets: See McGowan, Skeets.

MacKenzie, Shreve: Cau.—*The Sound and the Fury* (1929)— Bkg.—Quentin Compson's Harvard roommate; present on Bland picnic; cf. McCannon, Shrevlin.

Madden, Rufus: Cau.—*Soldiers' Pay* (1926)—Minor—Wounded veteran who lives in Donald Mahon's hometown; served under Capt. Green and Lt. Richard Powers.

Magdalen: Cau.—"New Orleans" (1925)—Major—States the reason she chose the prostitution profession.

Mahon, Donald: Cau.—*Soldiers' Pay* (1926)—Major—Central character; wounded, dying soldier who never recovers enough to adjust to being at home; Mrs. Margaret Powers marries him.

Mahon, Rev. Joseph: Cau.—*Soldiers' Pay* (1926)—Major— Donald's father; Episcopalian rector who spouts platitudes; tries to ignore the imminent death of his son.

Mahon, Mrs. Margaret Powers: Cau.—*Soldiers' Pay* (1926)— Major—Twenty-four-year-old war widow from Alabama who tries to help Donald Mahon; marries him and comforts him and his father until Donald dies.

Mallison, Charles (Charley) and Margaret Stevens: Cau. —*Intruder in the Dust* (1948)—Bkg.—Chick's parents; "Knight's Gambit" (1949)—Bkg.—She is mentioned as Charles Mallison's mother. *Requiem for a Nun* (1951)—Bkg.—Maggie is mentioned as Gavin Steven's twin sister. *The Town* (1957) —Minor—Parents of Chick (Charles) Mallison; she is Gavin's twin sister. *The Mansion* (1959)—Bkg.—Chick's mother who is Gavin Stevens' twin; he is not mentioned.

Mallison, Charles (Chick), Jr.: Cau.—"Monk" (1937)— Apparently the narrator; unnamed. "Tomorrow" (1940)—Minor —Gavin Stevens' unnamed messenger boy. *Intruder in the Dust* (1948)—Major—Initiator of the action which saved Lucas Beauchamp; nephew of Gavin Stevens. "An Error in Chemistry" (1946)—Major—Apparently the narrator; unnamed. "Knight's Gambit" (1949)—Major—Gavin's eighteen-year-old nephew who aids him; later he joins the military. *The Town* (1957)—Minor—Young nephew of Gavin Stevens who helps narrate the story. *The Mansion* (1959)—Minor— Gavin Stevens' nephew who attends Harvard; interested in Linda Snopes; joins U.S. Air Force; becomes German p.o.w.; helps narrate parts of the novel.

Mandy: Neg.—*Sartoris* (1929)—Bkg.—Cook for MacCallum family.

Mandy: Neg.—"That Will Be Fine" (1935)—Bkg.—Grandpa's cook.

Mannie: Neg.—"Pantaloon in Black" (1940)—Minor—Rider's wife who dies after only a few months of marriage.

Mannigoe, Nancy: Neg.—"That Evening Sun" (1931)—Major —Called Nancy; prostitute who fears that Jesus, her husband will kill her; Mr. Stovall is a white customer. *Requiem for a Nun* (1951)—Major—She, the Nun, killed the child of Temple and Gowan Stevens to prevent a divorce.

Mannock: Cau.—*A Fable* (1954)—Bkg.—R.F.C. hero.

Marchand: Cau.—*Pylon* (1935)—Bkg.—Employee of Ord-Atkinson Aircraft Corp.

Marders, Mrs. Sarah: Cau.—*Sartoris* (1929)—Bkg.—Fat, sociable woman; friend of Belle Mitchell.

Marengo (Ringo): Neg.—*The Unvanquished* (1938)—Major —Dependable companion who grows up with Bayard Sartoris (elder); smarter than Bayard; son of Simon; grandson of Joby and Louvinia. "My Grandmother Millard" (1943)—Minor— playmate of narrator [Bayard]; called Ringo.

Markey, Robert: Cau.—"Knight's Gambit" (1949)—Bkg.— Memphis lawyer-friend of Gavin Stevens; they met at Heidelberg.

Marsh: Cau.—"Two Soldiers" (1942)—Bkg.—Mrs. Grier's brother who fought in France in World War I.

Martel, General: Cau.—*A Fable* (1954)—Bkg.—A parchment mysteriously blows from his desk.

Martha, "Miss": Cau.—*The Wild Palms* (1939) in "Wild Palms" Bkg.—Wife of doctor from whom Harry Wilbourne and Charlotte Rittenmeyer rent a cabin.

Martino, Dr. Jules: Cau.—"Dr. Martino" (1931)—Major— Cardiologist with the failing heart; has strangely valuable relationship with Louise King.

Mary: Cau.—"The Kid Learns" (1925)—Major—Girl accosted by the Wop and rescued by the Kid.

Marya: Cau.—*A Fable* (1954)—Minor—She and her younger sister, Martha, take the Corporal's body for burial; mentally retarded.

Mason: Cau.—*Requiem for a Nun* (1951)—Bkg.—Rowdy fellow during Jefferson's early days.

Matthew: Cau.—"Hand Upon the Waters" (1939)—Bkg.— Paid part of Lonnie Grinnup's burial expense.

Maurier, Harrison: Cau.—*Soldiers' Pay* (1926)—Bkg.—Possible husband for Cecily Saunders.

Maurier, Mrs. Patricia: Cau.—*Mosquitoes* (1927)—Major— Wealthy widow who takes everyone for a cruise on her yacht, *The Nausikaa;* her husband, an old man whom she married in her youth for his money is mentioned.

Maxey: Cau.—"Hair" (1931)—Minor—Owner of the barber shop where Stribling worked in Jefferson; his brother-in-law owned the shop in Porterfield where Stribling had worked. *Light in August* (1932)—Bkg.—Mentioned in barbershop.

Maycox, Judge: Cau.—*Intruder in the Dust* (1948)—Bkg.— Judge in Lucas Beauchamp's case.

Maydew: Cau.—"Pantaloon in Black" (1940)—Minor—Sheriff who arrests Rider for killing Birdsong.

Mayes, Will: Neg.—"Dry September" (1931)—Major—Night watchman at the ice plant; accused and lynched for the rape of Minnie Cooper.

McAndrews: Cau.—"Pantaloon in Black" (1940)—Bkg.—Foreman of sawmill where Rider worked.

McCallum, Anse: Cau.—"The Tall Men" (1941)—Minor—He and Lucius, his twin, sons of Buddy McCallum join the Army; they have had a year at the state agricultural college. "Knight's Gambit" (1949)—Bkg.—Mentioned. *The Town* (1957)—Bkg. —Son of Buddy McCallum; fights Matt Levitt.

McCallum, Mr. and Mrs. Anse: Cau.—*The Hamlet* (1940)— Bkg.—He tamed his team of spotted horses. "The Tall Men" (1941)—Bkg.—Grandparents of the two boys to be arrested;

he occupies the same familial position that Virginius Mac-
Callum holds in *Sartoris;* she was a Carter.

McCallum, Henry: Cau.—*Sartoris* (1929)—Bkg.—Womanish,
fifty-year-old second son of Virginius MacCallum; maker of
excellent whisky for family consumption only.

McCallum, Jackson: Cau.—*Sartoris* (1929)—Bkg.—Fifty-two-
year-old eldest son of Virginius MacCallum. "The Tall Men"
(1941)—Bkg.—Buddy's eldest brother; about seventy.

McCallum, Lee: Cau.—*Sartoris* (1929)—Bkg.—Son of Virginius
MacCallum; singer; in his late thirties. "The Tall Men" (1941)
—Bkg.—Buddy's brother.

McCallum, Lucius: Cau.—"The Tall Men" (1941)—Minor—
He and his twin, Anse, join the Army because they have not
registered for selective service. "Knight's Gambit" (1949)—
Bkg.—Mentioned.

McCallum, Old Man Hundred-and-One: Cau.—*The Hamlet*
(1940)—Bkg.—Mentioned as figure of comparison.

McCallum, Raphael Semmes (Rafe): Cau.—*Sartoris* (1929)
—Minor—Forty-four-year-old son of Virginius MacCallum;
lover of horses and good whiskey; drinking friend of Bayard
Sartoris (young); twin to Stuart. "The Tall Men" (1941)—
Bkg.—Buddy's brother; about forty-five. "Knight's Gambit"
(1949)—Minor—Sold the intended murder stallion to Max
Harriss. *The Mansion* (1959)—Bkg.—Mentioned as seller of
stallion to Melisandre Harriss's son.

McCallum, Stuart: Cau.—*Sartoris* (1929)—Bkg.—Forty-four-
year-old son of Virginius MacCallum; unlike his twin, Rafe;
good farmer; canny trader. *As I Lay Dying* (1930) Bkg.
—Unnamed but mentioned as farmer, twin to Rafe. "The Tall
Men" (1941)—Bkg.—Buddy's brother.

McCallum, Virginius, Jr. (Buddy): Cau. *Sartoris* (1929)—
Minor—Twenty-year-old son of Virginius MacCallum by a
second marriage; friend to Bayard Sartoris (young); shamed
his father by joining the Yankee army in World War I;

received medal for bravery. "The Tall Men" (1941)—Major —Father of Anse and Lucius McCallum, the twins who did not register for selective service; he has his leg amputated. *Intruder in the Dust* (1948)—Bkg.—Traded Luger pistol to Crawford Gowrie. *The Town* (1957)—Bkg.—Mentioned as one-legged father of Anse.

McCallum, Virginius, Sr.: Cau.—*Sartoris* (1929)—Minor— Seventy-seven-year-old, twice widowed father of six sons, none of whom is married; an unyielding rebel; had walked from his home eighteen miles outside Jefferson to Lexington, Va., to enlist in Stonewall Jackson's brigade of the Confederate Army; spelled MacCallum.

McCannon, Shrevlin: Cau.—*Absalom, Absalom!* (1936)— Major—Canadian roommate of Quentin Compson at Harvard; imagines a lot of the action; born in Edmonton, Alberta, Canada, in 1890; cf. MacKenzie, Shreve.

McCarron, Mr. and Mrs. (Alison Hoake): Cau.—*The Hamlet* (1940)—Bkg.—Noted gambler who married Alison Hoake and settled down for a time; he was killed ostensibly in gambling dispute; parents of Hoake McCarron.

McCarron, Hoake: Cau.—*The Hamlet* (1940)—Minor— Triumphs over Eula's other beaux and she gives him herself; father of Linda Snopes. *The Town* (1957)—Bkg.—Mentioned as Eula's lover and father of her child. *The Mansion* (1959)— Minor—As Linda Snopes's natural father, he attends her wedding in New York.

McCaslin: Cau.—*The Reivers* (1962)—Bkg.—Uncle of Zack McCaslin; cousin of Lucius Priest; owner of the mare which foaled the racing mule.

McCaslin, Amodeus (Uncle Buddy): Cau.—*The Unvanquished* (1938)—Bkg.—Mentioned as the twin who went to Civil War; his and Buck's experiments in social relationships are stressed as far in advance of their times. "The Old People" (1940)—Bkg.—Twin brother of narrator's father. "Was"

(1942)—Major—Diffident twin brother of Theophilus; he wins
Tennie Beauchamp (Neg.) and Theophilus's freedom (from
Miss Sophonsiba Beauchamp) in a card game; son of L.Q.C.
McCaslin. "The Bear" (1942)—Bkg.—Mentioned as Theoph-
ilus's twin; cook; writer in the ledger; he and Buck began
freeing their slaves in 1830's. "Delta Autumn" (1942)—and
"The Fire and the Hearth" (1942)—Bkg.—Mentioned in same
role.

McCaslin, Delphine: Neg.—*The Reivers* (1962)—Bkg.—Cook
for Sarah Priest; fourth wife of Ned McCaslin.

McCaslin, Isaac (Uncle Ike): Cau.—"A Bear Hunt" (1934)
—Bkg.—Hunter. *The Hamlet* (1940)—Bkg.—Ab Snopes
wintered on his place. "The Old People" (1940)—Major—At
twelve he becomes a man and kills his first buck; son of
Theophilus McCaslin. "The Bear" (1942)—Major—Covering
various incidents from virtually all of Ike's life, this is the story
of his maturing and rejecting his patrimony; b. 1867; wife is
mentioned; McCaslin Edmonds gives him thirty dollars a
month. "Was" (1942)—Bkg.—Son of Theophilus McCaslin
and Sophonsiba Beauchamp; action concerns a situation in
which his parents nearly marry; his wife is mentioned. "Delta
Autumn" (1942)—Major—Very near eighty years old; wife is
mentioned; the elder statesman hunter; host at camp. "The
Fire and the Hearth" (1942)—Bkg.—Receives fifty dollars a
month from the plantation he rejected. *Intruder in the Dust*
(1948)—Bkg.—Ninety-year-old hunter; great-great-uncle of
Carothers Edmonds. "Race at Morning" (1955)—Bkg.—Mentioned as elder hunter. *The Town* (1957)—Bkg.—Owner of
hardware store in Jefferson; old hunter. *The Mansion* (1959)—
Bkg.—Partner in hardware store where Mink Snopes tried to
buy buckshot; once it was his; later Earl Triplett took over;
still later Jason Compson (IV) took it. *The Reivers* (1962)—
Bkg.—Cousin of Lucius Priest with whom Lucius pretended to

be staying when he left with Boon Hogganbeck to go to Memphis.

McCaslin, Lancaster: Cau.—*The Reivers* (1962)—Bkg.—According to Ned McCaslin, Lancaster is the father of L.Q.C. McCaslin.

McCaslin, Lucius Quintus Carothers: Cau.—"The Bear" (1942)—Bkg.—Father of the twins, Buddy and Buck, the mulatto Tomasina and her son Tomey's Turl, and grandfather of Lucas Beauchamp; bought the land from Ikkemotubbe. b. 1772 in Carolina—d. 27 June, 1837. Mentioned as patriarch in "The Old People" (1940), "Go Down, Moses" (1941), "The Fire and the Hearth" (1942), "Delta Autumn" (1942), "Was" (1942), *Intruder in the Dust* (1948), and *The Reivers* (1962).

McCaslin, Ned (Ned William McCaslin Jefferson Mississippi): Neg./Cau.—*The Reivers* (1962)—Major—Lucius Priest, Sr.'s, coachman; swaps the car for the race horse (Coppermine alias Lightning) and is the only one who can make the horse run; born a McCaslin in the McCaslin backyard in 1860; mother was the natural daughter of L.Q.C. McCaslin.

McCaslin, Mrs. Sophonsiba Beauchamp: Cau.—"Was" (1942) —Major—Hubert Fitz-Hubert Beauchamp's sister who tries to marry Buck McCaslin; later successful; mother of Ike. "The Bear" (1942)—Bkg.—Isaac McCaslin's mother who berates her brother for his Negro mistress.

McCaslin, Theophilus (Uncle Buck): Cau.—*Absalom, Absalom!* (1936)—Bkg.—At Thomas Sutpen's funeral he gives a rebel yell. *The Unvanquished* (1938)—Minor—Helped Bayard (old) and Ringo chase Grumby; lost chance to go to Civil War (Uncle Buddy outdrew him at cards); His and Buddy's experiments in social relationships and cooperative farming are discussed. *The Hamlet* (1940)—Bkg.—Mentioned as aiding Bayard Sartoris and Ringo avenge Miss Rosa Millard. "Was"

(1942)—Major—Accidentally engaged to Miss Sophonsiba Beauchamp; Buddy, in a game of poker, wins his freedom. "The Fire and the Hearth" (1942)—Bkg.—Father of Isaac McCaslin and twin to Buddy. "The Bear" (1942)—Bkg.— Referred to as father of Ike; Confederate soldier under N. B. Forrest; twin to Amodeus; manager of the farm. "Delta Autumn" (1942)—Bkg.—Mentioned. *The Reivers* (1962)—Bkg. —Ike's father who supposedly followed General Forrest into Gayoso Hotel trying to capture a Yankee general.

McCaslin, Thucydus (Thucydides): Neg.—"The Bear" (1942)—Husband of Eunice; son of Roscius and Phoebe; b. 1779—d. 17 February 1854.

McCord: Cau.—*The Wild Palms* (1939) in "Wild Palms"— Minor—Friend of Charlotte Rittenmeyer and Harry Wilbourne in Chicago; former New Orleans newspaperman.

McCudden: Cau.—*A Fable* (1954)—Bkg.—R. F. C. hero.

McDiarmid: Cau.—*The Reivers* (1962)—One of the judges in the horse races.

McEachern, Mr. and Mrs. Simon: Cau.—*Light in August* (1932)—Minor—Joe Christmas' stern Presbyterian foster parents; farm couple; he was extremely stern and she was a deceitful, beaten-down woman.

McGinnis, Second Lt. Darrel: Cau.—"Turnabout" (1932)— Minor—Sneering subordinate of Capt. Bogard.

McGowan, Skeets: Cau.—*As I Lay Dying* (1930)—Minor— Drugstore clerk in Jefferson who tricks Dewey Dell. *Intruder in the Dust* (1948)—Bkg.—Drugstore clerk. *The Town* (1957) —Bkg.—Soda jerk in Christian's drugstore. *The Mansion* (1959)—Bkg.—Soda jerk in Uncle Willy's drugstore.

McKellogg, Colonel and Mrs.: Cau.—"Two Soldiers" (1942) He is in the background; she is minor; she aids Pete Grier's younger brother.

McKie: Cau.—"Crevasse" (1931)—Major—Soldier who is lost with twelve others in the crevasse.

McLan: Cau.—"Victory" (1931)—Bkg.—Scottish soldier whom Capt. Alec Gray reprimands about his rifle.

McLendon, Mr. and Mrs. John (Jackson): Cau.—"Dry September" (1931)—Major—He, a hero of the French campaign of WWII, led the party to lynch Will Mayes; she is still up when he returns; called John. *Light in August* (1932)—Bkg. —In the barbershop; called Captain McLendon. *The Town* (1957)—Bkg. Called Jackson; World War I veteran. *The Mansion* (1959)—Bkg.—Captain of the Sartoris Rifles, World War I company of soldiers.

McNamara: Cau.—"Damon and Pythias Unlimited" (1925)— Minor—Tipster of sorts who tries to use his position as an ex-jockey to steal the narrator from another tipster.

McWilliams: Cau.—"Knight's Gambit" (1949)—Bkg.—Conductor on local train.

McWillie: Neg.—*The Reivers* (1962)—Bkg.—Acheron's jockey.

Meadowfill, Mr. and Mrs.: Cau.—*The Mansion* (1959)— Minor—Poor parents of Essie Meadowfill Smith; with Gavin Stevens's help they settle their feud with the Snopeses successfully.

Meek, Melissa: Cau.—Appendix to the Modern Library Edition (1946) of *The Sound and the Fury* (1929)—Bkg.—Librarian at Jefferson; wanted to save Candace.

Meeks, Doc: Cau.—*The Mansion* (1959)—Bkg.—Itinerant vendor of Watkins Products, patent drugs.

Melisandre, Cousin: See Backhouse, Mrs. Melisandre.

Merridew, Mrs.: Cau.—"Uncle Willy" (1935)—Major—Undertakes to "save" Uncle Willy Christian from dope and liquor addiction; seems to be interested in his money also.

Metcalf: Cau.—*Light in August* (1932)—Bkg.—Jailer in Mottstown.

Middleton, Captain: Cau.—*A Fable* (1954)—Minor—An American who thought he had buried the Corporal (whom he calls Brzewski) at sea.

Midgleston, Mrs. Martha: Cau.—"Black Music" (1934)—Bkg. —One of the reasons Wilfred Midgleston, her husband, does not return to New York; remarried.

Midgleston, Wilfred: Cau.—"Black Music" (1934)—Major— Became a tramp at 56 because he thought he had become a faun temporarily; resided in Rincon for twenty-five years. Apparently the same role though he is unnamed in "Carcasonne" (1931).

Mike: Cau.—*The Sound and the Fury* (1929)—Bkg.—Gerald Bland learned to box in Mike's gymnasium.

Milhaud, Madame: Cau.—*A Fable* (1954)—Bkg.—Operator of French restaurant.

Millard, Rosa: Cau.—*The Unvanquished* (1938)—Major— Widowed mother-in-law of Col. John Sartoris, granny to Bayard Sartoris (old), (and Ringo too); complimentary portrait of Southern lady; killed by horse thief with whom she was dealing. *The Hamlet* (1940)—Bkg.—Her horse-dealing with Ab Snopes is mentioned. "My Grandmother Millard and General Bedford Forrest and the Battle of Harrykin Creek" (1943)—Major—Central character; strong-willed Southern lady; her husband had owned a Memphis supply house. "Shall Not Perish" (1943)—Bkg.—Mentioned as Col. John Sartoris's mother-in-law who outwitted the Yankees.

Miller, Brother: Cau.—"Uncle Willy" (1935)—Bkg.—Teacher of the men's Bible class Willy Christian is forced into.

Miller, Mrs.: Cau.—*Soldiers' Pay* (1926)—Bkg.—Seamstress who first hires Emmy.

Millingham: Mentioned in *Intruder in the Dust* (1948) as family name of early Yoknapatawpha settlers.

Mink: ?—*The Sound and the Fury* (1929)—Bkg.—Driver of hack in which Jason holds Miss Quentin up as he drives rapidly past Caddy.

Minnie: Neg.—*Sanctuary* (1929)—Bkg.—Miss Reba Rivers's maid. *The Mansion* (1959)—Bkg.—Maid at Miss Reba Rivers's brothel; married to Ludus. *The Reivers* (1962)—Minor—Miss Reba's maid whose gold tooth tempts Otis.

Mitch: Cau.—*Sartoris* (1929)—Bkg.—Freight agent at the depot; drinks and goes serenading with Bayard (young) Sartoris; cf. Ewing, Mitch.

Mitchell: Cau.—"The Liar" (1925)—Bkg.—His horse was frightened by people who had just seen their first train.

Mitchell: Cau.—"Hand Upon the Waters" (1939)—Bkg.— Owner of store where Lonnie Grinnup had his burying money.

Mitchell, Mrs.: Cau.—*Soldiers' Pay* (1926)—Bkg.—Resident of Charlestown, Georgia.

Mitchell, Harry: Cau.—*Sartoris* (1929)—Minor—Amiable but dull cotton speculator whom Belle divorces to marry Horace Benbow; later Bayard (young) sees him drinking in a Chicago club. Mentioned in this role in *Sanctuary* (1931).

Mitchell, Hugh: Cau.—*The Hamlet* (1940)—Farmer in the gallery at the horse trade; recognized the horse Ab Snopes had gotten in a bad trade.

Mitchell, "little" Belle: Cau.—*Sartoris* (1929)—Bkg.— Daughter of Harry and Belle Mitchell. *Sanctuary* (1931)— Bkg.—Living with Horace and Belle M. Benbow; her actions reflect Temple Drake's past.

Mitchell, Uncle Few: Neg.—*The Unvanquished* (1938)— Bkg.—Referred to as deranged Negro.

Mohataha: Ind.—*Requiem for a Nun* (1951)—Bkg.—Mother of Ikkemotubbe; sister of Issetibbeha. *The Mansion* (1959)—Bkg. —Chickasaw matriarch (sister of Issetibbeha) who granted land to Quentin [Maclachan] Compson in 1821.

Moketubbe: Ind.—"Red Leaves" (1930)—Major—Son of Issetibbeha; New Chief; wearer of the red heeled shoes. "The Old People" (1940)—Bkg.—Son of Issetibbeha; became Chief and then abdicated in favor of Doom. Same role in "A Courtship" (1948). *The Reivers* (1962)—Bkg.—Mentioned as Chickasaw Chief.

Monaghan, Buck: Cau.—*Sartoris* (1929)—Bkg.—Aviator friend of young Bayard Sartoris. "Honor" (1930)—Major—Circus wingwalker who is in love with Mrs. Mildred Rogers. "Ad Astra" (1931)—Major—Shanty Irish-American soldier; captured a German flyer whose presence in a French cafe occasions a brawl. *A Fable* (1954)—Bkg.—American in the R.A.F.

Monckton: Cau.—"Divorce in Naples" (1931)—Bkg.—Sailor on the merchant ship with Carl.

Monk: Cau.—*Pylon* (1935)—Bkg.—Plane crewman at the New Valois meet.

Monk: See Odlethrop, S. J.

Montgomery, Jake: Cau.—*Intruder in the Dust* (1948)—Minor —Timber buyer murdered when he attempted to blackmail Crawford Gowrie.

Mooney: Cau.—*Light in August* (1932)—Bkg.—Foreman of the sawmill where Byron Bunch, Joe Christmas, and Joe Brown worked.

Moore, Brother: Neg.—*Sartoris* (1929)—Bkg.—Member of the deputation from Simon Strother's church; possessor of church financial records.

Morache: Cau.—*A Fable* (1954)—Bkg.—In the detail to find an Unknown Soldier's body.

Morowitz: Cau.—"Damon and Pythias Unlimited" (1925)— Major—Racing tout who takes the narrator to the races.

Mosby, Uncle Hogeye: Neg.—*Intruder in the Dust* (1948)— Bkg.—Mentioned as epileptic pauper.

Mose, Uncle: Neg.—"Fox Hunt" (1931)—Bkg.—One of Harrison Blair's grooms.

Moseley: *As I Lay Dying* (1930)—Bkg.—Fifty-six-year-old druggist in Mottson; refuses to help Dewey Dell Bundren have an abortion.

Mothershed: Cau.—"Beyond" (1933)—Major—Suicide atheist in Heaven (or Purgatory) against his will; he and Judge Allison had often discussed metaphysics.

Mulberry: Neg.—*Requiem for a Nun* (1951)—Bkg.—U.S. marshal in Jefferson during Reconstruction; bootlegged whisky from mulberry tree; cf. Sickymo.

Murrel, John: Cau.—*Requiem for a Nun* (1951)—Bkg.— Rowdy fellow during Jefferson's early days.

Meyers, Al: Cau.—*Pylon* (1935)—Bkg.—Flyer at the New Valois Meet.

Myrtle: Cau.—*Sartoris* (1929)—Bkg.—Dr. Alford's receptionist.

Myrtle: Cau.—*The Sound and the Fury* (1929)—Bkg.—Married daughter of the sheriff.

Myrtle, Miss: Cau.—*Sanctuary* (1931)—Bkg.—A fat, prostitute friend of Miss Reba Rivers; see Uncle Bud.

N

Nancy: See Mannigoe, Nancy.

Natalie: Cau.—*The Sound and the Fury* (1929)—Bkg.—Girl Caddy saw Quentin hugging in the barn.

Nate: Neg.—"Hand Upon the Waters" (1939)—Bkg.—He was to notify the sheriff if Gavin Stevens did not come out of Lonnie Grinnup's camp.

Nelson, Aunt Callie: Neg.—*Soldiers' Pay* (1926)—Bkg.—Old Negress who helped raise Donald Mahon.

Nelson, Loosh: Neg.—*Soldiers' Pay* (1926)—Bkg.—Grandson of Callie Nelson; a corporal.

Newberry, Col.: Cau.—*The Unvanquished* (1938)—Bkg.—Rosa Millard gets her last order of mules from him.

Nightingale, Mr.: Cau.—*The Mansion* (1959)—Bkg.—Cobbler; father of Tug whom he disowned when Tug joined the Yankee Army (McLendon's group).

Nightingale, Tug: Cau.—*The Mansion* (1959)—Bkg.—Joined McLendon's company of soldiers in World War I against his father's wishes; moronic hostler and house painter.

Nunnery, Mrs.: Cau.—*The Town* (1957)—Bkg.—Cedric's Mother.

Nunnery, Cedric: Cau.—*The Town* (1957)—Bkg.—Supposedly lost five-year-old whom Eck Snopes died hunting.

O

Odlethrop, Mrs.: Cau.—"Monk" (1937)—Bkg.—Supposedly Monk's paternal grandmother.

Odlethrop, Mr. and Mrs.: Cau.—"Monk" (1937)—Bkg.— Monk's parents.

Odlethrop, Stonewall Jackson (Monk): Cau.—"Monk" (1937)—Major—Moron; possibly a cretin, who is tricked into a murder and hanged for it.

Odum, Cliff: Cau.—*The Hamlet* (1940)—Bkg.—Helped Vynie Snopes get the milk separator.

Ord, Mr. and Mrs. Matt: Cau.—*Pylon* (1935)—Minor—Matt is a champion flyer; resident of New Valois; tries to prevent Roger Shumann from flying a dangerous plane. She is mentioned.

Oscar: Neg.—"The Fire and the Hearth" (1942)—Bkg.—An Edmonds' worker.

Osgood: Cau.—*A Fable* (1954)—Bkg.—R.A.F. hero.

Otis: Cau.—*The Reivers* (1962)—Minor—Fifteen-year-old protégé of Miss Corrie; steals Minnie's gold tooth.

Ott, Jimmy: Cau.—*Pylon* (1935)—Bkg.—Flyer at New Valois.

Otto: Cau.—"The Kid Learns" (1925)—Minor—Cohort of the Kid's and encourages him to challenge the Wop.

Owl-by-Night: Ind.—"A Courtship" (1948)—Bkg.—Mentioned.

P

Painter: Cau.—*Idyll in the Desert* (1931)—Bkg.—Apparently a rancher near the tuberculosis camp.

Paoli: Cau.—"Knight's Gambit" (1949)—Bkg.—Max Harriss's Italian fencing instructor.

Paralee: Neg.—*Intruder in the Dust* (1948)—Bkg.—Aleck Sander's mother; cook for the Stevens-Mallison group. Cf. Sander, Guster.

Parker: Cau.—*The Sound and the Fury* (1929)—Bkg.—Operator of a Jefferson restaurant where Jason eats breakfast.

Parsham: Cau.—*The Reivers* (1962)—Bkg.—Town is named for him.

Pate, Lucy (Mrs. Jack Houston): Cau.—*The Hamlet* (1940) —Minor—Helped Jack through school; later married him; killed by a stallion; cf. Bookwright, Letty.

Patterson: Cau.—*The Sound and the Fury* (1929)—Bkg.—Boy; partner of young Jason in kite business.

Patterson, Mr. and Mrs.: Cau.—*The Sound and the Fury* (1929)—Bkg.—Benjy and Caddy carried her a letter from Uncle Maury with whom she seems to have been having an affair.

Paul: Cau.—*A Fable* (1954)—Bkg.—Breton; follower of the Corporal.

Peabody, Lucius Quintus (Loosh): Cau.—*Sartoris* (1929)— Minor—The eighty-seven-year-old town doctor; long time friend of the Sartoris family; special friend of Mrs. Jenny S. Du Pre. *The Sound and the Fury* (1929)—Bkg.—Mentioned as fat. *As I Lay Dying* (1930)—Minor—Called Doc Peabody; fat seventy-year-old doctor who came to see Addie and later attended Cash Bundren's leg. "Beyond" (1933)—Bkg.—Attending physician at the death of Judge Allison. *The Hamlet* (1940)—Bkg.—Mentioned as source of whisky. *The Town* (1957)—Bkg.—Old town doctor. *The Reivers* (1962)—Bkg.— Attended those hurt in the Hogganbeck-Ludus fracas.

Peabody, Dr. L. Q., Jr.: Cau.—*Sartoris* (1929)—Bkg.—Son of Dr. L. Q. Peabody; engaged in medical research in New York.

Pearson: Cau.—"The Tall Men" (1941)—Major—Narrator for a large part of the story; sympathetic portrait of a misunderstanding government agent.

Peebles, E. E.: Cau.—*Light in August* (1932)—Bkg.—Joanna Burden's Memphis lawyer.

Pete: Cau.—"Home" (1925)—Bkg.—Jean-Baptiste ponders Pete's reaction to his refusal to participate in a crime.

Pete: Cau.—*Pylon* (1935)—Bkg.—Owner of restaurant where Reporter gets absinthe.

Pete: Cau.—*The Wild Palms* (1929) in "Wild Palms"—Bkg. —Mexican houseboy at San Antonio brothel.

Pete: Cau.—*Requiem for a Nun* (1951)—Minor—Brother to Alabama Red; tried to blackmail Temple D. Stevens.

Pettibone: Cau.—*Absalom, Absalom!* (1936)—Bkg.—Virginia planter.

Pettigrew: Cau.—"Beyond" (1933)—Bkg.—Mortician (or lawyer or executor) who allows the misplaced grave and the use of an automobile hearse.

Pettigrew, Thomas Jefferson: Cau.—*Requiem for a Nun* (1951)—Bkg.—Mail rider for whom Jefferson was named.

Peyton, George: Cau.—*The Reivers* (1962)—Bkg.—Famous dog trainer who attends quail season at Parsham.

Philadelphia (Philadelphy): Neg.—*The Unvanquished* (1938)—Wife of Loosh (Lucius). "My Grandmother Millard" (1943)—Bkg.—Younger Negro cook; wife of Lucius.

Philip: Cau.—"Elly" (1934)—Bkg.—Elly's fiance; Jefferson bank cashier.

Philip: Filipino—"Golden Land" (1935)—Bkg.—Houseboy of Ira Ewing, Realtor.

Phoebe: Neg.—"The Bear" (1942)—Bkg.—Wife of Roscius; mother of Thucydides; she and Roscius brought from Carolina by L. Q. C. McCaslin; d. and buried 1 August 1849.

Picklock: Cau.—*A Fable* (1954)—Minor—One of the soldiers who are looking for a body for the tomb of the Unknown Soldier.

Pinckski: Cau.—"Pennsylvania Station" (1934)—Minor—Undertaker who kept Mrs. Gihon's money.

Pinkie: Neg.—"Artist at Home" (1933)—Bkg.—Howes's cook courted for a time by Johnny Blair.

Ploeckner: Cau.—*Sartoris* (1929)—Bkg.—German aviator who shot John Sartoris's plane down in World War I.

Polchek: Cau.—*A Fable* (1954)—Minor—Betrayed the Corporal.

Poleymus: Cau.—*The Reivers* (1962)—Bkg.—Constable in Parsham; jails Butch Lovemaiden and Boon Hogganbeck.

Pomp: Neg.—*Light in August* (1932)—Bkg.—Slave to Gail Hightower (I); husband to nanny of Gail Hightower, D.D.

Popeye: See Vitelli, Popeye.

Pose: Cau.—"Hand Upon the Waters" (1939)—Bkg.—Contributed to Lonnie Grinnup's funeral expense.

Potter, Jack: Cau.—"Cheest!" (1925)—Major—Jockey who narrates this story of self-glorification.

Powell, John: Neg.—*The Reivers* (1962)—Bkg.—Chief hostler whose pistol Boon Hogganbeck borrows to shoot at Ludus.

Powers, Mrs. Margaret: See Mrs. Margaret Powers Mahon.

Powers, Richard: Cau.—*Soldiers' Pay* (1926)—Bkg.—Husband of Margaret Powers; Rufus Madden's company commander; shot in the face by one of his own men (Dewey Burney) in Europe.

Priest, Alexander; Maury, Jr.; and Lessep: Cau.—*The Reivers* (1962)—Bkg.—Younger brothers of Lucius Priest.

Priest, Lucius: Cau.—*The Reivers* (1962)—Major—Narrator; jockey for Coppermine (alias Lightning); tells the story in 1961 to his own grandson; eleven when the incidents occurred in 1905; son of Maury and Alison Priest.

Priest, Mr. Lucius and Mrs. Sarah Edmonds: Cau.—*The Reivers* (1962)—Major—Grandparents of Lucius Priest, narrator; called Boss Priest, he is the president of the Bank of Jefferson.

Priest, Mr. and Mrs. Maurice (Sallie Hampton): Cau.—*The Town* (1957)—Bkg.—Mrs. Priest received a corsage and Mr. Priest returned a fist.

Priest, Mr. Maury and Mrs. Alison Lessep: Cau.—*The Reivers* (1962)—Minor—Parents of Lucius Priest, the eleven-year-old narrator. Mr. Maury Priest operates the livery stable.

Pritchel, Wesley: Cau.—"An Error in Chemistry" (1946)—Minor—Ellie P. Flint's father who is murdered and then impersonated by his son-in-law, Joel Flint.

Provine, Lucius: Cau.—"A Bear Hunt" (1934)—Major—At the time of the story a worn out prankster; earlier known as Butch; butt of Ratliff's joke to cure hiccups. He, his unnamed brother, and Jack Bonds were known as the Provine gang. In the *Big Woods* (1955) version this role is given to Lucius Hogganbeck.

Provine, Mrs. Lucius: Cau.—"A Bear Hunt" (1934)—Bkg.— Seamstress; three children also mentioned. See Provine, Lucius.

Provine, Wilbur: Cau. *The Town* (1957)—Bkg.—Moonshiner from Frenchman's Bend.

Pruitt, Mr. and Mrs.: Cau.—"That Will Be Fine" (1935)— Minor—President of Compress Association; she is consort of Uncle Rodney.

Pruitt, Mrs.: Cau.—"Tomorrow" (1940)—Bkg.—Rufus Pruitt's mother who tells some interesting details about S. J. Fentry.

Pruitt, Rufus: Cau.—"Tomorrow" (1940)—Bkg.—Neighbor of S. J. Fentry.

Q

Quentin, Miss: See [Compson], Miss Quentin.

Quick, Uncle Ben: Cau.—*The Hamlet* (1940)—Bkg.—Owner of the goats Flem bought. "Tomorrow" (1940)—Bkg.—Owner of the sawmill where S.J. Fentry worked.

Quick, Isham: Cau.—"Tomorrow" (1940)—Major—Told Gavin Stevens the completing details about S.J. Fentry; son of Ben Quick.

Quick, Lon (Old): *As I Lay Dying* (1930)—Bkg.—Man from whom Jewel bought his spotted horse.

Quick, Lon (Young): *As I Lay Dying* (1930)—Bkg.—Son of (old) Lon; neighbor to Bundrens; found Doc Peabody's buckboard. *The Hamlet* (1940)—Bkg.—Owner of a sawmill; purchaser of spotted horse; left gate open so that spotted horses got out.

Quick, Solon: Cau.—"Shingles for the Lord" (1943)—Major—Started the business of work units that turned out to be "dog units." Shall Not Perish" (1943)—Bkg.—Owner and operator of school bus which Griers ride into Jefferson. *The Mansion* (1959)—Bkg.—Constable at Frenchman's Bend during Mink Snopes–Jack Houston controversy.

Quick, Mrs. Solon: Cau.—"Shall Not Perish" (1943)—Bkg.— Her husband makes her pay out of her egg money for the ride into Jefferson on his school bus.

Quick, Theron: Cau.—*The Mansion* (1959)—Bkg.—One of the trio courting Eula Varner when she became pregnant; left country.

Quinn, Doctor: Cau.—*Sanctuary* (1931)—Bkg.—Miss Reba Rivers's doctor who treated Temple Drake.

Quistenberry, Dink: Cau.—*The Town* (1957)—Bkg.—Operator of the Jefferson Hotel for his in-laws the Snopes.

R

Rachel: Neg.—*Sartoris* (1929)—Bkg.—Belle Mitchell's excellent cook.

Rachel, Aunt: Neg.—"That Evening Sun" (1931)—Bkg.— Supposedly Jesus's mother.

Rainey, Paul: Cau.—*The Reivers* (1962)—Bkg.—Wealthy landowner who is a hound expert.

Ralph: Cau.—*The Wild Palms* (1939) in "Wild Palms"—Bkg. —Brother to Charlotte Rittenmeyer.

Ratcliffe: Cau.—*Requiem for a Nun* (1951)—Bkg.—Greatgreat-grandfather of V.K. Ratliff.

Ratcliffe, (Ratliff), Nelly: Cau.—*The Mansion* (1959)—Bkg. —Married the first Vladimir Kyrilytch in the U.S. and he took her name.

Ratliff, V. K.: Cau.—"A Bear Hunt" (1934)—Major—Sewing machine salesman who tricks Butch Provine with the joke that backfires. *The Hamlet* (1940)—Major—Matches wits with Flem Snopes on the Frenchman's place; as a child he had been a friend of Ab Snopes; in addition to selling sewing machines, he barters; narrates many of the incidents, especially those dealing with Snopes background material; owner of house in Jefferson; kindly disposed man who does a little snopesing himself. *The Town* (1957)—Minor—He, Vladimir Kyrilytch Ratliff, is the confidant of Gavin Stevens; amiable realist. *The Mansion* (1959)—Major—Helps Gavin Stevens try to keep Flem Snopes in check; narrates parts of the novel; sells radios and televisions as well as sewing machines. See Suratt, V. K.

Reba, Miss: See Rivers, Miss Reba.

Red (Alabama): Cau.—*Sanctuary* (1931)—Bkg.—Popeye obtained gratification by watching him make love to Temple Drake; later killed by Popeye. *Requiem for a Nun* (1951)— Bkg.—Mentioned in same role as above.

Redlaw: See Redmond, Ben J.

Redmond, Ben J.: Cau.—*Sartoris* (1929)—Bkg.—Col. John Sartoris's political opponent and former railroad partner; a lawyer; murdered Col. Sartoris. Named Redlaw here. *The Unvanquished* (1938)—Minor—Killed Col. Sartoris and forced out of town by Bayard (elder). Called Ben J. Redmond; a lawyer; former railroad partner and political opponent of intolerant Col. Sartoris. *Requiem for a Nun* (1951)—Bkg.— Mentioned as carpetbagger who joined Col. Sartoris and General Compson in the railroad venture, but was ultimately squeezed out.

Reed, Susan: Cau.—"Hair" (1931)—Major—Orphan whom

Henry Stribling marries after she grows up; her reputation in Jefferson was bad.

Reeves: Cau.—"Turnabout" (1932)—Bkg.—Crew member of Hope and Smith's torpedo boat.

Reichmann: Cau.—*Mosquitoes* (1927)—Bkg.—A New Orleans businessman approached by Major Ayers about an investment in laxatives.

Reinhardt: Cau.—"Honor" (1930)—Bkg.—Owner of the auto agency from which Buck Monaghan is becoming unemployed.

Renfrow: Cau.—*The Town* (1957)—Bkg.—Employed Eck Snopes as night watchman for oil tank.

Reno: Neg.—*Sartoris* (1929)—Bkg.—Led the little band that Bayard (young) hired to serenade the girls.

Reporter: Cau.—*Pylon* (1935)—Major—The unnamed central character; newspaper reporter; becomes associated with the Shumanns and tries unsuccessfully to aid them; his mother is mentioned. Cf. Mr. and Mrs. Hurtz.

Res: Cau.—*Sartoris* (1929)—Bkg.—Cashier in Sartoris bank.

Rhodes, Miss: Cau.—*The Reivers* (1962)—Bkg.—Narrator Lucius Priest's school teacher.

Richard: Neg.—*Sartoris* (1929)—Bkg.—Mandy's helper in MacCallum kitchen.

Richardson, Dr.: Cau.—*The Wild Palms* (1939) in "Wild Palms"—Bkg.—Surgeon at hospital where Charlotte Rittenmeyer dies.

Richthofen: Cau.—*Sartoris* (1929)—Bkg.—German aviation instructor.

Riddell: Cau.—*The Town* (1957)—Bkg.—Little boy with polio which causes the Jefferson schools to close.

Rideout, Aaron: Cau.—*The Hamlet* (1940)—Bkg.—Ratliff's partner in Jefferson side-street restaurant. His cousin, also a Rideout, is mentioned.

Rideout, Dr.: Cau.—"The Fire and the Hearth" (1942)—Bkg. —Summoned to aid Aunt Molly Beauchamp.

Rider: Neg.—"Pantaloon in Black" (1940)—Major—Buries his wife and spends a tragic day trying to find peace; lynched by relatives of Birdsong whom he has slain over a crooked dice game; wife named Mannie.

Ringo: See Marengo.

Rittenmeyer, Ann: Cau.—*The Wild Palms* (1939) in "Wild Palms"—Bkg.—Younger daughter of Charlotte and Francis Rittenmeyer.

Rittenmeyer, Charlotte: Cau.—*The Wild Palms* (1939) in "Wild Palms"—Bkg.—Older daughter of Francis and Charlotte Rittenmeyer.

Rittenmeyer, Charlotte: Cau.—*The Wild Palms* (1939) in "Wild Palms"—Major—Left her husband and children to live with Henry Wilbourne, hoping to nurture the love they had found; dies in the hospital of a small Mississippi coastal town from an abortion Henry performed on her.

Rittenmeyer, Francis: Cau.—*The Wild Palms* (1939) in "Wild Palms"—Major—husband who refuses to give Charlotte a divorce though he permits her affair with Harry Wilbourne; tries to aid Harry after Charlotte's death.

Rivers, Lee: Cau.—*Soldiers' Pay* (1926)—Bkg.—An immature suitor of Cecily Saunders; had one year at Princeton.

Rivers, Miss Reba: Cau.—*Sanctuary* (1931)—Minor—Operated the Memphis brothel where Popeye took Temple; Virgil Snopes and Fonzo [Winbush] roomed there. *The Mansion* (1959)—Bkg.—Operated the bordel where potent Virgil Snopes boards. *The Reivers* (1962)—Major—Abets Boon Hogganbeck and Lucius Priest in their racing affairs. At her bordel where Everbe Corinthia works, Lucius Priest gets his education; shrewd; motherly; kind; lover of Mr. L. Binford, *q.v.*

Robert, Uncle: Cau.—"Uncle Willy" (1935)—Bkg.—Uncle of narrator.

Robyn, Gus: Gus is a name that Theodore and Patricia Robyn apply to one another.

Robyn, Henry (Hank): Cau.—*Mosquitoes* (1927)—Bkg.—Father of Theodore and Patricia Robyn.

Robyn, Patricia: Cau.—*Mosquitoes* (1927)—Major—Mrs. Maurier's niece who is amazingly perceptive and frank. She is sexually attractive to the men though she has an epicene figure; twin to Theodore.

Robyn, Theodore: Cau.—*Mosquitoes* (1927)—Major—Mrs. Maurier's nephew who is going to Yale in September; twin to Pat; causes yacht to go aground.

Rodney, Uncle: Cau.—"That Will Be Fine" (1935)—Major—Adulterous, thieving, maternal uncle to Georgie; killed.

Roebuck, John Wesley: Cau.—*The Town* (1957)—Bkg.—Young companion of Chick Mallison.

Rogers: Cau.—*The Sound and the Fury* (1929)— Bkg.—Operator of restaurant where Earl eats lunch. *Sartoris* (1929)—Bkg. —Mentioned as restaurant owner in Jefferson.

Rogers, Howard: Cau.—"Honor" (1930)—Major—Honorable husband of the woman Buck Monaghan has an affair with.

Rogers, Ken: Cau.—"The Liar" (1925)—Bkg.—Sheriff at Mitchell.

Rogers, Mrs. Mildred: Cau.—"Honor" (1930)—Major—Buck Monaghan's lover; she remains with her husband.

Roscius (Roskus): Neg.—"The Bear" (1942)—Bkg.—Slave whom L.Q.C. McCaslin brought from Carolina; husband of Phoebe; father of Thucydides. Died and buried 12 January 1841.

Rosie: Neg.—"That Will Be Fine" (1935)—Bkg.—Cook who accompanies Georgie and his parents to Mottstown.

Roskus: See Gibson, Roskus.

Ross, Frank and Martha: Cau.—"The Brooch" (1936)—Minor—Martha's phone call brings the marriage of Howard and Amy Boyd to a crisis.

Rouncewell: Cau.—"Go Down, Moses" (1941)—Bkg.—Owner of Jefferson store which S. W. Beauchamp broke into.

Rouncewell: Cau.—*The Reivers* (1962)—Bkg.—Gasoline dealer for Yoknapatawpha County and possibly the husband of boarding house keeper.

Rouncewell, Mrs.: Cau.—"Tomorrow" (1940)—Bkg.—Operator of boarding house in Jefferson. *The Town* (1957)—Bkg.—Florist. *The Mansion* (1959)—Bkg.—Operated the Commercial Hotel until it became Snopes Hotel. *The Reivers* (1962)—Bkg.—Operates a boarding house in Jefferson.

Rouncewell, Whit: Cau.—*The Town* (1957)—Bkg.—Son of Mrs. Rouncewell, the florist. *The Mansion* (1959)—Bkg.—Saw burglars in Uncle Willy Christian's drugstore.

Roxanne, Aunt: Neg.—"My Grandmother Millard" (1943)—Bkg.—Servant of Mrs. Jason Compson (II).

Roy: Cau.—*Mosquitoes* (1927)—Bkg.—Boy friend of Jenny Steinbauer's girl friend Thelma Frances.

Runner: Cau.—*A Fable* (1954)—Major—British soldier striving for peace; relinquished colonel's rank to become a runner, diplomatic courier.

Russell: Cau.—*Light in August* (1932)—Bkg.—Deputy sheriff in Mottstown.

Russell, Ab: Cau.—*The Sound and the Fury* (1929)—Bkg.—Farmer from whom Jason (IV) borrows an air pump.

Rust, Everbe Corinthia: Cau.—"The Leg" (1934)—Major—George's girl who died apparently of fright.

Rust, Jotham: Cau.—"The Leg" (1934)—Major—Everbe C. Rust's brother who tries to kill Davy; Jotham believes Davy caused his sister's death.

Rust, Simon: Cau.—"The Leg" (1934)—Bkg.—Father of Everbe C. Rust and Jotham Rust; lock keeper on the Thames.

Ryan: Cau.—"Frankie and Johnny" (1925)—Major—Considers Johnny a young tough. "The Kid Learns" (1925)—Minor—Johnny, long known to Ryan, takes the girl he has rescued to Ryan's home.

Ryan, Mrs.: Cau.—"The Kid Learns" (1925)—Bkg.—Policeman Ryan's wife.

S

Saddie: Neg/Cau.—"There Was a Queen" (1933)—Bkg.— Elnora's daughter.

Sales, Mac: Cau.—*Pylon* (1935)—Minor—Federal official who qualifies the plane Roger Shumann dies in.

Salmon: Cau.—*Light in August* (1932)—Bkg.—Owner of rental car in Mottstown.

Sam: Neg.—*The Hamlet* (1940)—Bkg.—Servant to the Will Varner Family.

Samson, Mr. and Mrs. (Rachel): Cau.—*Sartoris* (1929)— Bkg.—Farmer who lives near a bridge. *As I Lay Dying* (1930) —Bkg.—Neighborly farmers who shelter the Bundrens one night.

Samson: Neg.—*The Town* (1957)—Bkg.—Hotel porter.

Samuel: Cau.—*"The Leg"* (1934)—Bkg.—Helped Davy with the boat in the Thames.

Sander, Aleck: Neg.—*Intruder in the Dust* (1948)—Minor— Son of Paralee; companion who helped Chick Mallison and Miss Habersham in their investigation of the Gowrie grave. *The Town* (1957)—Bkg.—Son of Big Top and Guster; Chick Mallison's playmate.

Sarah: Cau.—"That Will Be Fine" (1935)—Minor—Mother of narrator; her shiftless brother Uncle Rodney, is killed.

Sartoris—daughters of Col. John: Cau.—*Sartoris* (1929)— Bkg.—Two daughters are mentioned; one older than Bayard (old) was twenty-two in 1869; one younger than Bayard was seventeen in 1869.

Sartoris, Bayard (infant): Cau.—*Sartoris* (1929)—Bkg.— Infant son of Bayard (young) and Caroline White; died at birth.

Sartoris, Bayard (of North Carolina): Cau.—*Sartoris* (1929) —Brother of Col. John Sartoris and Mrs. Virginia S. Du Pre who died at twenty-three before the second Battle of Manassas because he went back into an enemy camp for anchovies; aide to Jeb Stuart. *The Unvanquished* (1938)—Bkg.—Mentioned in same role.

Sartoris, Bayard (old): Cau.—*Sartoris* (1929)—Major—Grandfather of Bayard (young) around whom the story centers; president of the bank; son of Col. John Sartoris; dies December 1919 while riding in his grandson's car. "Rose for Emily" (1930)—Bkg.—Col. Sartoris is mayor of Jefferson in 1894; nature of the reference implies that Col. John Sartoris is intended but he died in 1876. "There Was a Queen" (1933)—Bkg.—Deceased son of Col. John Sartoris; nephew of Mrs. Jenny Du Pre, the Queen; half-brother to Elnora. *The Unvanquished* (1938) —Major—Narrator and perpetrator of much of the activity, which covers his life from twelve to twenty-four; this is the story of his maturing; son of Col. John Sartoris whose death he avenged in the final chapter; he had earlier revenged the murder of his grandmother Mrs. Rosa Millard. *The Hamlet* (1940)—Bkg.—Mentioned as son of Col. John Sartoris and avenger of Mrs. Rosa Millard. "The Bear" (1942)—Bkg.— Mentioned as camp visitor. "My Grandmother Millard" (1943) —Major—Young narrator; unnamed; Ringo is the companion with whom he fights Yankees. *Requiem for a Nun* (1951)— Bkg.—Banker in Jefferson. *The Town* (1957)—Bkg.—Banker who dies in his grandson's auto though he had fathered the edict that autos should be banned from the streets of Jefferson. *The Mansion* (1959)—Bkg.—First president of Merchants and Farmers Bank. *The Reivers* (1962)—Bkg.—President of Merchants and Farmers Bank; Lucius Priest (Sr.) gets an automobile to thwart Bayard's attempt to ban them.

Sartoris, Bayard (young): Cau.—*Sartoris* (1929)—Major— Twenty-six-year-old veteran of World War I who cannot reconcile himself to live without John, his younger twin brother; son of John (II) and Lucy Cranston Sartoris; first married to Caroline White who died in childbirth while he was still in the R. A. F.; later married to Narcissa Benbow and father of a son (Benbow); died in crash of an experimental plane he was testing; (March 16, 1893—June 11, 1920). "Ad Astra" (1931)—Minor—Disgruntled R. F. C. pilot. "There Was a Queen" (1933)—Long-dead husband of Narcissa B. Sartoris; father of Benbow Sartoris. *The Town* (1957)—Bkg.—Grandson of Col. Bayard Sartoris; noted for reckless driving which kills his grandfather. *The Mansion* (1959)—Bkg.—Great-grandson of Col. John Sartoris; killed in an airplane crash in Dayton; Bayard (old) dies of a heart attack while riding in his auto.

Sartoris, Benbow: Cau.—*Sartoris* (1929)—Bkg.—Son of Bayard (young) and Narcissa B. Sartoris; born near end of novel. *Sanctuary* (1931)—Bkg.—Mentioned as ten-year-old son of Narcissa. "There Was a Queen" (1933)—Minor—Twelve-year-old son of Narcissa; Aunt Jenny's pet; very independent. "Knight's Gambit" (1949)—Bkg.—Mentioned as soldier already on active duty in England (World War II). *The Town* (1957)—Bkg.—Mentioned as above. *The Mansion* (1959)—Bkg.—Excellent bird shot at nineteen.

Sartoris, Mrs. Caroline White: Cau.—*Sartoris* (1929)—Bkg.—Bayard (young) Sartoris's first wife who died in childbirth October 27, 1918; son was named Bayard nine months before birth.

Sartoris, Drusilla Hawk: Cau.—*The Unvanquished* (1938)—Major—Spirited young woman who fought for the Southern cause; engaged to Gavin Breckbridge who died at Shiloh; cousin by marriage to Col. John Sartoris whom she later married; Bayard (old) Sartoris's fourth cousin.

Sartoris, Colonel John: Cau.—*Sartoris* (1929)—Bkg.—Recalled here as gallant Confederate soldier, builder of a railroad, and politician. He had been killed by his former partner Redlaw long before the incidents of this novel. (1823–September 4, 1876). *The Sound and the Fury* (1929)—Bkg.—Mentioned as conversing with Quentin Compson's grandfather. *Light in August* (1932)—Bkg.—Mentioned as killer of Joanna Burden's grandfather and her half-brother. "There Was a Queen" (1933) —Bkg.—Appears in the genealogy as brother of Mrs. Virginia Sartoris Du Pre and Bayard (North Carolina); father of Bayard (old) and Elnora. *Absalom, Absalom!* (1936)—Bkg.— Mentioned as Confederate colonel whom Sutpen replaced in regimental election. *The Unvanquished* (1938)—Major—Daring Civil War hero; father of narrator (Bayard); son-in-law to Mrs. Rosa Millard; marries Drusilla Hawk; finally his erstwhile railroad partner, Ben J. Redmond, kills him. "Barn Burning" (1939)—Bkg.—Col. Sartoris (Sarty) Snopes, son of Ab, is his namesake. *The Hamlet* (1940) Bkg.—Mentioned as one who shot Ab Snopes in the heel when Ab tried to steal his stallion. "The Bear" (1942)—Bkg.—Mentioned as Confederate soldier. "My Grandmother Millard" (1943)—Minor—Came home to give the bride away; his wife had been Rosa Millard's daughter. "Shall Not Perish" (1943)—Bkg.—Mentioned as Confederate leader. *Requiem for a Nun* (1951)—Bkg.—He, Redmond, and General Compson built a railroad; Civil War exploits mentioned. *The Town* (1957)—Bkg.—Many details of his life add color to the background; commander of the group which reportedly hanged Ab Snopes for horse stealing. *The Mansion* (1959)—Bkg.—Mentioned as Civil War hero; railroad builder. *The Reivers* (1962)—Bkg.—Mentioned as hunter, soldier, railroader, father of banker.

Sartoris, Mrs. John (Colonel): Cau.—*The Unvanquished* (1938)—Bkg.—Mentioned as daughter of Rosa Millard; cousin of Drusilla Hawk; mother of Bayard; deceased at time of novel.

Sartoris, John (II): Cau.—*Sartoris* (1929)—Bkg.—Mentioned as son of Bayard (old)—father of twins, Bayard (young) and

John (young); husband of Lucy Cranston Sartoris; died of yellow fever and old bullet wound received in Spanish-American War. "There Was a Queen" (1933)—Bkg.—Mentioned as Bayard (old) Sartoris's son. "The Bear" (1942)—Bkg.—Mentioned as accompanying his father to de Spain's hunting camp on the day that Old Ben is killed.

Sartoris, John (Johnny) (young): Cau.—*Sartoris* (1929)—Bkg.—Killed in World War I; remembered here as the more illustrious of the twins; his spirit is a potent force in the life of his older twin brother, Bayard (young). (b. March 16, 1893—d. July 5, 1918). "All the Dead Pilots" (1931)—Major—Southerner in the R. F. C. who is killed fighting in France in World War I; defeated his amatory rival Spoomer. "There Was a Queen" (1933)—Bkg.—Mentioned as having died in France. *The Mansion* (1959)—Bkg.—Col. John Sartoris's great-grandson; twin to Bayard (young); killed in France.

Sartoris, Mrs. Lucy Cranston: Cau.—*Sartoris* (1929)—Bkg.—Wife of John Sartoris (II); mother of twins Bayard and John.

Sartoris, Mrs. Narcissa Benbow: Cau.—*Sartoris* (1929)—Major—Twenty-six-year-old sister of Horace Benbow; marries Bayard (young) Sartoris and gives birth to Benbow Sartoris on the day of his father's death. *Sanctuary* (1931)—Minor—Widow of Bayard (young) Sartoris for ten years; sister of Horace Benbow; cooperates with District Attorney Graham to defeat Horace in the Goodwin case. "There Was a Queen" (1933)—Major—Story centers around her (widow of Bayard and mother of Benbow) as "unquality" in the Sartoris home; redeems [Byron Snopes's] obscene love letters by committing adultery with a government agent, a Jewish Yankee. *The Town* (1957)—Bkg.—Mother of Benbow Sartoris; second wife of Bayard (young) Sartoris. *The Mansion* (1959)—Bkg.—Mentioned in same role as above.

Sartoris, Mrs. Virginia: See Du Pre, Mrs. Virginia S.

Saunders, Cecily: Cau.—*Soldiers' Pay* (1926)—Major—Donald Mahon's fiancee; very flirtatious; finally marries George Farr after trying to fulfill her commitment to Donald.

Saunders, Mr. Robert and Mrs. Minnie: Cau.—*Soldiers' Pay* (1926)—Minor—Parents of Cecily and Robert; father tries to get Cecily to visit Donald Mahon.

Saunders, Robert, Jr.: Cau.—*Soldiers' Pay* (1926)—Minor—Cecily's younger brother; type of the curious young boy.

Schluss: Cau.—*Soldiers' Pay* (1926)—Bkg.—Ladies' underwear salesman on the train to Charlestown, Georgia.

Schofield, Dr.: Cau.—"The Tall Men" (1941)—Minor—Physician who removes Buddy McCallum's leg.

Schultz, Rev. and Mrs.: Cau.—"Uncle Willy" (1935)—Major—Minister who tries to help cure Uncle Willy Christian; she is mentioned.

Secretary: Neg.—"Uncle Willy" (1935)—Major—Uncle Willy Christian's chauffeur for the car and the plane.

Semmes, Mr.: Cau.—"The Bear" (1942)—Bkg.—Memphis liquor dealer from whom Boon Hogganbeck and Ike McCaslin procure fresh supplies of whisky.

Shack: Cau.—*Sanctuary* (1931)—Bkg.—One of two college boys who trick the conductor.

Shegog, Reverend: Neg.—*The Sound and the Fury* (1929)—Bkg.—St. Louis preacher who preached at Dilsey Gibson's church on Easter Sunday, 1928.

Short, Herman: Cau.—*The Hamlet* (1940)—Bkg.—Former owner of horse Ab Snopes tries to trick Pat Stamper with.

Shumann, Dr. and Mrs. Carl: Cau.—*Pylon* (1935)—Bkg.—Parents of Roger; they take Jack Shumann; live in Myron, Ohio; he is a small town physician.

Shumann, Jack: Cau.—*Pylon* (1935)—Minor—Son of Laverne and either Roger Shuman or Jack Holmes; young boy.

Shumann, Roger and Laverne: Cau.—*Pylon* (1935)—Major—Pilot who races airplanes; Laverne's legal husband though neither of them knew whose child she had had; he is the son of a doctor; dies in the crash of a faulty plane; she is from Iowa; goes away with Jack Holmes after Roger's death.

Sibleigh: Cau.—*Sartoris* (1929)—Bkg.—R.A.F. comrade of Bayard and John Sartoris (the twins). *A Fable* (1954)—Bkg.—R.A.F. flyer.

Sickymo: Neg.—"The Bear" (1942)—Bkg.—Former slave; U.S. marshal during reconstruction; bootlegged whisky from sycamore tree. Cf. Mulberry.

Simmons: Cau.—*The Sound and the Fury* (1929)—Bkg.—Mentioned as possessor of key to Old Opera house where Jason (IV) found blank checks.

Simms: Cau.—*Light in August* (1932)—Bkg.—Owner of the sawmill where Byron Bunch, Joe Christmas, and Lucas Burch (alias Joe Brown) worked.

Simon: Neg.—"Race at Morning" (1955)—Bkg.—Cook at the hunting camp.

Simon: See Strother, Simon.

Skipworth: Cau.—*Intruder in the Dust* (1948)—Bkg.—Constable who arrests Lucas Beauchamp.

Smith, Lieutenant: Cau.—*A Fable* (1954)—Bkg.—British soldier who is knocked out by Runner.

Smith, Miss: Cau.—"Tomorrow" (1940)—Bkg.—Name S. J. Fentry gives for Buck Thorpe's mother; her maiden name was Thorpe.

Smith, Mrs.: Cau.—*Sartoris* (1929)—Bkg.—Receptionist in Dr. Brandt's office.

Smith, Essie Meadowfill: Cau.—*The Mansion* (1959)—Minor—Valedictorian of her high school class; employee of the Bank of Jefferson; gains wealth from Snopes-Meadowfill feud (with the aid of Gavin Stevens); marries McKinley Smith.

Smith, McKinley: Cau.—*The Mansion* (1959)—Minor—Married Essie Meadowfill; ex-Marine corporal; built home in Eula Acres.

Smith, Midshipman Ronnie Boyce: Cau.—"Turnabout"—
(1932)—Minor—British sailor; foil for Hope; commander of
the torpedo boat.

Smitty: Cau.—*Pylon* (1935)—Bkg.—Feature writer for newspaper that Reporter works for.

Snopes: Cau.—*As I Lay Dying* (1930)—Horse trading nephew
of Flem Snopes; trades Anse Bundren a pair mules.

Snopes: Cau.—"The Hound" (1931)—Bkg.—Clerk at Varner's
store; possibly Flem.

Snopes: Cau.—"Shingles for the Lord" (1940)—Bkg.—Farmer
who is to help rebuild the church.

Snopes, Abner (Ab): Cau.—*The Unvanquished* (1938)—
Minor—Helps Miss Rosa Millard steal mules from the Yankees
and then sell them back; he gets her involved with Major
Grumby. "Barn Burning" (1939)—Major—The barn-burning
father of Col. Sartoris Snopes; once a professional horse trader;
husband of Lennie Snopes. *The Hamlet* (1940)—Minor—
Father of Flem Snopes and two daughters; younger son is mentioned by Ratliff; soured on the world. "My Grandmother Millard" (1943)—Type character for low white trash; Col. John
Sartoris's independent horse-captain. *The Town* (1957)—Bkg.
—Owner of watermelon patch; Flem's father; report that Ab
Snopes hanged during Civil War by Confederates probably
arose from Bayard (old) Sartoris's whipping him for involvement in Mrs. Rosa Millard's death. *The Mansion* (1959)—
Minor—Probably Flem's father; once evicted by Will Varner
for non-payment of rent.

Snopes, Admiral Dewey: Cau.—*The Town* (1957)—Bkg.—
Eckrum Snopes's youngest son. *The Mansion* (1959)—Bkg.—
Younger brother of Wallstreet Panic Snopes.

Snopes, Bilbo: Cau.—*The Town* (1957)—Bkg.—Son of I. O.
Snopes and his illegal wife; twin brother of Vardaman. *The
Mansion* (1959)—Bkg.—Mentioned as a Snopes.

Snopes, Byron: Cau.—*Sartoris* (1929)—Minor—Cashier in the Sartoris bank; writes obscene letters to Narcissa Benbow; robs the bank and leaves town. "There Was a Queen" (1933)—Bkg.—His letters turn up in government possession. *The Town* (1957)—Bkg.—Son of schoolmaster; Virgil's brother; sent his wild children to Flem. *The Mansion* (1959)—Bkg.—Mentioned as thieving bank clerk; father of half-wild children; lives in Mexico; his father is called Uncle Wesley Snopes.

Snopes, Clarence Eggleston: Cau.—*Sanctuary* (1931)—Minor —State senator; whoremonger who told Horace Benbow where Temple Drake was; later sold same information to the Memphis lawyer. *The Town* (1957)—Bkg.—Oldest son of I. O. Snopes and his illegal wife. *The Mansion* (1959)—Bkg.—Puppet senator who is defeated by the dalliance with the dog thicket.

Snopes, Colonel Sartoris: Cau.—"Barn Burning" (1939)— Major—Son of Abner Snopes, but like his mother, he seems to have a good streak; runs away. *The Hamlet* (1940)—Bkg.— Unnamed but alluded to by Ratliff.

Snopes, Doris: Cau.—*The Mansion* (1959)—Bkg.—Youngest brother of Clarence E. Snopes; almost burned at stake by Byron's children. (1961 Vintage edition of *The Town,* 1957) reports this incident with Doris in the same role, though the earlier version does not mention Doris and depicts Clarence as almost getting burned.)

Snopes, Eckrum (Eck): Cau.—*The Hamlet* (1940)—Cousin of I. O. Snopes; apprentice blacksmith; helps pay for solution to Ike Snopes's sodomy problem; large family; rather too honest to be a good Snopes. *The Town* (1957)—Minor—Father of Wallstreet Panic and Admiral Dewey Snopes; his death (he was blown up when he put a lantern into a gas tank) provided the initial capital for the Snopes Grocery. *The Mansion* (1959) —Bkg.—Mentioned as not a true Snopes.

Snopes, Mrs. Eckrum: Cau.—*The Town* (1957)—Bkg.—Landlady at Snopes Hotel for a time; receives $1,000 compensation for the death of her husband.

Snopes, Mrs. Eula Varner: Cau.—*The Hamlet* (1940)—Major—Youngest child of Will Varner; wife of Flem Snopes; sex-personified; cause of combat among young men of Frenchman's Bend; Hoake McCarron earns her virginity. *The Town* (1957)—Major—Mother of Linda Snopes by Hoake McCarron; mistress of Mandred de Spain; commits suicide when Flem uses her affair to gain control of the de Spain bank. *The Mansion* (1959)—Minor—Friend of Gavin Stevens; same role as in prior works.

Snopes, Flem: Cau.—*Sartoris* (1929)—Bkg.—Mentioned as first Snopes in town; owner of side-street cafe; vice-president of Sartoris bank; sponsoring relative for other Snopeses; unseen in novel. *As I Lay Dying* (1930)—Bkg.—Named as one who brought spotted horses to Yoknapatawpha twenty-five years prior to action of the novel. "Centaur in Brass" (1932)—Major—Materialist who panders his wife (unnamed) for his own benefit; loses brass; infant daughter mentioned. "Barn Burning" (1939)—Bkg.—Apparently the unnamed elder brother of Colonel Sartoris Snopes. *The Hamlet* (1940)—Major—Ascends to wealth and importance by extreme shrewdness; son of Ab Snopes; marries Eula Varner when she becomes pregnant by Hoake McCarron; receives Frenchman's place as Eula's dowry; outwits everyone; at the end of the novel he moves on toward Jefferson. *The Town* (1957)—Major—Impotent himself, he panders his wife to influential people, thus gaining wealth and position; becomes president of the de Spain bank; aids other Snopeses as they enter Jefferson life; legal father of Linda Snopes. *The Mansion* (1959)—Major—Very successful banker in Jefferson; murdered by his cousin Mink Snopes. *The Reivers* 1962)—Bkg.—His affairs with Mink Snopes are mentioned here; hotel keeper in Jefferson about 1905.

Snopes, I. O.: Cau.—*The Sound and the Fury* (1929)—Bkg.— Mentioned as cotton speculator. "Mule in the Yard" (1934)— Major—Owner of the mule though he feared animals; Mrs. Hait really outwitted him about the mule killing business which he and Mr. Hait had conducted. *The Hamlet* (1940)— Minor—Took over the blacksmith shop; his relation to Flem is unknown; taught school a while after Labove left; his legal wife's sudden appearance causes him to leave Frenchman's Bend. *The Town* (1957)—Minor—Father of Clarence, Vardaman, and Bilbo; "Mule in the Yard" is included here. *The Mansion* (1959)—Bkg.—Father of Clarence and M. W. Snopes to whose mother he was not legally married.

Snopes, Mrs. I. O.: Cau.—*The Town* (1957)—Bkg.—Woman to whom I. O. is bigamously allied; mother of Clarence, Vardaman, Bilbo.

Snopes, Isaac: Cau.—*The Hamlet* (1940)—Minor—Idiot cousin of Flem Snopes; his sodomy is the subject of the most poetic section of the novel.

Snopes, Launcelot (Lump): Cau.—*The Hamlet* (1940)—Bkg. —Clerked while Flem went on his honeymoon. *The Mansion* (1959)—Bkg.—Same role as above.

Snopes, Lennie: Cau.—"Barn Burning" (1939)—Major—Wife of Abner Snopes; begs him not to burn Major de Spain's barn. *The Hamlet* (1940)—Bkg.—Mentioned and described in role of Ab's wife, but unnamed.

Snopes, Linda: Cau.—*The Town* (1957)—Minor—Teenage daughter of Eula Varner Snopes and Hoake McCarron; Gavin Stevens is trying to save her from Snopesism. For other information see Kohl, Mrs. Linda Snopes.

Snopes, Mink (M. C.): Cau.—*The Hamlet* (1940)—Bkg.— Flem Snopes's very poor cousin who murders Jack Houston; Ratliff uses him as a pawn trying to outwit Flem. *The Town* (1957)—Bkg.—Murderer of Zack Houston; sentenced to life imprisonment. *The Mansion* (1959)—Major—Poor farmer, crushed by circumstance, pushed down by Flem, and finally aided by Linda Snopes; murders Jack Houston and Flem Snopes. Mentioned but unnamed in same role in *The Reivers* (1962). Cf. Cotton, Ernest.

Snopes, Mrs. Mink (Yettie): Cau.—*The Hamlet* (1940)— Minor—Moved into Jefferson to try to help Mink; they have two daughters. *The Mansion* (1959)—Bkg.—Writes to Mink at Parchman; called Yettie.

Snopes, Montgomery Ward: Cau.—*Sartoris* (1929)—Bkg.— Mentioned as refused by the Army because he had put tobacco under his left arm pit; accompanied Horace Benbow to France as a Y.M.C.A. worker during World War I; proved unsatisfactory. *The Town* (1957)—Minor—Former Y.M.C.A. worker with Gavin Stevens in World War I; his Atelier Monty, a pornographic peepshow, is discovered, but Flem rescues him to save family name. *The Mansion* (1959)—Minor—Helped frame Mink Snopes at Parchman where he had been sent for illegal possession of whisky instead of peddling pornography.

Snopes, Net: Cau.—"Barn Burning" (1939)—Minor—One of the lazy twin daughters of Abner and Lennie Snopes. Ab has two lazy daughters, unnamed, in *The Hamlet* (1940).

Snopes, Orestes (Res): Cau.—*The Mansion* (1959)—Minor— Hog raiser whose fuss with Mr. Meadowfill costs him the deed to part of his land, thanks to Gavin Stevens.

Snopes, Saint Elmo: Cau.—*The Hamlet* (1940)—Bkg.—I. O. Snopes's son who steals candy.

Snopes, Vardaman: Cau.—*The Town* (1957)—Bkg.—Son of I. O.; twin to Bilbo. *The Mansion* (1959)—Bkg.—Mentioned as a full-fledged Snopes.

Snopes, Virgil: Cau.—*Sanctuary* (1931)—Minor—He and Fonzo [Winbush] boarded at Miss Reba Rivers's bordel while attending barber college in Memphis. *The Town* (1957)—Bkg. —Brother of Byron. *The Mansion* (1959)—Bkg. Boarded with

Miss Reba Rivers; youngest son of Wesley Snopes; exceptional sexual potency.

Snopes, Mrs. Vynie: Cau.—*The Hamlet* (1940)—Bkg.—She gets her milk separator by selling cow; Ab Snopes first wife whose father takes her home and threatens to shoot Ab Snopes; they had no children.

Snopes, Wallstreet Panic: Cau.—*The Hamlet* (1940)—Bkg.— Oldest son of Eck, the blacksmith; helps catch spotted horses. *The Town* (1957)—Minor—Prospers honestly and becomes the owner of a large wholesale grocery business covering parts of three states. *The Mansion* (1959)—Bkg.—Attends the funeral of Flem Snopes.

Snopes, Mrs. Wallstreet Panic: Cau.—*The Town* (1957)— Minor—Hates evil snopesism with a passion and is determined to rise above it.

Snopes, Watkins Products (Wat): Cau.—*The Mansion* (1959)—Bkg.—Carpenter who remodeled the de Spain home for Flem Snopes whose distant relative he is.

Snopes, Wesley: Cau.—*The Town* (1957)—Bkg.—Unnamed, but mentioned as father of Byron and Virgil; school teacher who is tarred and feathered for lechery. *The Mansion* (1959)— Bkg.—Father of Virgil; revival song leader who was tarred and feathered for lechery; named here.

Snopes, Yettie: See Snopes, Mrs. Mink.

Sol: Neg.—*Sartoris* (1929)—Bkg.—Railroad porter.

Sometimes-Wakeup: Ind.—"A Justice" (1931)—Bkg.—Brother of the Chief before Doom; Doom's uncle.

Son Thomas: Neg.—*The Reivers* (1962)—Bkg.—Driver at Priest's livery stable.

Spilmer: Cau.—*The Town* (1957)—Bkg.—Mrs. Hait kills I. O. Snopes' mule behind Spilmer's house.

Spintrius: See Brownlee, Percival.

Spoade: Cau.—*The Sound and the Fury* (1929)—Bkg.—Fellow student with Quentin Compson at Harvard.

Spoade: Cau.—*The Mansion* (1959)—Bkg.—Charles Mallison's fellow Harvardian; his father had been classmate of Gavin Stevens at Harvard.

Spoomer, Captain: Cau.—"All the Dead Pilots" (1931)—Major —Amatory rival whom Johnny Sartoris embarrasses into leaving his area.

Stamper, Pat: Cau.—*The Hamlet* (1940)—Bkg.—Really sharp horse trader who tricked Abner Snopes. *The Mansion* (1959)— Bkg.—Mentioned as super horse trader.

Starnes, Mr. and Mrs. Joe: Cau.—"The Liar" (1925)—Minor —The wife collaborates to have her husband killed in an accident. But he is killed in a fight with the lover.

Starnes, Sophie: Cau.—"Hair" (1931)—Bkg.—Fiancée of Henry Stribling; she died, leaving him to care for her mother.

Starnes, Mr. and Mrs. Will: Cau.—"Hair" (1931)—Minor— Parents of Sophie. They lived at Division.

Stefan: Cau.—*A Fable* (1954)—Major—To Colonel Beale he was Boggan; to Captain Middleton, he was Brzewski; central, Christ-figure of the book though he says and does little; son of Supreme Commander of the Allied Armies; half-brother to Marthe Dement and Marya; his body comes to occupy the tomb of France's Unknown Soldier.

Steinbauer, Mr.: Cau.—*Mosquitoes* (1927)—Bkg.—Jenny's father.

Steinbauer, Genevieve (Jenny): Cau.—*Mosquitoes* (1927)— Major—Teenager brought on the cruise unexpectedly by Pat Robyn. A flirtatious girl who excites all the men and thwarts Mr. Talliafero cruelly.

Stevens, Bucky: Cau.—*Requiem for a Nun* (1951)—Bkg.—Son of Gowan and Temple D. Stevens.

Stevens, Gavin: Cau.—[Phi Beta Kappa graduate of Harvard; Ph.D. from Heidelberg]—"Hair" (1931)—Bkg.—District attorney and friend of the narrator (probably V. K. Ratliff). *Light in August* (1932)—Bkg.—Put the Hineses on the train

and philosophized about the story. "Smoke" (1932)—Major—
Working like Sherlock Holmes or Perry Mason, Gavin brings
the case to an astonishing close; county attorney. "Monk"
(1937)—Major—Discovered the truth about Bill Terrell's part
in Monk's death; an idealistic gentleman. "Hand Upon the
Waters" (1939)—Major—Discovered the facts about Lonnie
Grinnup's death and almost got killed; county attorney.
"Tomorrow" (1940)—Major—Graduate of Harvard, Heidelberg, and state university law school; defended Bookwright for
killing Buck Thorpe. "The Tall Men" (1941)—Bkg.—Lawyer
who advises Buddy McCallum about crop allotments. "Go
Down, Moses" (1941)—Major—County attorney who arranges
for the body of Samuel Worsham Beauchamp to be brought
home after electrocution. *Intruder in the Dust* (1948)—Major
—Helps rescue Lucas Beauchamp; county attorney. "An Error
in Chemistry" (1946)—Major—Catches the clever murderer of
Ellie P. Flint. "Knight's Gambit" (1949)—Major—Gambled,
saved the life of Gualdres, and won the woman; fifty-year-old
country attorney; this is perhaps the most complimentary
portrait of Gavin; witty, clever, warmly human, effective.
Requiem for a Nun (1951)—Major—Defended Nancy Mannigoe and helped Temple Drake Stevens confess. *The Town*
(1957)—Major—City attorney; loved Eula V. Snopes and
Linda Snopes; wanted to save Jefferson from snopesism, but
only fairly effective; narrates parts of the novel. *The Mansion*
(1959)—Major—Defender of Linda Snopes Kohl and Jefferson
from the Snopeses; lawyer; son of Judge Lemuel Stevens; twin
brother to Mrs. Margaret S. Mallison; marries Mrs. Melisandre
B. Harriss.

Stevens, Gowan: Cau.—*Sanctuary* (1931)—Major—Proposes to
Mrs. Narcissa B. Sartoris, then takes Temple Drake to Lee
Goodwin's where he leaves her. *Requiem for a Nun* (1951)—
Major—Temple D. Stevens's husband; father of the child
murdered by Nancy Mannigoe; nephew of Gavin Stevens.

The Town (1957)—Minor—Young first cousin of Gavin Stevens; helps narrate through Chick Mallison's memory.

Stevens, Judge Lemuel: Cau.—"A Rose for Emily" (1930)—Minor—Eighty-year-old judge. "Tomorrow" (1940)—Bkg.—Offered advice to his son Gavin about the case; called Captain Stevens. "An Error in Chemistry" (1946)—Bkg.—Gavin's father is mentioned. *The Town* (1957)—Bkg.—Lived in semi-active retirement in Jefferson; father of Mrs. Margaret Stevens Mallison and Gavin Stevens. *The Mansion* (1959)—Bkg.—Appointed by Judge Dukinfield to hear the case against Mayor de Spain; father of Gavin. *The Reivers* (1962)—Bkg.—Tried the culprits in the Hogganbeck-Ludus fracas.

Stevens, Mrs. Lemuel: Cau.—"Knight's Gambit" (1949)—Bkg.—Mentioned as Gavin's mother.

Stevens, Mrs. Melisandre Backus Harriss: Cau.—*The Mansion* (1959)—Wealthy widow with two grown children; Gavin Stevens, a childhood sweetheart, finally marries her. See Backus, Melisandre; and Harriss, Mrs. Melisandre B.

Stevens, Mrs. Temple Drake: Cau.—*Requiem for a Nun* (1951)—Major—Confesses to her past crimes and perjury; wife of Gowan Stevens; mother of Bucky. See Drake, Temple.

Stillwell, Shuford H.: Cau.—*The Mansion* (1959)—Bkg.—Mink Snopes's fellow inmate in the penitentiary; escapes; later killed by a collapsing church.

Stokes: Cau.—"A Justice" (1931)—Bkg.—Managed the farm for Jason Compson (II).

Stone: Cau.—*The Town* (1957)—Bkg.—Oxford lawyer who drew up Linda Snopes's will.

Stovall: Cau.—"That Evening Sun" (1931)—Bkg.—Deacon, bank cashier, and customer of Nancy's who owes her money for services rendered; kicked her teeth out.

Straud, Dr.: Cau.—*Sartoris* (1929)—Bkg.—New York mentor to Dr. Lucius Peabody, Jr.

Stribling, Henry (Hawkshaw): Cau.—"Hair" (1931)—Major

—Jefferson barber who paid off the mortgage on his late fiancée's home; then married Susan Reed. "Dry September" (1931)—Major—Tried unsuccessfully to prevent the lynching of Will Mayes.

Strother, Caspey: Neg.—*Sartoris* (1929)—Bkg.—Dissatisfied son of Simon Strother; brother to Elnora; uncle to Isom. "There Was a Queen" (1933)—Bkg.—Elnora's husband who is in the penitentiary for stealing.

[Strother], Elnora: See Elnora.

Strother, Euphrony: Neg.—*Sartoris* (1929)—Bkg.—Mentioned as wife of Simon Strother.

Strother, Simon: Neg.—*Sartoris* (1929)—Minor—Sixty-year-old carriage driver for Bayard (old); husband to Euphrony; father of Elnora and Caspey; killed ostensibly for pursuing a young Negress. "There Was a Queen" (1933)—Bkg.— —Husband of Elnora's mother; simply called Simon. *The Unvanquished* (1938)—Bkg.—Father of Ringo; accompanied Col. John Sartoris to Civil War; called Simon.

Strutterbuck, Captain: Cau.—*The Mansion* (1959)—Bkg.— Two-dollar customer of Miss Thelma's.

Strutterbuck, Q'Milla: Cau.—*The Mansion* (1959)—Bkg.— Name signed to two dollar money order Capt. Strutterbuck gave Miss Thelma; probably his wife.

Studenmare, Captain: Cau.—"A Courtship" (1948)—Bkg.— Skipper of the boat that David Hogganbeck piloted to the Indian plantation.

Sue: Cau.—*Sartoris* (1929)—Bkg.—Mentioned by Hub; probably his sister.

Suratt, V.K.: Cau.—[Early name for the role later designated by V.K. Ratliff, q.v.] *Sartoris* (1929)—Minor—Drinking friend of young Bayard Sartoris. *As I Lay Dying* (1930)— Seller of phonographs. "Centaur in Brass" (1932)—Bkg.— Mentioned as duped by Flem Snopes.

Sutpen, Mrs. Ellen Coldfield: Cau.—"Wash" (1934)—Bkg.—

Mentioned as Col. Thomas Sutpen's wife. *Absalom, Absalom!*
(1936)—Minor—Col. Thomas Sutpen's wife who dies young;
mother of Judith and Henry; sister to Rosa Coldfield; b. 1818
—d. 1862.

[Sutpen,] Eulalia: See Bon, Eulalia.

Sutpen, Henry: Cau.—"Wash" (1934)—Bkg.—Unnamed but
mentioned as dying the same winter as Mrs. Sutpen. *Absalom,
Absalom!* (1936)—Major—Son of Colonel Thomas Sutpen and
Ellen Coldfield Sutpen; murders Charles Bon, his half-brother
to prevent his marriage to Judith; comes back to the plantation
to die. b. 1839—d. 1910.

[Sutpen], Clytemnestra: See Clytemnestra.

Sutpen, Judith: Cau.—"Wash" (1934)—Bkg.—Mentioned.
Absalom, Absalom! (1936)—Minor—Col. Sutpen's daughter
whom Charles Bon courts; engaged to Charles Bon until his
death; she bore the defeat of her hopes with Stoic reserve.
b. 1841—d. 1884.

Sutpen, Colonel Thomas: Cau.—"Wash" (1934)—Major—
Father of Wash Jones's great-granddaughter; killed by Wash
when he rejected the female child and its mother. *Absalom,
Absalom!* (1936)—Major—By sheer physical power and
strength of will he rose from the ranks of poor white trash to
owner of Sutpen's Hundred, a ten-mile square of land in
Yoknapatawpha; his father, brothers and sisters are mentioned; married to Eulalia Bon and later to Ellen Coldfield;
father of Charles Bon, Clytemnestra, Henry Sutpen, and Judith
Sutpen; he had a magnificent dream but his failure to understand people brought the devastation of that dream. *The Unvanquished* (1938)—Bkg.—Mentioned as aristocratic dreamer
who refused to join the Ku Klux Klan. "The Bear" (1942)—
Bkg.—Obtained the hunting land from the Indians; later
Major de Spain had acquired it from him. *Requiem for a Nun*
(1951)—Bkg.—Story of his acquisition of Sutpen's Hundred,

the plantation, is reported here. *The Reivers* (1962)—Bkg.—Mentioned in same role.

Sutterfield, Rev. Tobe (M. Tooleman): Neg.—*A Fable* (1954)—Friend of the Corporal; leader of the Les Amis Myriades et Anonymes à la France de Tout la Monde; the groom who helps Mr. Harry with the three-legged race horse. Unnamed but occupying the same role in *Notes on a Horsethief* (1950).

Sylvester's John: Ind.—"A Courtship" (1948)—Bkg.—Mentioned.

T

Talliafero, Ernest: Cau.—*Mosquitoes* (1927)—Major—Thirty-eight-year-old psychological misfit who is constantly attempting to seduce some female and always failing; talks to Dawson Fairchild about his plans; born Tarver.

Tennie's Jim: See Beauchamp, James Thucydides.

Terrel, Bill: Cau.—"Monk" (1937)—Major—Persuaded Monk to kill Warden Gambrell; pardoned by dishonest Governor.

Thelma Frances: Cau.—*Mosquitoes* (1927)—Bkg.—Friend of Jenny Steinbauer.

Thelma: Cau.—*The Mansion* (1959)—Bkg.—Miss Reba's new girl who entertained Capt. Strutterbuck.

Theodule: Cau.—*A Fable* (1954)—Bkg.—A woman claims that the unidentified body taken from Fort Valaumont is her son Theodule.

Thisbe, Aunt: Neg.—"The Fire and the Hearth" (1942)—Bkg. —An Edmonds' servant.

Thomas, Son: See Son Thomas.

Thompson: Cau.—*The Sound and the Fury* (1929)—Bkg.—Restaurant owner.

Thompson, Pappy: Neg.—*Light in August* (1932)—Bkg.—Old man who is abused by Joe Christmas in the Negro church.

Thompson, Roz: Neg.—*Light in August* (1932)—Bkg.— Pappy's grandson whom Joe Christmas knocks unconscious.

Thorndyke: Cau.—*The Town* (1957)—Bkg.—One of the ministers whom Gavin Stevens prevents from conducting Eula V. Snopes' funeral.

Thorpe: Cau.—"Tomorrow" (1940)—Bkg.—Two brothers who came to get Jackson and Longstreet Fentry, their nephew.

Thorpe: Cau.—*A Fable* (1954)—Bkg.—R.A.F. flyer.

Thorpe, Buck (Jackson and Longstreet Fentry): Cau.— "Tomorrow" (1940)—Minor—Murdered by Bookwright while trying to elope with Bookwright's daughter.

Thorpe, Mrs. Buck: Cau.—"Tomorrow" (1940)—Bkg.—She turned up mysteriously to claim the body.

Three Basket: Ind.—"Red Leaves" (1930)—Major—Sixty-year-old Indian hunting for Issetibbeha's Negro.

Tim: Cau.—"The Liar" (1925)—Bkg.—Ken Roger's "deppity."

Tobe: Neg.—*Soldiers' Pay* (1926)—Bkg.—Saunders's butler.

Tobe: Neg.—*Sartoris* (1929)—Bkg.—Hostler of the stallion which Bayard (young) Sartoris rode.

Tobe: Neg.—"A Rose for Emily" (1930)—Minor—Miss Emily Grierson's only servant; disappears at her death.

'Toinette: Cau.—"All the Dead Pilots" (1931)—Bkg.—French girl over whom Spoomer and Johnny Sartoris fought.

Tom: Cau.—"The Fire and the Hearth" (1942)—Bkg.—Deputy sheriff.

Tom: Cau.—*The Town* (1957)—Bkg.—Countryman who could not read the bank note Bayard (old) Sartoris had made out.

Tomasina: Neg./Cau.—"The Bear" (1942)—Bkg.—Daughter of L.Q.C. McCaslin and Eunice, a Negro slave; later she bore Tomey's Turl by L.Q.C. McCaslin; b. 1810—d. June 1833. "The Fire and the Hearth" (1942)—Bkg.—Mentioned as Aunt Tomey.

Tomey's Turl (Terrel): Neg./Cau.—"Was" (1942)—Major— McCaslin Negro slave; half-brother to Buck and Buddy; son of L.Q.C. McCaslin and Tomasina; constantly running away; later marries Tennie Beauchamp. "The Fire and the Hearth" (1942)—Bkg.—Three-quarters-white son of L.Q.C. McCaslin; father of Lucas Beauchamp. "The Bear" (1942)—Bkg.—Son of Tomasina and L.Q.C. McCaslin who bequeathed him one thousand dollars; the bequest which he never claimed devolved to his children by Tennie Beauchamp: Sophonsiba (Fonsiba) Beauchamp, Lucas Q. C. Beauchamp, and James Thucydides (Tennie's Jim) Beauchamp (who never claimed his portion either). "Delta Autumn" (1942)—Bkg.—Mentioned as the great-grandfather of the woman on whom Roth Edmonds has begot a child.

Tommy: Cau.—*Sanctuary* (1931)—Minor—Murdered by Popeye; Lee Goodwin convicted of the crime; mentally deficient young man who befriends Temple Drake.

Tom Tom: See Bird, Tom Tom.

Tony the Wop: Cau.—"Home" (1925)—Bkg.—Jean-Baptiste ponders his reaction to Jean-Baptiste's decision.

Tooleyman: See Sutterfield, Rev. Tobe.

Top, Big: Neg.—*The Town* (1957)—Bkg.—Husband of Guster; father of Little Top and Aleck Sander.

Top, Little: Neg.—*The Town* (1957)—Bkg.—Oldest son of Big Top and Guster.

Triplett, Earl: Cau.—*The Sound and the Fury* (1929)—Bkg.— Owner of the hardware store where Jason Compson (IV) works and pretends to his mother he has a $1,000 interest. *The Mansion* (1959)—Bkg.—He maneuvered Ike McCaslin out of ownership of the McCaslin Hardware Co.; later Jason Compson (IV) had maneuvered him out.

Trumbull: Cau.—*The Hamlet* (1940)—Bkg.—Varner's blacksmith; replaced by Flem Snopes's relatives. *The Town* (1957) —Bkg.—Re-instated as Varner's blacksmith after much quick-dealing by Flem Snopes.

Tubbs, Mr. and Mrs. Euphus: Cau.—*Intruder in the Dust*

(1948)—Bkg.—Keepers of the Jefferson jail. *Requiem for a Nun* (1951)—Bkg.—Keepers of the jail where Nancy Mannigoe was locked up. *The Mansion* (1959)—Bkg.—Keepers of the county jail where Montgomery Ward Snopes was incarcerated; she seems interested in the pornographic pictures peddled by M.W. Snopes.

Tucker Mr. and Mrs.: Cau.—"That Will Be Fine" (1935)—Bkg.—She was a paramour of Uncle Rodney; he is a cuckold.

Tull, Eula: Cau.—*As I Lay Dying* (1930)—Bkg.—Mentioned as daughter of Vernon and Cora Tull; interested in Darl Bundren.

Tull, Kate: Cau.—*As I Lay Dying* (1930)—Bkg.—Mentioned as daughter of Vernon and Cora Tull; interested in Jewel Bundren.

Tull, Mr. Vernon and Mrs. Cora: Cau.—*As I Lay Dying* (1930)—Minor—She, once a school teacher, is an overzealous Christian friend who sat up with Addie; he helped the Bundrens across the river. "The Hound" (1931)—Bkg.—Referred to as farming couple. *Sanctuary* (1931)—Bkg.—Ruby Lamar calls the sheriff from Tull's house; presumably Vernon and Cora. *The Hamlet* (1940)—He is a very hen-pecked, bkg. character; she, a minor character, really speaks out when she sues Eck Snopes for damages occasioned by his spotted horse. "Two Soldiers" (1942)—Bkg.—Pete Grier sparks Tull's girls; presumably daughters of Vernon and Cora. "Shingles for the Lord" (1943)—Bkg.—Res Grier's silent partner in the hunting dog. *The Town* (1957)—Bkg.—He is a farmer at Frenchman's Bend; her sister's niece is I. O. Snopes's illegal wife. *The Mansion* (1959)—Bkg.—He is a farmer; she probably wrote the letter Yettie Snopes sent Mink while he was at Parchman.

Turpin: Cau.—*The Mansion* (1959)—Bkg.—Gavin Stevens and V. K. Ratliff accidentally found a young man named Turpin hiding at Mink Snopes abandoned house; he was trying to evade the draft.

Turpin, Buck: Cau.—*The Sound and the Fury* (1929)—Some kind of town official in Jefferson; possibly mayor.

U

Uncle Bird: See Bird, Uncle.

Uncle Bud: See Bud, Uncle.

Uncle Henry: See Henry, Uncle.

Urquhart: Mentioned in *Intruder in the Dust* (1948) as family name of early Yoknapatawpha settlers. Now Workitt.

V

Van: Cau.—*Sanctuary* (1931)—Bkg.—One of Popeye's truck drivers; he beats Gowan Stevens up and tries to molest Temple Drake.

Van Dyming: Cau.—"Fox Hunt" (1931)—Bkg.—Supposed to be interested in a non-existent horse that Harrison Blair wants to buy.

Van Dyming, Mr. Carleton and Mrs. Mathilda Lumpkin: Cau.—"Black Music" (1934)—Bkg.—Wealthy people who bought the haunted place.

Van Tosch: Cau.—*The Reivers* (1962)—Bkg.—Owner of Coppermine (alias Lightning); intrigued with Ned McCaslin's ability to make Coppermine run.

Varner, Eula: See Mrs. Flem Snopes.

Varner, Jody: Cau.—*As I Lay Dying* (1930)—Bkg.—Mentioned as born in 1888. *Light in August* (1932)—Bkg.—Mentioned as storekeeper. *The Hamlet* (1940)—Major—Eula Varner's brother and protector, he thinks; easily outwitted by Flem Snopes; ninth of Will Varner's sixteen children; only son at home. *The Town* (1957)—Bkg.—Son of Will Varner; rather in eclipse after Flem's outdistancing of him. *The Mansion* (1959)—Bkg.—Uncle of Linda Snopes Kohl; son and helper of Will Varner.

Varner, Will: Cau.—*As I Lay Dying* (1930)—Bkg.—Horse

doctor neighbor who sets Cash Bundren's broken leg. "The Hound" (1931)—Bkg.—Varner's store mentioned. *Light in August* (1932)—Jody's father. *The Hamlet* (1940)—Major— Father of Jody and Eula and fourteen more; owner of the mansion at Frenchman's Bend, and most of the rest of Frenchman's Bend property; veterinarian of sorts; political and economical boss. "Tomorrow" (1940)—Bkg.—Justice of the peace to whom Bookwright surrendered. "Shingles for the Lord" (1943)—Bkg.—Had given Vernon Tull the hunting dog. *Intruder in the Dust* (1948)—Bkg.—Store owner; influential man in Frenchman's Bend. *The Town* (1957)— Minor—Wealthy father of Eula Varner Snopes; his indignation caused Eula's death and Flem's bank presidency. *The Mansion* (1959)—Minor—Justice of the peace at Frenchman's Bend with all kinds of political and financial ramifications.

Varner, Mrs. Will: Cau.—*The Hamlet* (1940)—Bkg.—Appears briefly and humorously as cooker, preserver, efficient housewife; unruffled by Eula's pregnancy. Once called "Miss Maggie." Mother of sixteen children. *The Town* (1957)—Bkg.— Mentioned as above.

Vatch: Cau.—"Mountain Victory" (1932)—Major—Yankee who cannot forgive Rebels; he kills Saucier Weddel, Jubal, and Hule, his younger brother.

Venturia, Juan: Cau.—"The Rosary" (1925)—Major—Mr. Harris's annoying neighbor who learned to mutilate the song "The Rosary" on a saxophone.

Vera: Cau.—*The Reivers* (1962)—Bkg.—Prostitute at Miss Reba's house in Memphis.

Vernon: Cau.—*The Sound and the Fury* (1929)—Bkg.—Myrtle's husband; son-in-law of sheriff.

Vernon: Cau.—"Death Drag" (1932)—Bkg.—Restaurant person who brings water to Jock.

Vidal, Francois: Cau.—"Mountain Victory" (1932)—Bkg.— Grandfather of Saucier Weddel.

Vines, Deacon: Neg.—*Light in August* (1932)—Bkg.—Present at Negro church which Joe Christmas disrupts.

Vinson, Mr. and Mrs.: Cau.—*Miss Zilphia Gant* (1932)—Bkg. —He is the oldish, pigeyed husband of young Mrs. Vinson who elopes with Jim Gant; she and Gant are shot by Mrs. Gant.

Virgil: Cau.—*The Reivers* (1962)—Bkg.—Clerk at the hotel where Miss Rivers stayed in Parsham.

Vitelli, Popeye: Cau.—*Sanctuary* (1931)—Major—Only called Popeye here; the smart crook who kills Tommy, rapes Temple Drake, and then takes her to Miss Reba Rivers's brothel as his girl; kills Red; finally hanged for a crime he did not commit. His mother, insane grandmother, father, and step-father are mentioned. *Requiem for a Nun* (1951)—Bkg.— Temple tells about him; full name given.

Vladimir Kyrilytch: Cau.—*The Mansion* (1959)—Bkg.— Hessian soldier who married Nelly Ratcliffe after the American Revolution; took her name; now Ratliff; ancestor of present V. K. Ratliff, q.v.

W

Waldrip: Cau.—"Honor" (1930)—Bkg.—Fellow pilot of Monaghan's during World War I.

Waldrip, Mrs. Vernon: Cau.—*The Wild Palms* (1939)—in "Old Man"—Major—The Tall Convict's young girl friend for whom he thought he was robbing the train; while he was in prison she married someone else.

Walker, Mr. and Mrs. Ed: Cau.—*Sanctuary* (1931)—Bkg.— She took Ruby Lamar in to stay with her at the jail; he probably did not approve her action; likely jail keepers.

Walkley: Cau.—"Victory" (1931)—Minor—Hospital friend of Alec Gray; his Canadian adventure serves to highlight Alec's ultimate condition.

Wallace, Captain: Cau.—"Sunset" (1925)—Bkg.—Commander

of the soldiers who destroy the pathetically confused Negro on whom the sketch focuses.

Waller, Mr. and Mrs. Hamp: Cau.—*Light in August* (1932)—Bkg.—They found Joanna Burden's body in the burning house.

Walter: Neg.—*Mosquitoes* (1927)—Bkg.—Mrs. Maurier's butler.

Walter: Neg.—*Mosquitoes* (1927)—Bkg.—Crewman of the tug that gets *The Nausikaa* off the sandbar.

Walthall, Parson: Cau.—*The Sound and the Fury* (1929)—Bkg.—Pastor of Methodist Church; did not want the pigeons killed.

Wardle, Mrs.: Cau.—*Soldiers' Pay* (1926)—Bkg.—Upperclass resident of Charlestown, Ga.

Warren, Captain: Cau.—"Death Drag" (1932)—Major—He, a veteran of the Royal Flying Corps, was a friend of Jock, the pilot. "Knight's Gambit" (1949)—Bkg.—World War I pilot hero who advises Chick Mallison about military glory.

Wattman, Jakeleg: Cau.—*The Mansion* (1959)—Bkg.—The Jefferson bootlegger.

Watts: Cau.—*Sartoris* (1929)—Bkg.—Watt's Hardware Store mentioned.

Watts: Cau.—"Turnabout" (1932)—Bkg.—Gunner on Bogard's plane.

Watts, Mr.: Cau.—"That Will Be Fine" (1935)—Bkg.—Sheriff of Jefferson.

Watts, Birdie: Cau.—*The Reivers* (1962)—Bkg.—Keeper of brothel near Miss Reba's house in Memphis.

Weddel, Francis (or Vidal): Ind./Cau.—"Mountain Victory" (1932)—Bkg.—Mentioned as the Chief of the Choctaws; son of Francois Vidal and Choctaw woman; owner of Contalmaison Plantation; father of Saucier Weddel; went to Washington to see President Andrew Jackson. "Lo" (1934)—Major—Chief of all the Chackasaws; he visits Washington, D.C., and annoys the President; only named character in this story.

Weddel, Grenier: Cau.—*The Town* (1957)—Bkg.—Former

lover of Mrs. Maurice Priest whose husband gives him a black eye.

Weddel, Saucier: Ind./Cau.—"Mountain Victory" (1932)—Major—A twenty-eight-year-old Confederate major who tries to return home to Mississippi and finds trouble in the Tennessee mountains. He is the son of Francis Weddel (who is the son of Francois Vidal, a Napoleonic general) and a Choctaw woman.

West, Dr.: Cau.—"Smoke" (1932)—Minor—Owner and druggist of West's Drugstore; provided some of the essential clues in the Holland-Dukinfield murder case.

West, Miss: Cau.—"Honor" (1930)—Minor—Secretary for Mr. Reinhardt, owner of the auto agency.

West, David: Cau.—*Mosquitoes* (1927)—Minor—The *Nausikaa* steward who runs away with Pat Robyn and later leaves the ship alone for good.

White, Mr. and Mrs.: Cau.—"Honor" (1930)—Bkg.—Fellow who lost to Monaghan at cards; she is mentioned.

White, Hank: Cau.—*Soldiers' Pay* (1926)—Bkg.—Drunken soldier on the first train; may or may not be the one who tries to jump out the window.

White, Jed: Cau.—*The Unvanquished* (1938)—Bkg.—He took the message of the Bayard (old) Sartoris—Ben J. Redmond confrontation to Sartoris plantation.

Whiteby: Cau.—"Victory" (1931)—Bkg.—An officer who, in a position similar to Alec Gray's, commits suicide.

Whitfield: Cau.—*Requiem for a Nun* (1951)—Bkg.—Minister in early Jefferson.

Whitfield, Rev.: Cau.—*As I Lay Dying* (1930)—Minor—Father of Jewel Bundren. *The Hamlet* (1940)—Bkg.—He provided the solution to Ike Snopes's problem. "Tomorrow" (1940)—Bkg.—Helped S. J. Fentry bury the woman to whom he had just married Fentry. "Shingles for the Lord" (1943)—Minor—Favorable portrait of a Protestant, possibly Methodist, preacher.

Widrington (Widdrington), Mr. and Mrs.: Cau.—"Carcassonne" (1931)—Bkg.—Mentioned as allowing a tramp [Wilfred Midgleston] to sleep in the garret of a cantina owned by the Standard Oil Company which they represent. "Black Music" (1934)—Bkg.—Same role as above; he is Standard Oil manager in Rincon.

Widrington, Mrs.: Cau.—*The Town* (1957)—Bkg.—One of Byron Snopes's off-spring took her dog's collar to wear.

Wilbourne, Henry (Harry): Cau.—*The Wild Palms* (1939) in "Wild Palms"—Major—The twenty-seven-year-old medical intern who falls in love with love and chucks his career for an adulterous association with Charlotte Rittenmeyer. His deceased father, also a doctor, and his sister are mentioned.

Wildermark: Cau.—*The Town* (1957)—Bkg.—Owner of dry goods store in Jefferson.

Wildermark (Senior): Cau.—*The Town* (1957)—Bkg.—Excellent chess player; possibly father of store owner above.

Wilkie: Neg.—*The Sound and the Fury* (1929)—Bkg.—Servant of Gerald Bland's grandfather.

Wilkins, Professor and Mrs.: Cau.—*The Unvanquished* (1948)—Bkg.—People Bayard (old) lived with while studying law in Oxford; also called Judge Wilkins.

Wilkins, George: Neg.—"The Fire and the Hearth" (1942)—Minor—Married Nathalie, youngest child of Lucas and Mollie Beauchamp; slow-witted.

Wilkins, Mrs. Nathalie Beauchamp: Neg./Cau.—"The Fire and the Hearth" (1942)—Daughter of Lucas and Mollie; helped get Lucas in trouble with the law.

Willard: Cau.?—*Soldiers' Pay* (1926)—Bkg.—Resident of Charlestown, Ga. who grew good fruit.

Willow, Colonel: Cau.—*Absalom, Absalom!* (1936)—Bkg.—Colonel of Henry Sutpen's regiment; Thomas and Henry Sutpen meet in his tent.

Wilmoth: Cau.—"Go Down, Moses" (1941)—Minor—Editor of

the Jefferson paper; helps Gavin Stevens make arrangements for the return of Sam Worsham Beauchamp's body.

Wilson, Sergeant: Cau.—*A Fable* (1954)—Bkg.—The Iowan considers Wilson the best sergeant in the army.

Winbush, Mrs.: Cau.—*The Mansion* (1959)—Bkg.—Probably Fonso's mother; told him to board with a motherly-looking woman in Memphis.

Winbush, Fonso: Cau.—*Sanctuary* (1931)—Bkg.—Simply called Fonzo here; he and Virgil Snopes rent a room at Miss Reba Rivers's brothel. *The Mansion* (1959)—Bkg.—Friend of Virgil Snopes with whom he roomed in Memphis; nephew of Grover Cleveland Winbush.

Winbush, Grover Cleveland: Cau.—*The Town* (1957)—Minor—Night marshal whose absence from duty leads to exposure of M.W. Snopes's pornography peddling. *The Mansion* (1959)—Bkg.—Night policeman who causes Montgomery Ward Snopes to be caught; watched the peep show in Atelier Monty while Christian's drugstore was robbed.

Winbush, Mack: Cau.—*The Reivers* (1962)—Bkg.—At his property Ludus was to have purchased whiskey.

Winterbottom: Cau.—*Light in August* (1932)—Bkg.—Poor farmer. *The Hamlet* (1940)—Bkg.—Frenchman's Bend farmer; Launcelot Snopes boards with him.

Winterbottom, Mrs.: Cau.—*Sartoris* (1929)—Bkg.—Operator of boarding house where two Missouri men, who came to Jefferson to register Negroes, lived.

Wiseman, Mrs. Eva Kauffman: Cau.—*Mosquitoes* (1927)—Minor—A pleasantly witty widow who goes on the cruise; sister of Julius Kauffman; author of book of poetry.

Witt: Cau.—*A Fable* (1954)—Bkg.—R.A.F. Flyer.

Wop: Cau.—"The Kid Learns" (1925)—Major—Boss of the petty gangsters, whose position the Kid covets.

Wordwin: Cau.—*The Reivers* (1962)—Bkg.—Cashier in the

Bank of Jefferson who went to Memphis and brought Mr. Lucius Priest's car home.

Workitt: See Urquhart.

Workitt, Uncle Sudley: Cau.—*Intruder in the Dust* (1948)— Bkg.—Cousin of Mrs. Nub Gowrie; in business with Crawford and Vinson Gowrie, his nephews.

Workman: Cau.—"An Error in Chemistry (1946)—Minor— Insurance adjuster who tipped Gavin Stevens off to Joel Flint.

Worsham, Doctor: Cau.—*The Unvanquished* (1938)—Bkg.— Episcopal rector in Jefferson before Civil War.

Worsham, Miss Belle: Cau.—"Go Down, Moses" (1941)— Minor—Owner of the once prosperous "Worsham Place" where Hamp Worsham is a servant; her grandparents had owned Mollie W. Beauchamp's parents.

Worsham, Mr. and Mrs. Hamp: Neg.—"Go Down, Moses" (1941)—Minor—Brother of Mollie W. Beauchamp; wife is mentioned; servants to Miss Belle Worsham

Worsham, Samuel: Cau.—"Go Down, Moses" (1941)—Bkg.— Father of Belle Worsham; Mollie Beauchamp named her grandson for him.

Worthington, Mrs.: Cau.—*Soldiers' Pay* (1926)—Bkg.— Wealthy widow; family friend of the Mahons; sends her car to take Donald riding.

Wright, Doc: Cau.—*The Sound and the Fury* (1929)—Bkg.— Mentioned as cotton speculator.

Wutherspoon, Jamie: Cau.—"Turnabout" (1932)—Bkg.—British torpedo boat seaman.

Wyatt, Old Lady: Cau.—"A Rose for Emily" (1930)—Bkg.— Emily Grierson's great aunt who went insane.

Wyatt, George: Cau.—*The Unvanquished* (1938)—Minor— Friend of the Sartoris family; offered to help Bayard kill Redmond; formely one of Col. John Sartoris's soldiers.

Wyatt, Henry: Cau.—"Delta Autumn" (1942)—Minor— Hunter in the party.

Wyatt, Aunt Sally: Cau.—*Sartoris* (1929)—Bkg.—Sixty-five-year-old neighbor spinster who moved in to help keep Narcissa Benbow company while Horace was away in World War I.

Wyatt, Miss Sophia: Cau.—*Sartoris* (1929)—Bkg.—Older sister of Aunt Sally Wyatt; another sister younger than Aunt Sally is mentioned.

Wylie, Ash (old): Neg.—*Big Woods* (1955)—In this version of "A Bear Hunt" he is the father of Old Man Ash.

Wylie, Old Man Ash: Neg.—*Big Woods* (1955) In this version of "A Bear Hunt" he is called Old Man Ash Wylie. Cf. Ash, Old Man.

Wylie, Job: Neg.—"Uncle Willy" (1935)—Major—Uncle Willy Christian's servant; faithful; sensible.

Wyott: Cau.—*The Reivers* (1962)—Bkg.—Family friend of the Priests'; Ned McCaslin is discovered as a stowaway while Boon and Lucius are passing Wyott's.

Wyott: Cau.—*The Reivers* (1962)—Bkg.—Built store and ferry at Wyott's Crossing which later became Ballenbaugh's Ferry.

Wyott, Miss Vaiden: Cau.—*The Town* (1957)—Bkg.—Wall-street Panic Snopes's second grade teacher.

Y

Yaphank: See Gilligan, Joseph.

Yo Ho: Mongoloid—"Yo Ho and Two Bottles of Rum" (1925)—Major—Chinese mess boy who is accidentally killed by Mr. Ayers.

Z

Zilich, Mrs. Sophie: Cau.—"Pennsylvania Station" (1934)—Minor—Mrs. Gihon's helpful neighlor.

[Zsettlani], Piotr: Cau.—*A Fable* (1954)—Bkg.—A Judas figure; denies Corporal at last supper, tries unsuccessfully to rejoin Corporal in prison.

Zsettlani seems to be a tribal name of some sort, rather than a family name.

Selected
Bibliography

I. BOOKS BY FAULKNER

The Marble Faun. Boston: The Four Seas Co., 1924.

Soldiers' Pay. New York: Boni and Liveright, 1926. Also New York: Liveright Publishing Co., 1954.

Mosquitoes. New York: Boni and Liveright, 1927.

Sartoris. New York: Harcourt, Brace and Company, Inc., 1929. Reissued, 1951.

The Sound and the Fury. New York: Jonathan Cape and Harrison Smith, 1929. New York: The Modern Library, 1946 (with *As I Lay Dying*).

As I Lay Dying. New York: Jonathan Cape and Harrison Smith, 1930. New Edition, New York: Random House, 1964.

Sanctuary. New York: Cape and Smith, 1931. New York: The Modern Library, 1932.

Idyll in the Desert. New York: Random House, Inc., 1931.

These Thirteen. New York: Cape and Smith, 1931.

Salmagundi. Milwaukee: The Cassanova Press, 1932.

Light in August. New York: Harrison Smith and Robert Haas, 1932. New York: The Modern Library, 1950.

Miss Zilphia Gant. Dallas, Texas: The Book Club of Texas, 1932.

A Green Bough. New York: Smith and Haas, 1933.

Doctor Martino and Other Stories. New York: Smith and Haas, 1934.

Pylon. New York: Smith and Haas, 1935.

Absalom, Absalom! New York: Random House, Inc., 1936. New York: The Modern Library, 1951.

The Unvanquished. New York: Random House, Inc., 1938.

The Wild Palms. New York: Random House, Inc., 1939.

The Hamlet. New York: Random House, Inc., 1940. New York: The Modern Library, 1956. Third Edition. New York: Random House, Inc., 1964.

302

Go Down, Moses and Other Stories. New York: Random House, Inc., 1942. New York: The Modern Library, 1955. (*and Other Stories* omitted after first printing)

Intruder in the Dust. New York: Random House, Inc., 1948.

Knight's Gambit. New York: Random House, Inc., 1949.

Collected Stories of William Faulkner. New York: Random House, Inc., 1950.

Requiem for a Nun. New York: Random House, Inc., 1951.

Notes on a Horsethief. Greenville, Mississippi: The Levee Press, 1951.

Mirrors of Chartres Street. Minneapolis, Minnesota: The Faulkner Studies, 1953.

A Fable. New York: Random House, Inc., 1954.

Big Woods. New York: Random House, Inc., 1955.

New Orleans Sketches by William Faulkner. Tokyo: The Hosuseido Press, 1955.

The Town. New York: Random House, Inc., 1957.

New Orleans Sketches. New Brunswick, New Jersey: Rutgers University Press, 1958.

The Mansion. New York: Random House, Inc., 1959.

The Reivers. New York: Random House, Inc., 1962.

II. CRITICAL WORKS

Backman, Melvin. "The Wilderness and the Negro in Faulkner's 'The Bear,'" *PMLA,* LXXVI, No. 5 (December 1961), 595–600.

Blotner, Joseph, comp. *William Faulkner's Library—A Catalogue.* Charlottesville: University Press of Virginia, 1965.

Buckley, G. T. "Is Oxford the Original of Jefferson in William Faulkner's Novels?" *PMLA,* LXXVI (September 1961), 447–454.

Campbell, Harry M. and Ruel E. Foster. *William Faulkner: A Critical Appraisal.* Norman, Oklahoma: University of Oklahoma Press, 1951.

Coughlan, Robert. *The Private World of William Faulkner.* New York: Harper and Brothers, 1954.

Cowley, Malcolm, ed. *The Portable Faulkner*. New York: Viking Press, 1946.

Fant, Joseph L., III, and Robert Ashley, eds. *Faulkner at West Point*. New York: Random House, 1964.

Gwynn, Frederick L. and Joseph L. Blotner, eds. *Faulkner in the University*. New York: Vintage Books, 1965.

Hagopian, John V. and Martic Dolch. "Faulkner's 'A Rose for Emily,' " *The Explicator*, Vol. XXII, No. 8 (April 1964), note 68.

Hoffman, Frederick J. *William Faulkner*. Vol. I of Twayne's United States Authors Series. Ed. Sylvia E. Bowman. New York: Twayne Publishers, Inc., 1961.

Hoffman, Frederick J. and Olga W. Vickery, eds. *William Faulkner: Three Decades of Criticism*. East Lansing: Michigan State University Press, 1960.

———. *William Faulkner: Two Decades of Criticism*. East Lansing: Michigan State University Press, 1951.

Howe, Irving. *William Faulkner: A Critical Study*. 2nd Ed. New York: Vintage Books, 1962.

Hunt, John W. *William Faulkner: Art in Theological Tension*. Syracuse, New York: Syracuse University Press, 1965.

Jelliffe, Robert A., ed. *Faulkner at Nagano*. Tokyo: Kenkyusha Ltd., 1956.

Kirk, Robert W. and Marvin Klotz. *Faulkner's People*. Berkeley: University of California Press, 1963.

Longley, John Lewis, Jr. *The Tragic Mask: A Study of Faulkner's Heroes*. Chapel Hill, N.C.: University of North Carolina Press, 1963.

Meriwether, James B. *The Literary Career of William Faulkner: A Bibliographical Study*. Princeton, New Jersey: Princeton University Library, 1961.

———. *Essays, Speeches and Public Letters of William Faulkner*. New York: Random House, Inc., 1965.

O'Connor, William Van. *William Faulkner*. (Pamphlets on American Writers, No. 3) Minneapolis: University of Minnesota Press, 1959.

O'Donnell, George Marion. "Faulkner's Mythology," *Kenyon Review*, I (Summer, 1939), 285–99.

Poirer, William R. "Strange Gods in Jefferson, Mississippi," *Sewanee Review*, LIII (Summer, 1945), 44–56.

Robb, Mary Cooper. *William Faulkner: An Estimate of His Contribution to the American Novel*. Pittsburgh: University of Pittsburgh Press, 1957.

Slatoff, Walter J. *Quest for Failure: A Study of William Faulkner*. Ithaca: Cornell University Press, 1960.

Sleeth, Irene Lynn. *William Faulkner: A Bibliography of Criticism*. The Swallow Pamphlets No. 13. Denver: Alan Swallow, 1962.

Stein, Jean. "William Faulkner: An Interview," in *William Faulkner: Three Decades of Criticism*. Ed. F. J. Hoffman and Olga Vickery. East Lansing: Michigan State University Press, 1961. Pp. 67–81.

Swiggart, Peter. *The Art of Faulkner's Novels*. Austin: The University of Texas Press, 1962.

Thompson, Lawrence. *William Faulkner: An Introduction and Interpretation*. New York: Barnes & Noble, Inc., 1963.

Utley, F. L., Lynn Z. Bloom, and A. F. Kenney, eds. *Bear, Man, & God*. New York: Random House, 1964.

Vickery, Olga W. *The Novels of William Faulkner, A Critical Interpretation*. Rev. ed. Baton Rouge: Louisiana State University Press, 1964.

Webb, James W., and A. Wigfall Green, eds. *William Faulkner of Oxford*. Baton Rouge: Louisiana State University Press, 1965.

INVENTORY 1983